Perfect Day

NEW ZEALAND

WITHDRAWN

Map Included

www.marco-polo.com

Contents

⭐ **TOP 10** 4

That New Zealand Feeling 6

For chapters: See inside front cover

Not to be missed!
Our TOP 10 hits – from the absolute No. 1 to No. 10 –
help you plan your tour of the most important sights.

★ 1 FIORDLAND ➤ 170

This remote mountainous region is our number one destination thanks to its magnificent fiords, majestic waterfalls and thrilling hiking routes through mysterious jungles.

★ 2 BAY OF ISLANDS ➤ 52

This beautiful bay sprinkled with almost 150 islands (image left) is an enchantingly idyllic subtropical paradise where the nation of New Zealand was born. Don't leave without experiencing a boat tour over to the Hole in the Rock.

★ 3 WEST COAST ➤ 148

The west coast is where the mighty, glacier-filled Southern Alps meet a tangle of rainforest by the raging Tasman Sea. It's a wonderfully wild region that's home to some un-conventional individuals.

★ 4 THERMAL AREAS ➤ 86

Rotorua is the centre of a thermal wonderland filled with bubbling waters, gurgling mud pools, pictur-esque silica terraces and geysers that shoot high into the air.

★ 5 QUEENSTOWN ➤ 173

Take to the land, water and skies for thrills and spills at this veritable adventure playground in the upland region of Central Otago.

★ 6 DUNEDIN & OTAGO PENINSULA ➤ 175

Check out the pioneers' historic buildings before heading to the enchanting peninsula nearby to come face to face with penguins and rare royal albatrosses.

★ 7 ABEL TASMAN NATIONAL PARK ➤ 130

Many hikers maintain that New Zealand's smallest national park is also its prettiest – explore the Coast Track that runs alongside the stunning beaches of Tasman Bay.

★ 8 TE PAPA ➤ 110

New Zealand's national museum in Wellington gives visitors an imaginative, often tongue-in-cheek insight into the characteristics of the country and its inhabitants.

★ 9 COROMANDEL ➤ 55

The eastern side of this peninsula is a real paradise for beach fans. Don't leave without paying a visit to Hot Water Beach with its warm springs right beneath the sand.

★ 10 KAIKOURA ➤ 132

This lovely harbour town offers some spectacular whale watching tours – the massive marine mammals venture close to the coast in the deep, nutrient-rich waters nearby.

THAT
NEW ZEALAND

Find out what makes New Zealand tick and experience its unique flair – just like the Kiwis themselves.

BREAKFAST & BRUNCH

Kiwis like to head out on Saturdays for a hearty breakfast that lasts well into the afternoon. Join them for such classic dishes as bacon & eggs or Eggs Benedict, all washed down with a frothy cappuccino or a tasty latte. Brunch is taken particularly seriously in the capital of **Wellington** (➤ 105), where a variety of cafés and bistros offer appetising morning menus. **Caffe L'affare** (➤ 121), **Floriditas** (161 Cuba St.) and **Mojo** (33 Customhouse Quay) are all highly recommended. The latter roast their own coffee.

A VIVID HISTORY LESSON

Whether you're a patriotic Kiwi or an interested tourist, you simply can't visit the **Bay of Islands** without heading to the **Waitangi National Reserve** (➤ 53). Don't miss the historic Treaty House, the magnificent Maori meeting house, or the lawn above the bay – this well-tended patch of grass was where the British and the Maoris signed a treaty to found the new nation on 6 February 1840.

A REAL THERMAL TREAT

New Zealand's countless thermal springs are healthful, sociable places where you can sink into steaming pools, soak your bones after a hike and chat with your fellow bathers. The entry price often includes all manner of health and beauty treatments. The **Polynesian Spa** (➤ 97) in **Rotorua** and the **Hanmer Springs Thermal Pools and Spa** approximately 130km/81mi north of Christchurch (➤ 137) are among the most popular resorts.

FRESH FROM THE FRYER

Fish & chips are a popular treat in NZ: the freshly caught fish is encased in delicate batter, and the chips are crispy on the outside and deliciously soft within. Go to a fish & chip shop and they'll wrap it up in paper for you to take away. Copy the locals and tuck in with your fingers, preferably sitting out by the water. The best fish & chips in the Northland Region can be found at **Doubtless Bay**: foodies come from far and wide to visit the **Mangonui Fish Shop** (Beach Rd., 8:30–9, A210 B5).

FEELING

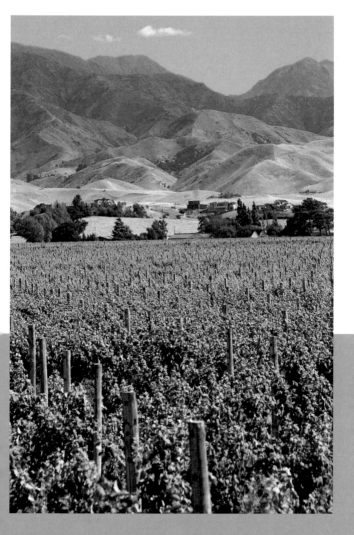

Grapevines fill the landscape near Blenheim

That New Zealand Feeling

HIKING WITHOUT THE HASSLE

Make like a Kiwi and explore the nation's islands on foot along its vast selection of excellent trails. Multi-day hikes lead you into the protected natural surroundings of the national parks. Some guided tours – e.g. along the 54km/33mi **Milford Track** to **Milford Sound** (➤ 170) – provide full-board accommodation and will even transport your bags!

AN ISLAND-HOPPING MINI-CRUISE

Car ferries (➤ 38) take just over 3 hours to sail between New Zealand's North and South Islands. It's a lovely trip in good weather – you can sit up on deck, doze in the sun and get some tips from the other passengers. Keep your eyes peeled for dolphins in **Cook Strait** (➤ 134), admire the views of **Wellington Harbour** (➤ 105), and enjoy passing through **Queen Charlotte Sound** (➤ 135).

CHEERS!

Once a die-hard beer-drinking nation, the Kiwis switched their allegiance to locally grown wines a long time ago. Try tasting some of their full-bodied reds and quaffable whites on a guided tour of a winery (or two!) Guides offer tours near **Blenheim** (➤ 136; image ➤ 7), where you can also enjoy a delicious meal at the **Twelve Trees Restaurant** (➤ 140) run by the renowned vintner, Allan Scott. Tourist information centres also have maps to help you plan a route round the different wineries yourself. If you'd rather drink beer, head to **Dunedin** (➤ 175) and take a tour of the traditional **Speight's Brewery** (tours several times a day, 200 Rattray St., tel: 03 4 77 76 97).

THRILLS MADE IN NZ

Inspired by a daring tradition from the island of Vanuatu, **bungy jumping** (➤ 182) was actually popularised by two New Zealanders. The Kiwis are real adrenaline junkies who seem to like nothing better than jumping from great heights with an elastic rope tied to their feet. If you want to experience this ultimate thrill (and live to tell the tale!), head to **Queenstown** (➤ 173) and take the plunge in **Nevis Valley** (134m/440ft high), from **Bob's Peak** (47m/154ft), or from the **Kawarau Suspension Bridge** (43m/141ft).

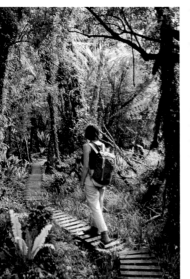

A hiker on Stewart Island

The Magazine

SHAKY ISLES

New Zealand is perched on the Pacific Ring of Fire, a collision zone between two gigantic chunks of the Earth's crust. Here, the Pacific and Indo-Australian tectonic plates grind against each other to create unique landscapes and at times their force is released with devastating consequences.

A Dynamic Land

The boundary between the tectonic plates runs right down the country – from the Bay of Plenty through Wellington and along the South Island. The plates move at approximately the same rate as fingernails and hair grow: about 30–60mm (1–2in) per year.

In the North Island, this friction has caused volcanic eruptions and earthquakes, but it has also created the extraordinary thermal areas of the Central Plateau (►86) and the spectacular peaks of Tongariro National Park (►93). The South Island also experiences regular tremors and landslides, the most recent being the tragic earthquake that hit Christchurch in early 2011 (see below). The Alpine Fault (which runs along the length of the Southern Alps and continues to push up the mountains) has formed snow-topped peaks, glaciers, lakes and fjords.

The Human Cost

On 22 February 2011, the destructive force of nature was experienced by the inhabitants of Christchurch as an earthquake reaching 6.3 on the Richter scale hit the country's second city with shattering results. While

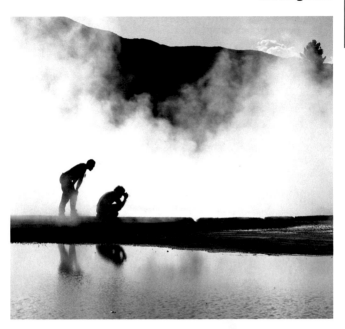

Bubbling and steaming mud pools are just one of the fascinating formations caused by tectonic plate movement

memories of the devastation and human losses caused by the 1931 Napier earthquake (▶ 99) still linger, and scars in the landscape are testimony to a powerful 1987 tremor at Edgecumbe in the Bay of Plenty, this most recent quake is the worst to have hit the country in over 80 years. You can still see lasting signs of the damage it caused in the town and its surroundings today. The tragic loss of life in that fateful year will be felt by the families affected for generations to come.

With growing cities sitting alongside fault lines and volcanoes, the reliance on technology and geologists to monitor the mood of each active volcano is essential. Even the sleeping volcanoes dotting Auckland's cityscape

The Magazine

The impressive crater of Mount Tarawera and Lake Rotomahana

(►57) are under constant scrutiny. The current cones are considered extinct, but the volcanic field below them is only dormant and could well open up new vents. New Zealand's capital, Wellington, is bracing itself for a spectacle of another kind. The city straddles a fault line that last caused a major earthquake in 1855. The quake, which registered 8.2 on the Richter scale, was felt from Auckland to Dunedin, and added a strip of new land to Wellington's entire southern coastline, uplifting some 5,000km² (2,000mi²) of land. The capital is now having to face the growing likelihood of another "big one" sometime soon.

Four Seasons in One Day

As if the threat of earthquakes and volcanoes wasn't enough for its inhabitants to contend with, New Zealand also experiences extremes in weather. The long and narrow islands can suffer freezing hailstorms on one coast at the same time as sunshine burns down on the other. From the subtropical climate of the far north to the freezing southern regions, the difference in temperature can be several degrees. The islands' maritime climate also means that the weather changes with amazing rapidity, and so visitors should come prepared for four seasons in one day.

THE LEGEND OF THE VOLCANOES

Maori mythology offers a beautiful and poetic explanation for New Zealand's volcanoes: Ngatoroirangi, an ancient priest and explorer, was caught in a blinding blizzard while climbing Mount Ngauruhoe. He called on his sisters, in the distant homeland of Hawaiki, to send him fire to keep him warm. The glowing embers sent by his sisters landed first at White Island (►97), and then where Ngatoroirangi was standing to form the volcanoes of the Central Plateau.

PEOPLE WITH MANA

"Haere mai, haere mai" are some of the first words you're likely to hear on arriving in New Zealand, welcoming you to Aotearoa, the Land of the Long White Cloud. A renaissance of Maori language and culture is happening.

No official event is complete without a Maori ceremony. Te Reo Maori, the Maori language, is taught in schools and used in parliamentary debates, and many of its words have entered New Zealand English. This renewed interest comes after Maori traditions were discouraged for generations.

A Proud Celebration of Maori Culture

Today, however, the goal is to embrace cultural diversity and to find a way for Maori and Pakeha (people of European descent) – and the many other ethnic groups of New Zealand – to live together in a fairer society. The process is not without tensions: Maori are still disadvantaged in many ways. But they are proud to celebrate the achievements of their cultural heroes – people with mana (spiritual authority).

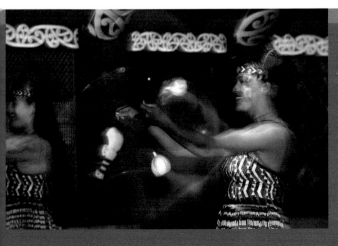

The traditional *Poi* dance performed at the New Zealand Maori Arts and Crafts Institute

The Magazine

Rebellion

Hone Heke Pokai (*c.*1810–50) became the first tribal chief to add his name to the Treaty of Waitangi in 1840 (► 53). Before long, though, Maori began to fear that the Europeans would observe the treaty's principles of partnership only until they could seize the land. Hone Heke regretted his role and expressed his growing resentment of British sovereignty by cutting down one of its symbols, a shipping-signal flagstaff on Maiki, overlooking Russell, not once but four times.

In 1887, **Horonuku Te Heuheu Tukino IV** (*c.*1821–88) gave away one of his tribe's most precious possessions – the three sacred peaks that form Tongariro National Park (► 93). The far-sighted paramount chief of the Ngati Tuwharetoa people realized that giving the land to the government would prevent it being sold off in small slices. The area became New Zealand's first national park.

In 1893, **Sir Apirana Ngata** (1874–1950) became the first Maori to graduate from a New Zealand university. He had grown up in the Ngati

---

THE TREATY OF WAITANGI

The Treaty of Waitangi was drawn up in 1840 and eventually signed by more than 500 tribal chiefs. Under its terms, chiefs ceded their sovereignty to the British Queen in exchange for protection and the same rights as British citizens.

However, the meaning of "sovereignty" was muddled in translation and the document remains controversial. The treaty guaranteed Maori the possession of their land and resources, but land was in fact confiscated and relations between the chiefs and the Crown quickly deteriorated.

A lively demonstration of stick dancing

Porou communities of the East Coast and saw it as his mission to save his people from social disintegration and eventual extinction. He helped them to develop and farm their land, while also encouraging them to preserve their culture and maintain their own identity.

More Leading Figures
Dame Whina Cooper (1895–1994) founded the Maori Women's Welfare League. She became a national representative of peaceful protest in her 80s. For two months in 1975 she headed the Maori land march from Northland to Parliament in Wellington (▶ 112), to dramatize the Maori's determination to retain their land and culture.

    Dame Te Atairangikaahu (1931–2006) was the very first Maori Queen and the sixth monarch of the Kingitanga movement on the North Island. She campaigned for the preservation of the Maori language and culture, while also encouraging Maoris to integrate into New Zealand society. Her widely admired efforts won her the respect of the entire nation.

MAORI GLOSSARY

Aotearoa New Zealand   *Kai* food, eat   *Maunga* mountain
Aroha love   *Karakia* prayer   *Moana* lake, sea
Awa river   *Kia ora* a common greeting   *Pa* fortified village
Haere mai welcome   *Kaumatua* male elder   *Pakeha* person of
Haka dance   *Kuia* female elder   European descent
Hongi pressing noses   *Mana* spiritual power,   *Pounamu* greenstone
   in greeting   authority   *Waka* canoe
Iwi people, tribe   *Marae* meeting place

A traditional Haka Otaki Te Rahui group in full dress

No More
MEAT & THREE VEG

From being a gastronomic wilderness up until the 1980s, New Zealand's culinary scene has since undergone a dramatic transformation, to the extent that its chefs are now in great demand around the world.

New Zealand has always produced some superb ingredients – including meat, poultry, vegetables, seafood and fruit – but New Zealanders have not always been as open to new culinary ideas as they are today. There was a time when roast lamb with bland vegetables was the most exciting meal on the menu. Meat and three veg is still a classic, but after simmering in their conservative juices for a long time, the Kiwis are now whipping up a fusion of flavours, with the strongest influences coming from Asia, the Pacific Islands and the Mediterranean.

Cosmopolitan Dining

The number of New Zealand's fully licensed restaurants has more than tripled since the early 1990s, supplemented by hundreds of smaller eateries. From fine dining to sandwich bars, there are plenty of culinary temptations in the cities.

Menus often feature local produce, and most eateries usually offer at least a couple of vegetarian options. Dishes that are sure to please include pan-fried fish such as blue cod, tarakihi or snapper; roast venison (sometimes called cervena) or lamb; crayfish (especially in Kaikoura, ► 132); and whitebait fritters.

INSIDER INFO

Held around March each year in the small West Coast town of Hokitika (► 149), the wildly popular **Wildfoods Festival** (www.wildfoods.co.nz) is certainly not for people with a timid palate. More than a hundred food stalls assemble to dish up "bush tucker" delicacies to crowds of around 22,000 adventurous gourmets during what has become a gastronomic highlight of the local social calendar. Old favourites include possum burgers, crouching grasshoppers, mountain oysters and huhu grubs – 5cm (2-inch)-long insect larvae that taste of peanut butter. To help the digestion, how about a worm slammer (earthworms pickled in vodka)?

WINES 101
White Wines
- Sauvignon Blanc: New Zealand's most famous wine, especially when it's from Marlborough. Typically, it has a gooseberry character with a dry style.
- Chardonnay: These range from big, buttery and full of oak to lighter styles designed to go with food.
- Riesling: A brilliant food wine, excellent value, and best made in the South Island. Canterbury is a leader in the variety.
- Sparkling: New Zealand sparkling wines range from cheap sweet fizz to traditionally made, bottle-fermented brut in the Champagne style.

Red Wines
- Pinot Noir: New Zealand produces world-class Pinot Noir, which tends to be relatively full-bodied. It's hard to grow and make, so quantities are small and it's expensive. The best comes from Martinborough and Central Otago.
- Cabernet Sauvignon/Merlot: Hawke's Bay is one of the few regions in New Zealand able to ripen Cabernet Sauvignon consistently to produce the distinctive fruity red. Merlot is often blended in to soften it.

Maori Cuisine

Traditionally, Maori gathered food from the land and sea, and also farmed such staples as *kumara* (sweet potato). Favourite dishes include tuna, eel, *kina* (sea urchin) and other *kai moana* (seafood), *titi* (muttonbird) and wild pork, while accompaniments and seasonings include *puha* (a spinach-like vegetable), *horopito* (a peppery-tasting shrub), *kawakawa* (also called bush basil) and *pikopiko* (fern frond, sometimes used in a pesto). These are often barbecued or stewed, or for special occasions are cooked in a *hangi* (earth oven). This is a pit dug in the ground and lined with stones heated in a fire. Leaves are then placed over the stones, and meat, seafood and vegetables layered on top. Finally, the *hangi* is covered over with more leaves and earth, and the food is left to steam. Try a *hangi* at Rotorua (►92, 97).

Weird and Wonderful
WILDLIFE

The kea is a breed of parrot

New Zealand is a favourite among wildlife tourists, who arrive armed with binoculars, under-water goggles, cameras and high hopes of catching a glimpse of some extraordinary creatures. Few realize that their first wild-life encounter is likely to be with a possum stretched out flat on the road.

Dolphin cruises are very popular

New Zealand is home to some of the world's rarest animals: kakapo – plump, bizarrely sweet-smelling parrots that have forgotten how to fly; tuatara – ancient, wrinkly reptiles that once shared the planet with dinosaurs; weta – heavily armoured insects the size of mice; and fluffy, flightless kiwi, the national symbol.

When New Zealand broke off from the super-continent Gondwana millions of years ago, its only animals were birds, reptiles and insects. The only land mammals were bats. Without the threat of predators or competition from oppo-nents, birds didn't need to fly and insects could grow to palm size. But there are now a number of stowaways like the possum.

The Possum Problem

Possums are a real pest. These cute critters were introduced from Australia

A yellow-eyed penguin

in 1837 to launch a fur trade, and are now found across more than 90 per cent of the country today. The standard joke about New Zealand is that the nation has more sheep than people – but possums outnumber both combined.

More than 70 million emerge from their sleeping holes each night to crunch on 19,000 tonnes of vegetation, mostly the shoots of indigenous trees. Australia's eucalyptus trees contain natural toxins, but New Zealand's trees have no defence mechanisms. Apart from stripping native forests, possums also rob birds of their food supplies.

While the public roadkill effort may initially come as a rather unpleasant and unusual surprise to visitors, it is but a small part of a huge plan to keep such undesirables in check. At a cost of around NZ$80 million per year, a variety of methods, including poisoning and trapping, are used to keep pests at bay.

A kea at the Willowbank Wildlife Reserve

Feathered Favourites

One of the most memorable wildlife experiences is watching penguins come ashore after their day's fishing. If you are in the right place at the right time, you'll see some of them waddle ashore or perform an elaborate ritual with their mate.

The Otago Peninsula (➤ 177) is a good place to see yellow-eyed penguins and at Milford Sound (➤ 170) you might encounter Fiordland crested penguins.

There are several other peculiar birds. The cheekiest is the kea (alpine parrot), which you're likely to encounter around Arthur's Pass (➤ 160), where it breeds in rocky crevices.

The night-active kiwi is almost impossible to see in the wild, unless you venture as far south as Stewart Island; because they nest on the ground, their eggs and chicks are sitting targets for predators, and all five endemic species are threatened with extinction. But there

A seal basks at Milford Sound

The Magazine

A bird makes its mark in the Awaroa inlet of Abel Tasman National Park

are several kiwi houses in the country – for example at the Whakarewarewa Thermal Valley in Rotorua (▶86) and at the Willowbank Wildlife Reserve in Christchurch (▶158) – and they've been reintroduced to the Zealandia Karori Sanctuary in Wellington (▶110).

New Zealand is surrounded by hundreds of offshore islands. They provide safe havens for endangered species. Kapiti (▶117) is one of the most accessible island reserves, where you can see rare bird species such as the kokako, as well as vivacious kaka (forest parrots) and parakeets.

Marine Mammals

Whales, dolphins and seals live around New Zealand's 15,000km (9,300mi) of coastline. The best place to see all three is Kaikoura (▶132) on the east coast of the South Island. Sperm whales are abundant here year-round. Dolphins cruise the bays around Kaikoura in large pods, and they are also reliably found in the Bay of Islands (▶52).

Hector's dolphins, the smallest species, regularly visit Kaikoura and Akaroa Harbour (▶153) in summer to have their young. If you're looking for seals, follow your nose. The grey torpedoes are hard to spot, but their fishy smell gives them away.

Above: New Zealand's famous kiwi is at risk from non-native predators but several reserves are helping its survival. Below: Bottlenose dolphins swimming just off Stewart Island

Wellington is a hotspot for film producers and actors

From
Mansfield to
Middle Earth

Not so long ago, New Zealand writers and painters were convinced that the only way to find fame and fortune was by leaving their island home behind. But things have changed and now movie stars and directors flock to New Zealand, and Kiwi writers and artists are fêted both at home and on the international stage.

Authors in the Limelight

Katherine Mansfield (1888–1923) is regarded as one of New Zealand's finest literary exports and the achievements of her short life continue to be celebrated at her birthplace in Wellington (► 115). Also held dear to New Zealanders is Janet Frame (1924–2004), whose autobiographical *An Angel at My Table* (1984) was subsequently turned into an award-winning film by Kiwi director Jane Campion in 1990.

The Magazine

Ruapehu, an active volcano, was used as a location in *The Lord of the Rings*

Keri Hulme is best known as the author of the Booker Prize-winning novel *The Bone People* (1984), but she has also produced many short stories and volumes of poetry. Another Maori writer who is creating waves internationally is Witi Ihimaera. The former diplomat and New Zealand consul to the United States became the country's first Maori writer to publish a novel in English. Since *Tangi* in 1973, he has become a prolific chronicler of social issues affecting Maori through such works as *The Whale Rider* (1987). A more recent Kiwi winner of the Booker Prize is Lloyd Jones, for his *Mister Pip* (2006). This novel tells the harrowing tale of a small community on the Papua New Guinean island of Bougainville caught up in the 1990s civil war.

The Visual Arts

The country's most internationally famous artist is Frances Hodgkins (1869–1947), whose watercolours and oil paintings are part of the permanent exhibitions at galleries in Wellington and Dunedin. Other renowned painters include Colin McCahon (1919–87); Rita Angus (1908–70), famed in particular for her landscapes and self-portraits; Charles Goldie (1870–1947), whose paintings of high-ranking Maori are tinged with sadness; and Ralph Hotere (*b.*1931), one of the most respected living artists.

Film Friendly

Filming by Peter Jackson of the successful *Lord of the Rings* trilogy in New Zealand in 1999 and 2000 put the country firmly on the cinematic map, and it continues to be used for its spectacular landscapes growing movie-production expertise. In 2002, Witi Ihimaera's *Whale Rider* was filmed at Whangara, north of Hawke's Bay (➤ 99), gaining Keisha

Soprano Kiri Te Kanawa during a performance of Mozart's *Don Giovanni*

Castle-Hughes, its 11-year-old star, an Oscar nomination for her role. Since then, the locally produced *In My Father's Den* (2004), based on the novel by Kiwi author Maurice Gee, was released to critical acclaim, and Peter Jackson went on to film his remake of the classic *King Kong* in 2005. New Zealand is also tipped to be the location used for Jackson's *The Hobbit* (2011).

The international films *The Chronicles of Narnia: The Lion, the Witch and the Wardrobe* (2005) and *Prince Caspian* (2008), based on CS Lewis's children's books, were filmed in New Zealand, using the country's spectacular scenery to great effect. In 2010 *Boy*, about growing up in New Zealand in the Michael Jackson-crazed 1980s, became New Zealand's highest-grossing film ever. Written and directed by Taika Waititi, it was shot in Waihau Bay.

MUSICAL KIWIS

Soprano **Dame Kiri Te Kanawa** is perhaps New Zealand's best-known singer. Although Dame Kiri has retired from the operatic stage, she still appears at concert halls and open-air venues in New Zealand and abroad. Another Kiwi soprano is Hayley Westenra, who gained international recognition at the age of just 16 in 2003 with the release of her album *Pure*.

Pop music stars include Bic Runga, of Chinese and Maori descent, a singer-songwriter renowned for her haunting ballads; Maori-Nuiean hip hop artist Che Fu; and the band Crowded House. The Grammy Award-winning comedy music act, *The Flight of the Conchords,* aka Bret McKenzie and Jermaine Clement, have gained success in the UK and US as a result of their television show.

The New Zealand EXPERIMENT

As a small nation of resourceful people far away from the rest of the world, New Zealand can afford to swim against the stream and try things others might not dare to consider.

Nuclear Free

When New Zealanders decide to tackle an issue, they aren't afraid to stand up and be counted. This can be seen in the country's controversial decision to declare itself nuclear free in 1987, and to spearhead protests against the testing of atomic bombs in the Pacific. Opposition to French nuclear testing at Mururoa and to visits by US nuclear-powered and armed ships culminated in the sinking of Greenpeace's *Rainbow Warrior* by French secret service agents in 1985. Outrage over the incident is still felt today, and the nation remains staunchly nuclear free.

In a bid to curb climate change New Zealand recently introduced a controversial Emissions Trading Scheme tax to discourage pollutants, and to encourage investment into forests and research.

Necessity is the Mother of Invention

The ingenuity of Kiwis is summed up by the saying that, given a piece of No. 8 fencing wire, they can fix or make just about anything. This stems from the days when spares were hard to come by and farmers had to make do and mend as best they could.

The film *The World's Fastest Indian* (2005) celebrates this inventiveness, telling the story of Burt Munro (1899–1978) and his 1920 Indian motorcycle. Munro

The sinking of *Rainbow Warrior* shocked the world. *Rainbow Warrior II* remained in service until 2011.

modified the machine over a period of 46 years in his garden shed, eventually taking it to the Bonneville Salt Flats in Utah and setting a world speed record that still stands today.

Another well-respected motorbike engineer was John Britten (1950–95), who designed and built record-making machines using exceptional materials; you can see his V1000 model at Te Papa in Wellington (below, ► 110). Other famous Kiwi inventors include South Island farmer Richard Pearse (1877–1953), who built his own plane and apparently flew before the Wright brothers did; and the "father of nuclear physics", Sir Ernest Rutherford (1871–1937), who split the atom – rather ironic for nuclear-free New Zealand.

LEADING THE FLOCK

1893 New Zealand is the first country to give women the vote.

1948 Major protests against the exclusion of Maori players from a rugby tour of South Africa.

1985 New Zealand's anti-nuclear policy leads to the refusal of a visit by the USS *Buchanan* warship.

1994 New Zealand ratifies the Protocol on Environmental Protection to the Antarctic Treaty, banning mining for at least 50 years.

2007 Prime Minister Helen Clark announces plans to make New Zealand the world's first totally carbon-neutral country by 2040.

2010 Prime Minister John Key introduces an Emissions Trading Scheme.

2025 New Zealand aims to produce 90 per cent of its energy from renewable sources by 2025.

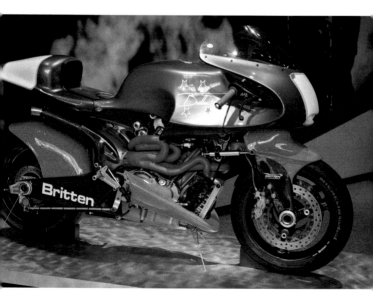

SWEATY JERSEYS and the Auld Mug

Sport is part of everyday life in New Zealand and a major source of national pride. Winning athletes are treated to a hero's welcome when they return, whereas failure to win a coveted trophy sends the nation into collective mourning.

Rugby

Rugby union is the main national sport – some would say obsession – with 150,000 Kiwis playing the game. The professional season starts in February with the Super 15 competition and ends with the National Provincial Championships in late October. The national team, the All Blacks, is among the most successful in the world: they managed to take home the Rugby World Cup for a third time in 2015. The players' every moves are recorded in the nation's memory, and many New Zealanders can recite the names of All Blacks players going back decades. Like film stars elsewhere, rugby players fill the tabloid pages, especially since the sport turned professional in 1995. The team is famous for performing the haka, a Maori dance, before each match, a tradition dating from the 19th century (▶ box).

> "Kiwis are natural competitors"

Yachting

One of New Zealand's biggest sporting coups took place in 1995 when a group of yachties took home the America's Cup, the world's oldest sporting trophy. In 144 years, the "Auld Mug" had left its case in the USA on only one other occasion – to spend a season with the Australian team in 1983. Five years after their historic 1995 win, Team New Zealand defended the title in the Hauraki Gulf (▶ 69), and Auckland's Viaduct Basin was the place to be for every self-respecting Kiwi. Again, New Zealand won the race, this time against the Italian Prada team in what was the first final in the cup's history without American competitors.

Software billionaire Larry Ellison's Oracle Team USA reclaimed possession of the America's Cup in 2010. They also managed to defend their title in a regatta off the coast of California on 25 September 2013 after making a spectacular comeback and edging ahead of their New Zealand competitors.

The racing yachts' designs have changed again and again throughout the history of the Cup, increasing their speeds each time. 2013 was

THE ALL BLACKS' HAKA

The haka performed by the All Blacks was composed by the famous Maori chief Te Rauparaha (c.1760–1849) to commemorate the occasion in 1810 when he escaped his enemies by hiding in a food pit. On emerging from the pit, Te Rauparaha was confronted by another chief, who to his relief turned out to be friendly. Following instruction from the haka leader, All Blacks players join in the actions and words of the chant:

Ka mate, ka mate	I die, I die
Ka ora', ka ora'	I live, I live
Ka mate, ka mate	I die, I die
Ka ora', ka ora'	I live, I live
Tenei te tangata puhuruhuru	This is the hairy man
Nana i tiki mai whakawhiti te ra	Who caused the sun to shine again for me
Upane, upane	Up the ladder, up the ladder
Upane, kaupane	To the top
Whiti te ra!	The sun shines!

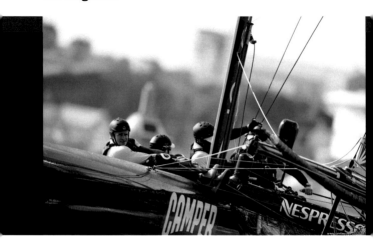

the year of the super catamaran – the Kiwis' boat measured 26m/85ft in length. With its massive wingsail that reached a height of 50m (164ft), the vessel could accelerate to 40 knots (74km/h/46mph) in no time and seemed to almost fly over the water.

NEW ZEALAND'S SPORTING HEROES

- Jean Batten smashes Amy Johnson's solo flight time between England and Australia by six days in 1934. In 1935, the "Garbo of the Skies" becomes the first woman to make the return flight. In 1936 she makes the first direct flight between England and New Zealand and then the fastest trans-Tasman flight.
- Jack Lovelock wins Olympic gold in the 1,500m at Berlin in 1936.
- Sir Edmund Hillary climbs Mount Everest in 1953.
- Yachtsman Sir Peter Blake wins the Whitbread Round the World Race in 1969, and leads Team New Zealand to victory in the America's Cup in 1995 and 2000.
- Mark Todd wins Olympic gold in three-day eventing in 1984 and 1988, and bronze in 2000.
- Hamish Carter wins an Olympic gold in the men's triathlon in 2004.
- Golfer Michael Campbell wins the US Open in 2005.
- Caroline and Georgina Evers-Swindell win Olympic gold in 2004 in the women's double sculls. The pair of identical twin sisters then manage to repeat this feat in Beijing in 2008.
- Valerie Vili takes the women's shot put record at the 2006 Commonwealth Games, wins the World Championship in 2007, and adds gold at the 2008 Olympics.
- 2012 was the most successful Olympic year to date for New Zealand's athletes, particularly in sailing, kayaking/canoeing, the shot-put (Valerie Adams) and rowing.

Outdoor Life

Easy access to wilderness areas and the ocean is one of the reasons for most Kiwis' sporting passion. It would be difficult to grow up in New Zealand without spending significant amounts of time hiking or riding the surf. Another reason is that Kiwis are natural competitors. It's perhaps not surprising that some of the most challenging outdoor competitions and adventure sports began in New Zealand. Whether it's bungy jumping, sailing or extreme races, chances are that a Kiwi holds the record.

CYCLE TOURING

The New Zealand Cycle Trail (Maori: Nga Haerenga), a national cycleway that will stretch from one end of the country to the other, is gradually taking shape. The government has invested NZ$50 million in the initiative. The first finished portion was the Ruapehu-Whanganui Trails Ngā Ara Tūhono, and 20 sections of the gargantuan route have been completed.

NEW ZEALAND'S SPORTING HEROES

Bungy jumping veteran AJ Hackett is one of the driving forces behind New Zealand's reputation as an adventure sports destination. However, bungy jumping is no New Zealand invention. On Pentecost, one of the islands in Vanuatu (in the South Pacific), men have been jumping off high wooden towers for centuries – with their feet attached to elastic vines. In the 1970s, this ancient ritual inspired the Oxford University Dangerous Sports Club to try it for themselves. AJ Hackett saw a video and was hooked. He spent some time testing latex rubber cords before making a series of jumps, first from a ski-field gondola 91m (298ft) above the snow, and then, in June 1987, from the Eiffel Tower, launching an entire industry.

TranzAlpine
TRAIN ADVENTURE

The coast-to-coast traverse of the Southern Alps is one of the great rail journeys of the world. From the Pacific to the Tasman Sea, the TranzAlpine route runs through 224km (139mi) of the South Island's rugged scenery.

The Modern Journey

Today, the TranzAlpine is still popular with regular travellers between the lush and wild West Coast (➤ 148) and the orderly Canterbury Plains, but the comfort level of the modern carriages reflects the growing number of travellers and rail buffs on the train. About 200,000 people have travelled on the TranzAlpine every year since it was launched as a tourist attraction in 1987.

For the first 20 minutes of the half-day journey to Greymouth, the train speeds – relatively speaking – through suburbia and the city's rural out-skirts to Rolleston, where it leaves the main south line to veer west towards the mountains. The train then rumbles through the flat alluvial Canterbury Plains, passing rolling pastures and small rural townships until reaching Springfield, a former railway service centre about an hour from Christchurch, which marks the start of the long alpine haul to Arthur's Pass (➤ 160).

TranzAlpine trains run through spectacular scenery

Here, the bush-clad foothills start stretching beyond the tree line, exposing the first raw rock faces and bare summits.

As the TranzAlpine enters a labyrinth of gorges and hills, it crosses the first viaduct, which spans more than 200m (650ft) across the dry shingle bed of the Kowai River.

Valleys Deep and Mountains High

For the next hour, the journey becomes a spectacular, scenic slide show. No fewer than sixteen short tunnels interrupt the stupendous vistas of magnificent deep-cut river canyons and soaring mountains. About 85km (53mi) from Christchurch, the rust-coloured "T" of the Staircase Viaduct connects two tunnels. At 73m (239ft) (3m/10ft higher than late Christchurch Cathedral), it's the highest of a sequence of tall steel bridges the TranzAlpine has to cross before it can emerge into the broad valleys of the Waimakariri and Bealey rivers. In summer, the braided Waimakariri (Maori for "cold water") runs through its wide gravel bed in trickles and streams, but after a storm it swells to a thunderous river that carves up the landscape.

INSIDER INFO

TranzAlpine Tips:
- Christchurch's railway station is to the southwest of Hagley Park and is not very well connected by public transport. The easiest and most inexpensive way to get there is to take one of the 10-seat shuttle buses that provide a door-to-door service throughout the city. *Insider Tip*
- There is a licensed buffet on board the train.
- There is an outdoor viewing platform on the TranzAlpine, a spartan affair but a perfect place to get good views and take photographs. *Insider Tip*
- Book ahead and arrive early for the train: seats are allocated when you check-in, not when you book.

The Magazine

Arthur's Pass, 737m (2,417ft) above sea level, is the end point of the climb and provides a brief stopping point on the journey. As the train starts its steep downhill ride to the West Coast, it disappears into the 8.5km (5mi) Otira Tunnel for more than 10 minutes.

The Other Side

At the other end the landscape is very different. Dense rainforest hangs over the track and huge flax bushes push against the embankment. Gems on the western leg include the Otira Hotel, the Taramakau River, rich in fish and greenstone, vast patches of rainforest and Lake Brunner.

Upon arrival at Greymouth most passengers opt to stay on for a few days to explore the West Coast. For those eager to experience the stunning views again, the train departs just one hour later for the return journey.

Stunning views of Arthur's Pass can be enjoyed from the train

INSIDER INFO

Planning your journey:
- The train leaves Christchurch at 8:15am, reaches Greymouth at 12:45, begins the return journey an hour later and arrives back in Christchurch at 6:05pm.
- Bookings can be made by calling 0800 872 467 (toll free) or 00 64 4 495 0775 from overseas. You can also visit www.kiwirailscenic.co.nz or buy tickets in person from the reservations centre at the station (open daily 6:30am–3pm). Advance reservations are recommended in summer.

Finding Your Feet

First Two Hours

New Zealand's three main international airports are at Auckland, Wellington and Christchurch. Some flights from Australia also land at Queenstown, Dunedin, Hamilton and Rotorua.

Travelling by Air

- All passengers arriving on international flights have to clear customs and immigration and undergo **biosecurity checks**. Fill in an arrival card and declaration form on the plane. Sniffer dogs at the baggage claim area monitor luggage for **animal and vegetable products**. They're extremely thorough, so don't bring anything with you – including any fruit they gave you during the flight! Officers from the Ministry of Agriculture and Forestry (MAF) will check your declaration form and luggage if necessary. Packaged foods are usually acceptable, but if you're unsure it's best to declare what you are bringing in and **check with the MAF officers**. Failure to declare risk goods carries an instant fine of NZ$400, while knowingly or accidentally bringing in such goods can cost you up to NZ$100,000.
- You can buy **Duty Free** on arrival in Auckland airport. Visitors can import 250g (8.8oz) of tobacco, 3.37 litres (118.6oz) of spirits, and 4.5 litres (158.3oz) of wine or beer. Check online at www.customs.govt.nz.

Arriving in Auckland

- About 80 per cent of all flights into New Zealand arrive at **Auckland International Airport** (www.aucklandairport.co.nz), 23km (14mi) south of the city.
- **Once you exit customs** on the ground floor, there are information and foreign exchange desks, luggage storage facilities, a domestic transfer check-in counter and car hire desks.
- The best way to get to downtown is on the **Airbus** (tel: 0800 103 080 toll free; www.airbus.co.nz, $$), which leaves from the forecourt of the arrivals area. It departs daily every 15 minutes 6am–6pm, every 20 minutes 6pm–8pm, then every 30 minutes until 10pm. The journey takes about 45 minutes to get to the city, stopping at all major hotels and landmarks along the way. It may make extra stops on request if they are en route. Buy your ticket on the bus.
- Some hotels have **free shuttle services** – check if yours does, too!

Insider Tip
- Small **door-to-door shuttle buses** (**Supershuttle:** tel: 0800 748 885 toll free; www.supershuttle.co.nz, $$$), which wait for passengers outside the terminal, are only slightly more expensive than the Airbus but can be faster.
- **Taxis** ($$$$) and shuttle buses depart from in front of the terminal.
- If you are **transferring to a domestic flight**, the domestic terminal is about 800m away. Follow the blue lines painted on the pavement outside the international terminal, or catch the free inter-terminal bus, which departs daily 6am–10:30pm from the arrivals end of the forecourt.
- Any of the transport options from the airport will take you to the city centre and Queen Street, the **main artery** that stretches from Quay Street at the waterfront to the junction of the city's main motorways.

Ground Transport Fares

$ under NZ$10	$$ NZ$11–$20	$$$ NZ$21–$30	$$$$ over NZ$30

Auckland Visitor Information Centres

- The centre at the international terminal is **open daily** while flights are arriving or leaving. The domestic terminal office is open daily 6am–10pm.
- **Inner-city information centres**: Sky City at the corner of Victoria and Federal streets focuses on the capital and is open daily 8–8; the Viaduct Basin branch, 137 Quay Street, Princes Wharf, covers the whole country and is open Nov–April daily 8–7; May–Oct 9–5:30 (tel: 0800 AUCKLAND or 0800 2825 5263; www.aucklandnz.com).

Arriving in Wellington

- **Wellington International Airport** (www.wellingtonairport.co.nz) is about 10km (6mi) from the inner city. The **domestic and international terminals** are housed in the same building.
- International passengers arrive on the **ground floor of the terminal building**. Car hire desks and luggage storage facilities are near the baggage claim carousels, and an information desk, shops and cafés are on the first floor.
- The best way to get to the city is on the **Airport Flyer** (tel: 0800 801 700 toll free; www.metlink.co.nz; $) which connects the airport with central Wellington and the Hutt Valley. It departs from the southern end of the airport terminal every 15 minutes on weekdays (6:20am–9:30pm).
- **Taxis** ($$$) and **shuttles** ($$) depart from bays opposite the main exit.
- **Wellington's inner city** stretches along the waterfront, between Mount Victoria (overlooking Oriental Parade) and the Parliament complex. The main downtown hubs are Lambton Quay and Courtenay Place.
- Wellington can be **confusing for drivers** because the streets don't follow a regular grid and the inner city is circumnavigated by a one-way system. The motorway runs through Wellington. Beyond the city centre it forks into SH1, going north to the Kapiti Coast, and SH2, to the Hutt Valley.

Wellington Visitor Information Centre

- The **main centre** is at the corner of Victoria and Wakefield streets, Civic Square (tel: 0800 933 5363 toll free or 04802 4860; www.wellingtonnz. com). The centre has free maps and information about attractions, accommodation and regional transport. Open Mon–Wed, Fri 8:30–5, Thu 9:30–5, Sat–Sun 9:30–4:30, public holidays 11–4:30, with extended hours in peak season (Dec–April).

Arriving in Christchurch

- International flights arrive at **Christchurch International Airport** (www. christchurchairport.co.nz), about 12km (7mi) northwest of the city centre. The **domestic and international terminals** are close together. Both have information and car hire desks.
- The **Metro Airport Bus** (www.metroinfo.org.nz; $) departs from outside the international terminal, on weekdays every 30 minutes 6:35am–6:35pm and hourly 7:20pm–1am. On weekends buses run every 30 minutes noon–5pm and hourly Sat 8:10am–noon, 5pm–12:55am and Sun 8:40am–noon, 5pm–12:55am. Routes and timings may be subject to change, see details online.
- **Taxis** ($$$$) and **shuttles** ($$) depart from a lane beginning outside the domestic and international terminals.
- Christchurch is laid out in a **grid pattern**, with Colombo Street as the main north–south thoroughfare. Hagley Park is a dominant feature, separating the inner city from the western suburbs.
- Tourist Information: ➤ 152.

Getting Around

New Zealand's major cities all offer a good network of public transport but there are also domestic flights, long-distance bus services and train services connecting the cities and larger towns. For longer journeys, plan and book ahead for the best prices.

In Auckland

- Auckland has an integrated public transport system that comprises buses, trains and ferries. Contact **MAXX** (tel: (09) 366 6400 or 0800 103080 toll free; www.maxx.co.nz) for all routes and timetables.
- At visitor information centres you can get the **Auckland Busabout Guide**, which lists all destinations, their bus route number and departure point.
- The **Link bus** ($), travelling clockwise and anticlockwise on a loop that includes most of the inner-city attractions, runs every 10 minutes at peak times (Mon–Fri 6:30am–8pm) and every 15 minutes off peak (Mon–Fri 8pm–11pm, Sat 6:30am–11pm, Sun and public holidays 7am–11pm).
- The Link and other buses often connect with **ferries** to Auckland's northern suburbs ($$) and to the Hauraki Gulf islands ($$$$). Ferries depart from the berth between Princes and Queens wharfs. The most frequent connections are the 12-minute ferry to Devonport (every 30 minutes or hourly Mon–Thu 6:10am–11:30pm, Fri–Sat 6:15am–1am, Sun and holidays 7:30am–10:30pm), Birkenhead (every 30 minutes or hourly Mon–Fri 7:15am–11:10pm, Sat–Sun and holidays 7:40am–5:40pm) and Bayswater (every 30 minutes or hourly Mon–Fri 7:15am– 10:40pm, Sat–Sun and holidays 7:40am–5:40pm) in the north, and to Waiheke Island (every 30 minutes or hourly Mon–Fri 5:20am–11:45pm, Sat 6:30am–11:45pm, Sun and holidays 7am–9:30pm). Contact **Fullers** (tel: (09) 367 9111; www.fullers.co.nz) for timetables.
- The metropolitan **commuter train service** (MAXX; tel: (09) 366 6400; www.maxx.co.nz, $–$$) runs west to Waitakere and south to Papakura.

In Wellington

- Wellington has an **excellent public transport network**, with buses running frequently and late into the night. The visitor information centre has maps of the bus network; or contact Metlink (tel: 0800 801 700 toll free; www.metlink.org.nz) for route and timetable details.
- **Buses** connect the inner city with all the suburbs, including the Hutt Valley.
- The **Stadium Shuttle** ($) is a special service linking the central city with the Westpac Stadium. For most major events, services commence approximately two hours prior to the start and continue to leave from the stadium about every 10–15 minutes.
- The **cable car** ($) runs from 28 Lambton Quay up to the Botanic Gardens, every 10 minutes Mon–Fri 7am–10pm, Sat 8:30am–10pm, Sun and public holidays 9am–9pm.

City Transport Fares
$ under NZ$5   **$$** NZ$6–$10   **$$$** NZ$11–$20   **$$$$** over NZ$20

Intercity Transport Fares
$ under NZ$30   **$$** NZ$31–$50   **$$$** NZ$51–$100   **$$$$** over NZ$100

- **Tranz Metro** operates a metropolitan commuter train service ($–$$) in Wellington, connecting the inner city with Upper Hutt in the Hutt Valley and Paraparaumu on the Kapiti Coast north of the capital (tel: 0800 801 700 toll free; www.tranzmetro.co.nz).

In Christchurch

- Most **buses** ($) depart from Central Station (50 Lichfield Street), where the Metroinfo counter (tel: (03) 366 8855; www.metroinfo.org.nz) has all route plans and timetables. Staff members will book door-to-door **shuttle buses** ($) to destinations not covered by the bus network.

Insider Tip

Visitor Information Network

There are more than 80 official visitor information centres *(i-site)* in New Zealand, indicated by the green "i" logo. Most of them are open daily, with opening hours depending on the season; www.newzealand.com. Most **telephone numbers beginning 0800** are free within New Zealand.

Intercity Connections

Domestic Flights

- **Air New Zealand** (tel: 0800 737 000 toll free; www.airnewzealand.com; special fares: www.grabaseat.co.nz) is the country's international and main domestic airline, providing daily domestic connections between 26 destinations. The main hubs are Auckland, Wellington, Christchurch and Queenstown, and flights are available to most cities in New Zealand. Booking via the Internet is quick and easy. Careful: there's a luggage limit of 23kg (50.7lbs) per person.
- **Jetstar** (tel: 0800 800 995 toll free; www.jetstar.com), a subsidiary of Quantas, operates flights between Auckland, Wellington, Christchurch and Queenstown. They're extremely fussy about their baggage rules.
- **Air New Zealand Link** Smaller national airlines operating under this brand carry out regional and feeder flights for Air New Zealand.
- **Soundsair** (tel: (03) 520 3080, 0800 505 005 toll free; www.soundsair.com) flies from Wellington to Picton, Blenheim and Nelson, and from Blenheim to Nelson.
- **Air2there.com** (tel: 0800 777 000 toll free; www.air2there.com) offers flights from Wellington to Blenheim, Nelson, New Plymouth, Palmerston North and Paraparaumu.

Buses

- Long-distance buses travel along all major routes ($–$$). The main company is **Intercity** (tel: (09) 583 5780; www.intercity.co.nz), which also operates **Newmans** (tel: (09) 583 5780; www.newmanscoach.co.nz). Both bus services offer a range of travel passes.
- Some bus companies offer special **backpacker deals** that are somewhat lighter on the wallet (e.g. www.magicbus.co.nz, www.kiwiexperience.com, www.straytravel.com, and www.nakedbus.com).

Trains

- New Zealand's train system, operated by **KiwiRail Scenic** (tel: 0800 872 467 toll free; www.kiwirailscenic.co.nz), runs along the main trunk from Auckland to Wellington and Picton to Christchurch, with the TranzAlpine branching to Greymouth (►30).
- Trains are comfortable and about as fast as buses, but more expensive.

Finding Your Feet

Ferries

- **Kiwi Rail** also operates ferry services across Cook Strait (tel: 0800 802 802 toll free; www.interislander.co.nz). It has three car and passenger Interislander ferries; the trip takes three hours.
- Bluebridge sails across the Cook Strait between Wellington and Picton four times daily (tel: 0800 844 844 toll free; www.bluebridge.co.nz).

Shuttles

- Several small door-to-door shuttle bus companies offer useful **regional services**. Ask at a visitor information centre for details.

Driving

- Highways (single or dual carriageway; SH) link major cities; rural roads are usually single-carriageway links between smaller centres; and you'll find unsealed roads in remote areas. Distances are measured in kilometres.
- Outside the main centres, **traffic is light**.
- The usual minimum legal age to **hire a car** in New Zealand is 21, in some cases 25. Most companies require an international driver's licence. Because hire car accidents are common in New Zealand, insurance premiums are relatively high.
- Check with your hire company whether any roads are excluded from your **insurance policy**. Most companies don't cover the road to Skippers Park (➤ 173), and don't allow you to drive on Ninety Mile Beach (➤ 73).
- For up-to-date **road reports**, go to www.maps.aa.co.nz/traffic.
- **Regular road signs** give the frequency for the local tourist radio station. Tune in to hear the hourly news bulletins, which usually end with a traffic and weather report for the area.
- If you are a member of a motoring organization affiliated to the Alliance Internationale de Tourisme (AIT), then you are entitled, for a period up to six months, to reciprocal services from the **New Zealand Automobile Association (NZAA)**. If you break down, call 0800 500 222 toll free.

Road Rules

- **Drive on the left**. On a motorway, keep left unless overtaking.
- **Speed camera checks** are extremely common on New Zealand's roads. During the main tourist season, the police operate an unpopular "no tolerance" policy that punishes anyone who exceeds the speed limit by 4km/h (2.5mph) (usually 10km/h or 6.2mph). The heavy fines are payable on the spot.
- **Traffic signals** are red, amber and green, and you cannot turn left at a red light unless there is a green arrow pointing left.
- All occupants must wear **seatbelts**.
- The normal **maximum speed** on the open road is 100kph (62mph); in urban areas 50kph (31mph); in a Limited Speed Zone (LSZ) it is 50kph (31mph) in adverse weather conditions, 100kph (62mph) in normal conditions.
- **One-lane bridges** are common on rural roads.
- The **legal limit for alcohol** is 30mg alcohol per 100ml blood (blood alcohol content 0.03) for drivers under 20, and 80mg alcohol per 100ml blood (0.08) for drivers aged 20 and over. There is no insurance cover for drivers over the legal limit.
- All **cyclists must wear helmets**.

Accommodation

Choose between luxurious country lodges, campsite chalets, bed & breakfast in a character villa, sharing life on a farm, the privacy of a self-catering apartment or the conviviality of a backpacker hostel.

Hotels

- In smaller towns and rural areas, some pubs offer simple accommodation with lots of character, but they can be noisy.
- Most **hotel chains** are represented in the main cities and resorts.
- **Rates in city hotels** range from around NZ$150 to $700 for a double room. In business areas, hotels may offer discounted rates at weekends.
- Good hotel chains include: **InterContinental Hotels** (Crowne Plaza, InterContinental, Holiday Inn; tel: 0800 801 111 toll free; www.ichotels group.com) and **Choice** (Comfort, Quality Hotels; tel: 0800 692 464 toll free; www.choicehotels.com.au).

Lodges

- From heritage buildings furnished with antiques to exclusive sporting retreats with fishing, hunting or golf, lodges offer **top-class facilities** in beautiful surroundings, usually in the countryside and often with excellent food (from NZ$500 to $2,000 per person per night).
- **New Zealand Lodge Association** Website: www.lodgesofnz.co.nz (book online – you'll find links to the homepages of each individual lodge on the site).

Motels

- Motels are popular with families and travellers who want to drive to the door of a unit and cater for themselves. They tend to be **designed for convenience** rather than charm, but are reasonably priced and generally well appointed, with telephone, television, ensuite bathroom and cooking facilities. Laundry facilities may be located in a separate block. Some complexes have swimming pools and children's playgrounds. Rates are around NZ$120 to $200 per double room.
- Most motels offer **breakfast**, delivered to the unit at an extra cost.
- Good motel chains include: **Best Western** (tel: 0800 237 893 toll free; www.bestwestern.co.nz) and **Golden Chain** (tel: 0800 80 465 336 toll free; www.goldenchain.co.nz).

Serviced Apartments

- Self-catering apartments are increasingly popular in the larger cities. **Centrally situated**, they may be in converted offices or heritage buildings and range from studios to spacious suites, at prices to match. You can pay anything from NZ$100 to $350 per night, though prices are often reduced at weekends and for stays of several days.
- Self-catering apartments usually have **fully equipped kitchens and laundry facilities**, and are serviced daily or according to your needs. They may also have a shared gym, spa, pool and sauna facilities.
- Good companies for finding serviced apartments are: Quest (tel: 0800 944 400 toll free; www.questapartments.com.au); or, in Auckland, Gatehouse Management (tel: (09) 302 1458; www. gatehouse.co.nz).

Finding Your Feet

Bed & Breakfast

- This covers **hosted accommodation** in private homes ("homestays"). The proprietors live on the premises and you can expect a personal welcome.
- Rooms may have **private or shared bathrooms**. There is usually a guest lounge. Some places offer evening meals as well as breakfast.
- **Prices** range from NZ$80 to $200, with dinner extra.
- For more details contact: **New Zealand Federation of Bed & Breakfast Hotels** (tel: (06) 358 6928; www.nzbnbhotels.com) or Heritage and Character Inns of New Zealand (www.heritageinns.co.nz).

Home and Farm Stays

- **Staying with a family** at their home or farm for a couple of days is a popular way to meet the locals. Guests share family meals.
- The **cost** is likely to be around NZ$80 to $150 per double for bed and breakfast, with dinner extra.
- These organizations can help: **Rural Holidays New Zealand** (tel: (03) 355 6218, 0800 883 355 toll free; www.ruralholidays.co.nz), **New Zealand Farm Holidays** (tel: (09) 412 9649; www.nzaccom.co.nz; or www.home stays.co.nz or www.homestays.net.nz).

Budget Accommodation

- **Backpacker hostels** are booming in New Zealand, with about 450 purveyors offering anything from dormitories at NZ$15 per night to double rooms with private bathrooms at around $90. There are **communal** cooking facilities and a lounge. Bed linen may be provided at an extra charge.
- **Campsites and holiday parks** are often in beautiful locations. Many have chalets, ranging from basic units with four bunks and little else at around NZ$50, to more comfortable ones with kitchens at around NZ$120.
- Contact **Budget Backpacker Hostels** (www.bbh.co.nz – note bookings can only be made by phoning individual hostels listed on the website) or **YHA New Zealand** (tel: (03) 379 9970, 0800 278 299 toll free; www.yha. org.nz), **Holiday Accommodation Parks New Zealand** (tel: (04) 298 3283; www.holidayparks.co.nz).

Practical Tips

- **Prices tend to be higher in the main cities** and may climb steeply in the main tourist resorts during the high season.
- **Pre-book in peak season** (Dec to March), and in ski resorts in the winter.
- **Tourism New Zealand's** website; www.newzealand.com, is useful. AA New Zealand Accommodation Guides (PO Box 101 001 North Shore Mail Centre, Auckland; www.aatravel.co.nz), published annually, include detailed accommodation directories, especially of motels and campsites.
- The **Qualmark** rating and classification system, a joint venture by Tourism New Zealand and the NZAA, awards stars to hotels, motels, hostels and holiday parks, based on annual assessments.

Accommodation Prices

Expect to pay for two people sharing a double room per night:

$ under NZ$200   **$$** NZ$200–$350   **$$$** over NZ$350

Food and Drink

With a plentiful supply of fresh, local seafood, meat and vegetables, choices for eating out are endless. Dining tends to be casual compared with Europe, and award-winning chefs are as likely to be found in bustling brasseries and vineyard restaurants as they are in top hotels.

New Zealand Food

- New Zealand's **European heritage** is largely British, with a culinary tradition strong on roast meat, baking and hearty breakfasts. You may still get this sort of food at farm and homestays and country pubs, but nowadays a family meal is more likely to be a barbecue.
- **Modern New Zealand chefs** draw on influences from Asia, the Mediterranean and the Pacific, developing a cuisine that reflects the climate and New Zealand's position in the world, sometimes called "Pacific Rim" food. Menus often focus on regional products, such as beef, lamb, scallops, oysters, wines and cheeses. Many vineyards have restaurants offering food to match their wines.
- Although New Zealand is still largely a nation of meat eaters, most restaurants offer **vegetarian** options, and there are some specialist vegetarian establishments.

Fine Dining

Fine dining in a formal sense is not common in New Zealand. The surroundings may be spectacular and the food exquisitely presented, but Kiwis are informal people. You can get a good three-course set menu for around NZ$50 per head.

Four of the Best

- The Grove, Auckland (➤ 77)
- Logan Brown, Wellington (➤ 121)
- Herzog's, Blenheim (➤ 140)
- Pescatore at The George Hotel, Christchurch (➤ 162)

Cafés

Stylish and quirky, often with deli bars and a reputation for excellent coffee, these are popular meeting places and offer good value. A main course usually costs less than NZ$20; a coffee around NZ$3.50.

Ethnic Restaurants and Takeaways

Informal ethnic restaurants offer some of the least expensive eating options. Japanese sushi bars and Thai, Chinese, Mexican and Indian restaurants are common. Chinese *yum cha* (also known as *dim sum*) is popular at weekend lunchtimes – a range of Cantonese hors d'oeuvres, washed down with copious amounts of Chinese tea.

Hangi

Many places, especially in Rotorua, offer the opportunity to try a Maori *hangi*. Traditionally, this is a simple meal of meat and vegetables cooked over hot stones in an underground oven. Although a version can be tasted at some hotels, for a more authentic experience it's best to go to a *marae* (area around a meeting house) or other Maori venue, such as Tamaki Maori Village (➤ 97) or Te Puia (➤ 87).

Finding Your Feet

Bring Your Own (BYO)

Some restaurants still allow you to bring your own wine to drink with the meal, but they charge corkage (NZ$5–$8).

Pubs

Cheap, hearty meals are available in many country pubs. Pubs serve draught and bottled beer, spirits and a limited range of wine. Boutique breweries offering interesting local beers are increasingly popular, especially in the cities. Smoking is banned in all indoor public areas.

Practical Tips

- **Restaurant hours** are usually noon–2:30 for lunch, and 6:30–10:30 for dinner, although many **cafés** offer all-day dining, and **bar snacks** may be served until the early hours.
- **Service charges and government taxes** are included in menu prices. Tipping is not traditional, although it is becoming more widespread.
- When travelling, **take a picnic** – there may be long distances between refreshments. Places in country towns close early and may not open at the weekend.

The Best for...

...**Location**: Dining Room, Duke of Marlborough Hotel, Russell (➤ 77)
...**View:** Panorama Restaurant at the Hermitage, Aoraki/Mount Cook (➤ 77)
...**Breakfast**: 50 on Park at The George Hotel, Christchurch (➤ 161)
...**Vineyard lunch**: Twelve Trees Restaurant, Blenheim (➤ 140)
...**Afternoon tea**: The Bathhouse, Queenstown (➤ 186)
...**Seafood**: Martin Bosley's Wellington (➤ 121)
...**West Coast tavern**: Lake Mahinapua Hotel, Hokitika (➤ 150)
...**Heritage building**: Chambers, County Hotel, Napier (➤ 102)
...**Country café**: Colenso Café, Coromandel Peninsula (➤ 78)

Kiwi Specialities

- **Kumara:** sweet potato.
- **Manuka honey:** distinctively flavoured from manuka tree blossom.
- **Feijoas:** an egg-shaped fruit with green skin and aromatic, cream-coloured flesh. You'll find it fresh, stewed, pickled or juiced.
- **Tamarillos (tree tomatoes):** egg-shaped fruit with gold or crimson skin and dark seeds. Eat fresh, as a sweet or savoury sauce, or as a chutney.
- **Greenshell mussels:** native New Zealand mussels, with green lipped shells.
- **Bluff:** (deep sea) oysters, crayfish, rock lobster and scallops.
- **Kina:** sea urchins (also called sea eggs), usually eaten raw.
- **Whitebait:** juvenile freshwater fish, mixed with a batter and fried in fritters.
- **Paua:** abalone, with meaty black flesh, usually eaten as steaks or fritters.
- **Pavlova:** meringue and fruit dessert, the subject of much friendly rivalry between New Zealand and Australia as to which country invented it.
- **Hokey-pokey:** honeycomb toffee.
- **Milo:** a popular malted milk energy drink.

Restaurant Prices

Expect to pay per person for a three-course meal, excluding drinks:

$ under NZ$45 $$ NZ$45–$60 $$$ over NZ$60

Shopping

New Zealand is fast losing the sleepy hollow reputation that caused wits to quip that they had visited, but it was closed. Liberalized trading hours mean it's now possible to shop every day in many places. You can find a range of shopping, from chic boutiques and old-fashioned department stores to markets, craft co-operatives and fashion retailers. In the suburbs, traditional shops are being replaced by undercover one-stop shopping centres. Goods posted to overseas destinations are free of the 15 per cent government tax normally imposed, and many stores offer mailing and shipping services.

Arts and Crafts

■ Everywhere you go, no matter how small the community, there's likely to be a **gallery** or **co-operative** selling paintings or pottery, woodcarving or jewellery. Ventures like the Nelson craft trail and the Christchurch Arts Centre (currently closed) let you meet and buy direct from the artists. In Northland, look out for items made from swamp kauri – wood that was buried after an ancient natural disaster. Up to 50,000 years later, it's being unearthed and turned into all manner of objects.

■ **Pictures of native birds, flowers and woods** decorate souvenirs, from mugs to ashtrays, T-shirts and corkscrews to placemats. Paua (abalone) are used to cultivate iridescent pearls, which command top prices.

■ **Maori art** is unique to New Zealand: intricate wood carvings on canoes depict ancestors and tell traditional stories. Paua shell, used for the eyes of *tiki* (human figures), and greenstone (pounamu), used for weapons and symbolic gifts, are now turned into jewellery and ornaments in traditional and modern designs.

■ Also popular are **bone carvings** in fish-hook and symbolic designs – you can even carve your own. Rotorua is a good place to watch Maori artists and hear explanations of their work (➤ 82, 103).

■ **Antiques shops** often turn up bargains for collectors, especially 19th-century furniture and silver brought over by early European settlers. Browse around High Street in Christchurch, Broadway in Dunedin, and Cuba Street in Wellington.

Sheep Products

■ With an estimated 10 sheep to every person, it's not surprising that sheepskin turns up in many guises, from hats, gloves and coats to rugs.

■ The wool is made into handspun jerseys, rugged Swanndri bush jackets, gossamer-soft merino underwear and trans-seasonal fashion knitwear.

■ Lanolin is used in a range of skincare products.

Clothing

■ New Zealand's funky young **fashion designers** are making a splash on international catwalks with labels such as Karen Walker, Nom*D, Zambesi, Zana Feuchs and Kate Sylvester. Their designs are often available here at a fraction of the price you would pay overseas.

■ Some designers have their own outlets in Auckland, but each of the main centres has a fashion quarter worth exploring: High Street and Merivale in Christchurch, Lambton Quay and Willis Street in Wellington, High Street and Newmarket in Auckland.

Finding Your Feet

- **Dress Smart** operates multiple factory outlet shopping malls in Auckland, Hamilton, Wellington and Christchurch (www.dress-smart.co.nz).
- **Outdoors enthusiasts** head to Christchurch – home to such specialist manufacturers and importers as Macpac, Kathmandu, Bivouac and Earth Sea Sky (high quality products made in New Zealand) – to stock up on all kinds of high-tech sports and climbing gear. Christchurch is also home to the Canterbury leisurewear brand, which has outlets in the main tourist centres.
- **All Blacks** rugby shirts and other paraphernalia associated with New Zealand's sporting heroes are available from most souvenir shops.

Wine

- New Zealand wines have a growing **international reputation**, particularly Marlborough's distinctive Sauvignon Blanc, but the range exported is limited, so wine lovers will enjoy the opportunity to discover labels and grape varieties produced by the more than 500 wineries dotted around the country.
- Marlborough and Hawke's Bay are the **main wine-producing areas**, but fine wines can also be found in the Auckland region, Martinborough, Nelson, Canterbury and Otago.
- Many wineries are open for **tastings**.
- **Dessert wines**, affectionately known as "stickies", are particularly good value compared with prices in Europe.
- Specialist shops such as Glengarry in Auckland and Wellington, and Vino Fino in Christchurch have a **wide selection of top labels**.
- For descriptions of individual wines, ➤ 17.
- For more details on **wine trails**, ➤ 46. For tours in a particular region, see the relevant Where to…Go Out sections of this guide.

Food

- In country areas, **roadside stalls and farms** sell local produce, from organic fruit and vegetables to lavender.
- **Native flower honeys** such as rata and manuka make attractive gifts. They are available prettily packaged at souvenir shops.
- **Apricots, cherries, apples** and **kiwi fruit** are turned into fruit brandies, chocolates and preserves – even kiwi fruit wine.
- **Markets** are great sources of fresh food for picnics. Try Auckland's **Otara Market** for Polynesian specialities (Sat 6–noon), or the **Marlborough Farmer's Market** in Blenheim (Oct–April Sun 9–noon) for the best locally grown supplies.

Shopping Hours

- **Shopping hours** are generally 9am–5:30pm, with a late night, usually Friday, until 9pm.
- **In smaller towns**, shops may close at 1pm on Saturday and all day Sunday.
- **In large cities,** supermarkets are often open daily 8am–9pm, and sometimes operate longer hours.

Methods of Payment

Most city shops are geared up for EFTPOS (Electronic Funds Transfer at Point of Sale) and accept major credit cards. Be prepared to pay cash at markets and in some rural areas. Travellers' cheques can be exchanged at most banks.

Entertainment

Outdoor Activities

- **All the major cities are at or near the sea** – Auckland and Wellington spectacularly so – and unspoiled countryside is never far away. Local councils and the Department of Conservation maintain a range of footpaths, and guide maps are available from visitor centres.
- The most popular **swimming beaches** are manned by lifeguards during the summer.
- **Horse racing** is also a popular day out. Each racecourse has regular meetings: phone the local harness racing or jockey club for details.
- **Golf** is very popular, and many courses are in spectacular sites.
- Salmon and trout **fishing** are popular, especially around Taupo and the South Island rivers. Guides there can supply equipment. Sea fishing trips are on offer at all seaside resorts. You always need a permit (which you'll have to pay for).
- Surfing, windsurfing, sailing, parasailing, kayaking, kite surfing, water skiing, scuba diving – whatever **water sport** takes your fancy, someone will be offering to hire out the gear and teach you what to do.
- **Skiing** may be less glamorous in New Zealand than in Europe but, particularly in the South Island, it's accessible, and relatively in-expensive. During the ski season, usually June to September, you can hire equipment on the field or from shops in town.

Adventure Sports

- To many travellers, New Zealand is synonymous with adventure sports such as bungy jumping, jet boating, sea kayaking, white-water rafting, zorbing, sky diving and variations of such activities.
- Make sure the risks you take don't extend to your insurance – it's imperative that your policy is extended before you go to cover named "dangerous sports". The slight extra cost could save you thousands of dollars in medical bills (➤ 204).

Performing Arts

- New Zealand's national symphony **orchestra and ballet** company, both based in Wellington, perform regularly and there are plenty of theatres, opera companies, choirs and orchestras elsewhere.
- At festivals and during the long summer holidays, the **arts move outdoors**, with opera staged under the stars, theatre in the park, concerts held in vineyards, buskers in the street and free programmes filled with family entertainment.

Festivals & Shows

From art deco in Napier (February) to wild foods in Hokitika (March), New Zealanders love **any excuse** for a festival.

- In February, you could also catch the start of the month-long **International Festival of the Arts** in Wellington, and **wine and food** festivals in Marlborough, Hawke's Bay, Canterbury, Devonport and Whangarei. Nelson's Hooked on Seafood festival is held in March.
- Most of the main centres hold annual **arts, music and literary festivals** at different times of the year.
- **Pacific Island culture** is celebrated with Pasifika in March, held in Auckland. For many, the most significant national event is **Waitangi**

Finding Your Feet

Day, on 6 February, when the birth of the nation is celebrated in Waitangi and on *marae* all over the country.

■ **Agricultural shows** (A+P shows) are important events in each region, with funfairs and food stalls alongside the prize cattle, sheep-shearing and wood-chopping competitions. Auckland's Royal Easter Show (April), and Christchurch's Cup and Show Week (November) are among the most popular.

■ New Zealand's major horticultural event, the **Ellerslie Flower Show**, is held at Christchurch's North Hagley Park in March.

■ See also recommendations in the Where to…Go Out sections.

Wine Trails

■ Going to a vineyard for a **wine tasting** or a spot of lunch is a popular pastime, especially during the warmer months of the year. Many wineries welcome visitors and have built attractive cellar-door facilities, which often include a restaurant.

■ **There are eight main wine regions** and each has its distinctive personality but as a rough guide, Marlborough is the biggest, Nelson and Waiheke are the prettiest, Waipara and Martinborough are so compact that you can walk between some vineyards, Hawke's Bay has the best range of reds, and Central Otago has the most spectacular sites.

■ **Wine trail maps** of most regions are available from wineries or visitor centres. Wine trail tours range from small, education-oriented groups to party buses.

Nightspots

■ Apart from the nightclubs on Auckland's Karangahape Road (known as K Road, ► 74) and Wellington's Courtenay Place (► 118), nightlife in most New Zealand centres is focused on restaurants and bars.

■ Several of the cities and resorts have **casinos** that stay open late, or even 24 hours. Some, like Sky City in Auckland, are large and purpose built, with restaurants, bars and several gaming rooms; others are boutique affairs in heritage buildings. Dress codes and age restrictions may apply.

Making Reservations

Many theatres, concert halls and sporting venues use booking agencies such as Ticketek (tel: 0800 842 538 toll free), which can advise on the availability of tickets and make the booking. Check the local phone book.

Gay Scene

New Zealand doesn't boast the outrageous nightlife you can find in some cities, but there are a lot of gay bars and clubs, especially in Auckland.

■ The main area for bars and clubs in Auckland is on K Road and Parnell Road. The busiest nightclub (on Fridays and Saturdays only) is **Family Bar** for a younger crowd. **Naval & Family** has two drag shows on Friday and Saturday nights, and **Urge** is mainly for older guys. **Finale** and **Caluzzi** are drag cabaret/restaurants.

■ If you're in Wellington, try **Club Ivy**. In Christchurch, the quake-damaged **Cruz** on 77 Victoria Street has opened its doors once again (check online at http://cruz.co.nz).

Auckland &
the Far North

 Little Treats

Harbour Tours in a Hurry
Take the passenger ferry to Devonport for some great harbour views as you float over to the **ferry building** (➤ 70).

A Polynesian Bazaar
Otara Market (➤ 79) in the south of the city is filled with vibrant, colourful exotica.

Mail from the Northern Cape
Send your postcards from **Cape Reinga** (➤ 73), home to the northernmost post office in the land.

Getting Your Bearings

Auckland is New Zealand's only truly big city, but size has not diminished its charms. The "City of Sails" is regularly voted one of the world's top 10 cities for its cosmopolitan lifestyle and exhilarating recreational opportunities.

Set between two harbours, Auckland's heart is the waterfront, with its busy wharf, attractive marinas and an inviting café scene. In the Maori language, Auckland is known as *Tamaki Makau Rau* – "the spouse of a hundred lovers" – and Aucklanders certainly are passionate about their city. 1.4 million people – almost a third of all New Zealanders – call Auckland home. Many can't understand why anybody would want to live south of the Bombay Hills, which form an imaginary boundary line south of the city.

Aucklanders have good reason for their local patriotism. Their metropolis blends modern city life with an easily accessible outdoor playground. Even the bustling downtown breathes easily, courtesy of countless parks that cover the city's dramatic volcanic landscape.

Auckland is also home to the world's largest concentration of Polynesian people, who add an eclectic mix of languages and traditions, and who make the city pulsate to the rhythm of the Pacific. The city is the ideal gateway to subtropical Northland and the Bay of Islands, or the Coromandel peninsula. And mountain ranges, rainforests and the glistening Hauraki Gulf with its myriad islands are all within reach.

Cape Reinga **22**

North Cape

Cape Maria van Diemen

23 Te Paki Stream

Ninety Mile Beach **21**

•Houhora

•Kait...

Omape...

Waipoua Tane...

Waitemata Harbour

Auckland Harbour Bridge

Auckland Harbour 12

Auckland City 11

AUCKLAND

PARNELL

Auckland Art Gallery 15 **13**

Auckland War Memorial Museum

REMUERA

Mount Eden 17

EPSOM

BALMORAL

One Tree Hill 16

ROYAL OAK

The Bay of Islands is a popular sailing and boating destination

Getting Your Bearings

Five Perfect Days

You should plan to spend five days exploring Auckland and the north of New Zealand. Follow our itinerary and you won't miss any of the highlights. For more information see the main entries (➤52–74).

Day 1

Morning
From **①Downtown**, get your bearings from the viewing platform of the **Sky Tower** (above, ➤58) before strolling down **Queen Street** from **Aotea Square** (➤57). Collect brochures and bus timetables from the visitor information centre at the Viaduct Basin (➤60), where you can also pick up a map for the Link bus (➤36). The **New Zealand National Maritime Museum** (➤62) is located at the **⑫Harbour**.

Afternoon
Catch the free shuttle from Sky City to the **Kelly Tarlton's Sea Life Aquarium** (➤62). Afterwards, take a short stroll along Tamaki Drive for vistas of Devonport and the **⑭Hauraki Gulf** (➤69). Enjoy views of the **Harbour Bridge** (➤61) on the ferry ride back to the city.

Evening
Return to the **Sky Tower** for night views of Auckland and to try **Orbit**, the revolving restaurant, for dinner (➤58). Ponsonby Road is another good place to eat.

Day 2

Morning
Plan at least two hours to explore **⑬Auckland War Memorial Museum** (➤64) and the Auckland Domain, then walk to the historic **Parnell village** (➤79) for lunch and shopping.

Afternoon

Explore the **⑭ Hauraki Gulf** islands (▶ 69). A "coffee cruise" will give you good views of the islands and some of the best views of the city's skyline. If you are interested in natural history, go for a walk on **Rangitoto Island** (▶ 69). If your tastes are more for arts, fine food and wine, explore **Waiheke Island** (▶ 69). On your way back, catch a ferry that stops at Devonport for a walk and your evening meal.

Day 3

Get up early to fly to Kerikeri. Then hire a car or catch a shuttle for the short distance to Paihia, to start your visit of the ⭐ **Bay of Islands** (▶ 52). In the afternoon visit historic **Waitangi National Reserve** (▶ 53) and explore its historic grounds, the Treaty House and the meeting house.

Day 4

Take a day cruise of the sun-drenched Bay of Islands and the spectacular Hole in the Rock or join a boat cruise to see or ⑳ **swim with dolphins** (▶ 72). Explore the historic township of **Russell** (▶ 63) in the afternoon and evening.

Day 5

Fly back to Auckland, drive to ⭐ **Coromandel peninsula** (▶ 55) and explore Hot Water Beach. If you have any extra days to spare, visit Cathedral Cove and the sandy bays, rugged hills and charming seaside towns in the region.

⭐2 Bay of Islands

The Bay of Islands is one of New Zealand's most popular destinations and a boat-lover's paradise. What you see from the beach is a mere hint of the turquoise and blue wonders further offshore. Sprinkled with almost 150 mostly uninhabited islands, the bay is a subtropical haven of secluded coves, forest-clad hills and unspoiled sandy beaches.

The area is historically significant, as it was here that Europeans first settled in New Zealand. **Pahia**, a small resort that grew from one of New Zealand's first Christian mission stations, established in 1823, is the base for most operators and is the hub for many tourist activities. It has plenty of amenities and is a good starting point for explorations.

Cruising the Island

Insider Tip

The most popular cruises are the **dolphin-watching trips** (➤ 72) during which you may be able to swim with the marine mammals if conditions are suitable, or all-day excursions to the **Hole in the Rock**, an impressive natural arch at the tip of **Cape Brett**. The rugged tunnel cuts through **Piercy Island**, at the entrance to the Bay of Islands, and is just wide enough for a catamaran to travel through on a calm day. The cruise catamarans double as goods-delivery boats and make brief stops at most inhabited islands. Only the farm managers are permitted to build here, and the houses nestle in palm groves or pockets of native forest. It's often impossible to tell whether anybody lives there at all until an excited farm dog bursts forth to meet the boat at the jetty.

A bird's-eye view of the Bay of Islands

Beautiful and detailed carvings can be found in the meeting house, Whare Runanga at Waitangi

Sheltered **Otehei Bay**, on **Urupukapuka Island**, is a popular lunch stop for cruise ships and private yachts. American writer Zane Grey camped here in the 1920s and used the island for his fishing expeditions, but today people come to swim in the clear water or to explore the numerous Maori archaeological sites found here. Urupukapuka is the largest island in the bay and from its summit, about 15 minutes from the beach, there are panoramic views of the surrounding islands and the deeply fissured coastline leading to Cape Brett. The bumpy ride through the Hole in the Rock is an imposing finale, within view of the cape's lighthouse and with the entire bay unfolding before you.

On your return, you can disembark at **Russell**, the first European settlement in the area. Today, it's a small seaside town with whitewashed weatherboard houses and cottage gardens. The waterfront is dotted with cafés and restaurants, which spill out onto the sunny promenade. The town's present tranquillity belies its turbulent past as the "hell-hole of the Pacific". It started out as a destination for 19th-century sailors, whalers and traders looking for provisions, rum and fun after months at sea. The first Europeans to settle were not usually idealists hoping for a new life but largely ship deserters and time-expired convicts from New South Wales, who did nothing to enhance the town's reputation.

Birthplace of the Treaty

It's a short ferry ride back to the bustle of Paihia and from there to one of New Zealand's most significant historic sites. It was in the Bay of Islands that 45 Maori chiefs gathered in February 1840 to discuss and sign the **Treaty of Waitangi**, a document that remains the lynchpin of race relations in New Zealand (▶ 14). So you shouldn't miss the **Waitangi National Reserve**, about 2km (1mi) from Paihia.

The Waitangi grounds include the **Georgian-style Treaty House**, originally built as the home of James Busby, whose job it was to protect British commerce in the embryonic colony, and a magnificent **Maori meeting house**, Whare Runanga. Completed in 1940 to commemorate the centenary of the treaty, 14 carved panels in the meeting house represent the major Maori tribes. This symbolizes the unity of the tribes under the treaty, as meeting houses usually show carvings that relate only to a particular tribe or region. Walk across the sweeping lawns to see two war canoes, launched every year on 6 February for the Waitangi Day celebrations.

TAKING A BREAK

If you want to avoid the buzzing activity of Paihia, there are several **Insider Tip** cafés along the waterfront at Russell. The **Waikokopu Café** at Waitangi is also a good option.

➕ 210 C4

Bay of Islands i-SITE Visitor Centre
✉ The Wharf, Marsden Road, Paihia
☎ (09) 402 7345; www.northlandnz.com
🕐 Dec–Feb daily 8–8; March 8–7; April 8–6; May–Oct 8–5

Fullers GreatSights Bay of Islands
✉ The Maritime Building, waterfront, Paihia
☎ (09) 402 7421; www.dolphincruises.co.nz
🕐 Nov–March daily 7am–8pm; April–Oct 7am–10pm for phone reservations

Most day cruises will include a trip to the Hole in the Rock

Waitangi National Reserve
✉ 1 Tau Henare Drive, Paihia ☎ (09) 402 7437; www.waitangi.net.nz
🕐 Nov–March daily 9–6; April–Oct 9–5
🍴 Waikokopu Café ($) 💰 NZ$25

Pompallier
✉ The Strand, Russell ☎ (09) 403 9015; www.pompallier.co.nz
🕐 Nov–April continuous tours daily 10–5, rest of year hourly tours 10–4 💰 NZ$8

INSIDER INFO

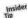

- **Kerikeri**, a charming town surrounded by citrus orchards, is worth exploring for its historic buildings and replica Maori village.
- When in Russell, wander through the 19th-century graveyard around **Christ Church**, the country's oldest, still scarred with bullet holes – legacies of a clash between a group of Maori and the British navy in 1844.
- Explore the Bay of Islands by kayak, underwater or on a tall ship. To **hire a kayak** or join a guided kayaking tour, contact Coastal Kayakers in Waitangi (Te Karuwha Parade; tel: (09) 402 8105, 0800 334 661 toll free; www.coastalkayakers.co.nz). Dive the wreck of the *Rainbow Warrior* (▶ 24), the Greenpeace flagship sunk in 1995, or the HMNZS *Canterbury* with Paihia Dive HQ (tel: 09 402 7551; www.divenz.com). Or cruise in style on board the tall ship the *R. Tucker Thompson* (tel: 09 402 8430, 0800 882 537 toll free; www.tucker.co.nz), which departs for day trips from Russell.

⭐9 Coromandel

Escape from the city to the Coromandel peninsula, with its dramatic coastline and forested mountains. With a history of relentless logging and gold mining, the peninsula has become the cradle of New Zealand's environmental movement, and inspires those seeking an alternative lifestyle.

Much of the peninsula's spine is covered with pockets of regenerating bush and remnants of kauri trees, which were logged almost to extinction during the pioneer period. Its rugged interior is fringed with fine surfing beaches, sheltered inlets and estuaries, and impressive coastal scenery. The shoreline landscape is especially striking on its eastern side.

Natural Beauty and Gold Mines

The gateway to the Coromandel is its main town, **Thames**, on the shallow Firth of Thames about 90 minutes from Auckland, where rich saltwater shallows and mud flats provide a habitat for migratory and wading birds. Thames is the hub of the peninsula. Some of the town's old wooden houses were built during its gold rush heyday. The main attraction is the **Goldmine Experience**, a tour of a gold mine with a rock-crushing stamper battery at its northern end.

Pretty bays and golden beaches line the Coromandel peninsula

The road between Thames and **Coromandel town** hugs the coastline, offering exquisite views over pretty bays and calm beaches. The 55km (34mi) journey is particularly scenic during December and January when the pohutukawa trees are in flower. Coromandel town also showcases its gold-mining history – it was just north of here, at **Driving Creek**, that New Zealand's first gold discovery was made in 1852.

From Coromandel, you can cross to the east coast by either taking the longer (41km/25mi) but more scenic SH25, or the 32km (20mi) unpaved "309 Road", which passes a waterfall and a grove of kauri trees. The state highway winds around estuaries, through holiday towns and past beaches, offering great views of the **Mercury Islands** before reaching **Whitianga**, the peninsula's main holiday resort. It's a pleasant town from which to explore **Mercury Bay**. The bay and the islands were named by James Cook, who dropped anchor here in 1769.

Auckland & the Far North

The peninsula's most popular beaches are south of Whitianga, near **Hahei**. Just north of Hahei is **Cathedral Cove**, a gigantic, arched limestone cavern that connects two sandy beaches but is accessible only at low tide; it appears in the film *The Chronicles of Narnia: Prince Caspian* (▶ 21). To the south of Hahei is **Hot Water Beach**, where thermal waters boil up just below the surface.

TAKING A BREAK

Café Nina (20 Victoria Street, Whitianga; tel: (07) 866 5440) offers home-cooked food in a 100-year-old miner's cottage.

✚ 211 F2

Thames Visitor Information Centre
✉ 206 Pollen Street, Thames ☎ (07) 868 7284; www.thamesinfo.co.nz
🕐 Mon–Fri 9–5, Sat–Sun noon–4

Coromandel Information Centre
✉ 355 Kapanga Rd, Coromandel ☎ (07) 866 8598; www.coromandeltown.co.nz, www.thecoromandel.com 🕐 Mon 9–5, Sun 10–2

Whitianga Information Centre
✉ 66 Albert Street, Whitianga ☎ (07) 866 5555; www.whitianga.co.nz
🕐 26 Dec–end Jan daily 8–6; rest of year Mon–Fri 9–5, Sat 9–4, Sun 9–4

Goldmine Experience
✉ Main Road (SH25), Thames ☎ (07) 868 8514; www.goldmine-experience.co.nz 🕐 Daily 10–4 (phone in winter as hours may be limited) 🎟 NZ$15

Natural thermal waters lie just beneath the sand at Hot Water Beach

INSIDER INFO

■ Be careful if you want to take a swim in the ocean at Hot Water Beach: there are some **dangerous currents** there and several tourists have drowned. You might also want to bring a bucket with you to wash yourself off after a warming dip.

■ Life is altogether less hazardous in Coromandel Town. At Driving Creek, local potter Barry Brickell has built a 2.5km (1.5mi) 🚂 **narrow-gauge railway**, originally to transport clay from one end of his property to his kiln. The railway travels up steep grades, across trestle bridges, along two spirals and through two tunnels.

⓲ Auckland City

Unlike the planned settlements of Wellington, Nelson, Christchurch and Dunedin, Auckland had a slow start. It was not long, however, before its mild climate and scenic maritime setting soon attracted thousands of new migrants. Their vibrant mix of cultures is still obvious as you walk along Queen Street, Auckland's main artery, to the harbour.

Start your downtown explorations in **Aotea Square**, the focal point for Auckland's performance venues and civic offices. In one corner is the **Town Hall**, with its Oamaru limestone facade. On the other side of the square, the low **Aotea Centre** was built at the request of opera singer Kiri Te Kanawa, and is now the country's foremost concert hall.

Head in the Clouds

The three public observation decks at the **Sky Tower** all offer stunning views of Auckland's urban sprawl. Think twice if you're afraid of heights – ascending the tower and standing on the glass floor in the main deck isn't everyone's cup of tea! The map that comes with your entry ticket points out all the landmarks you can see from the top, and there are explanation panels in the observation deck itself. Look for the Harbour Bridge (➤ 61) and Westhaven marina. Then survey Auckland's northern suburbs and cast your eyes across to **Devonport**, the Hauraki Gulf islands (➤ 69) and the Auckland War Memorial Museum (➤ 64) in the Auckland Domain. The distant ranges behind the Hauraki Gulf islands are part of the Coromandel peninsula (➤ 63–64).

Back on terra firma, continue on Queen Street towards the harbour, wandering down the narrow side streets, such as **Vulcan Lane**, **High Street** and **O'Connell Street**, to window shop for gifts and fashion.

Volcanoes on View

The top of the tower also offers views of some of the 48 extinct volcanoes in the area. **Mount Hobson**, named after New Zealand's first governor and Auckland's founder Captain William Hobson, looks like a giant armchair, and

---

SPRINGING FROM THE SKY TOWER

In 1998, AJ Hackett (➤ 29) used the Sky Tower to set a new height record for bungy jumping. Leaping from the observation deck, he fell 180m (590ft) at 130kph (81mph), breaking his own record, set (illegally) in 1997 at the Eiffel Tower. Now you can do the same, with the SkyJump – a 192m (630ft) freefall off the Sky Tower (tel: (09) 368 1835, 0800 759 586 toll free; www.skyjump.co.nz).

Views from a Great Height

There are two ways to reach the largest observation deck of the Sky Tower in the North Island metropolis of Auckland – you can walk up its grand total of 1,029 steps or hop aboard one of its speedy glazed elevators. The choice is yours!

❶ **Sky Tower Gift Shop** Buy some souvenirs for your loved ones back home after your visit.

❷ **Stairs** The winner of a competition held in 2002 managed to climb the tower's stairs in just 5 minutes and 7 seconds. How long will it take you…?

❸ **Elevators** Three glass-fronted elevators with glazed floors shoot 225 people up to the observation level every 15 minutes. The trip takes just 40 seconds at 18km/h (11mph). If you're feeling brave, walk out onto the clear glass floor at the top – it's 186m (610ft) above the city below!

❹ **Main Observation Level** Download the Sky Tower app to learn a whole host of technical facts and figures about the Tower. You can also go analogue and send your family and friends an old-fashioned postcard from the highest post box in the southern hemisphere.

❺ **Orbit** Kiwi cuisine, served 190m (623ft) up in the air: head to Orbit to enjoy a big cooked breakfast or a salad at midday while admiring the 360° view. Go back in the evening to revolve round the whole of Auckland while you eat your dinner.

❻ **Sky Lounge** Fancy a lighter bite? Check out this café with its selection of coffee and snacks.

❼ **Sky Jump** Who dares, wins: thrill seekers who jump from the Sky Tower attached to an elastic cord plummet towards the city of Auckland at speeds of up to 75km/h (46mph) for a grand total of sixteen seconds (► 57).

For another kind of adventurous kick, try the Sky Walk for size: participants don a special suit, attach themselves to ropes and walk out along the edge of the platform at a height of 192 metres (630ft).

❽ **The Observatory** The buffet at this altitudinous eatery specialises in a wide variety of fish dishes.

Enjoy the breath-taking views from the Sky Tower with the entire city at your feet

Simply unforgettable: it takes a lot of nerve to jump from the platform at the top and hurtle head-first towards the earth…

The Sky Tower rises up majestically in Auckland's cityscape

Auckland's evening skyline, featuring the Sky Tower

although **One Tree Hill** (➤ 65) has lost its lone pine tree, it is still easily recognized by the tall obelisk. All volcanic cones are reserve land,.

TAKING A BREAK

If, after your heady trip up the Sky Tower, you feel in need of refreshments, try the rotating **Orbit Restaurant** (tel: (09) 363 6000; Mon–Fri 11:30–2:15, Sat, Sun 11–4:30, daily 5:30–9:30; ➤ 58) or, for a lighter snack, the **Sky Lounge**.

✚ 211 D2

Visitor Information Centres
✉ Viaduct Basin; corner of Quay and Hobson streets and corner of Victoria and Federal streets
☎ (09) 367 6009, 0800 282 552 toll free; www.aucklandnz.com
🕔 For both centres: Nov–April daily 8:30–6:30; May–Oct daily 9–5
ℹ Also at the airport (➤ 34)

Sky Tower
✚ 222 A4 ✉ Corner of Victoria and Federal streets
☎ (09) 363 6000, 0800 759 2489 toll free; www.skycity.co.nz
🕔 Sun–Thu 8:30am–10:30pm, Fri–Sat 8:30am–11:30pm.
Last lift leaves 30 mins before closing time
🚌 Link bus (➤ 34) 🎟 Sky Deck and observation desks: NZ$30

INSIDER INFO

Insider Tip

The **Sky Tower** is open late into the evening – the **views** are particularly spectacular **at night**. **Albert Park**, accessible from Kitchener Street or Wellesley Street East, provides an oasis of calm in the bustling city centre during the day.

⑫ Auckland Harbour

One fifth of Aucklanders own a boat, so the waterfront is where it's all happening. Walk along Quay Street, between Queens Wharf and the Viaduct Basin, to see luxury yachts, tall ships, steamboats, ferries, fishing dinghies and enormous cruise liners all plying the waters of the Waitemata Harbour.

Flung across the narrow Tamaki isthmus, Auckland is surrounded by the sea: the Waitemata Harbour and Hauraki Gulf (►69) to the north and east, and the Manukau Harbour and Tasman Sea to the south and west. The largest of Auckland's six marinas, Westhaven marina, at the southern end of the Harbour Bridge, bobs with more than 2,000 masts, most metamorphosing into full sail every summer weekend.

A focal point of the waterfront is the **Viaduct Basin**, home to Auckland's fishing fleet since the 1930s but extensively rebuilt for New Zealand's defence of the America's Cup in 2000 (►26). The basin is a short walk downhill from the Sky Tower (►58), and only a few metres from the old ferry building opposite the harbour end of Queen Street.

Races on the Waves

The cup races brought the basin alive again in early 2003 but between races the **Viaduct Basin** comes to life in the evenings with bars and restaurants around the water's edge. But you can still get a taste of cup fever: as you walk towards the basin, you will see the *KZ1*, the New Zealand boat in the 1988 America's Cup challenge, strung up across the entrance. And you can book a two-hour turn around the harbour on the 1995 America's

The Auckland Harbour Bridge is over a kilometre (0.62 mi) in length

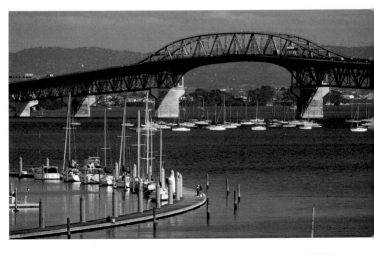

Auckland & the Far North

Cup boat *NZL-40* or a three-hour match race on **NZL-40** or **NZL-41**.

The history of New Zealand yachting and the country's America's Cup victories takes up a whole gallery in the **New Zealand National Maritime Museum**, with the winning yacht *NZL-32 (Black Magic)* forming the centrepiece. You can see the darker side of the sea in the Edmiston Gallery, where there is an exhibition on the sinking of the HMS *Orpheus* on 7 February 1863. In what is still New Zealand's worst maritime disaster, 189 men and boys lost their lives after the ship struck a sandbar at the entrance to Manukau Harbour in fine conditions.

Stories of Discovery and Settlement

The Polynesian discovery of New Zealand is brought to life in a 10-minute video, *Te Waka: Our Great Journey,* while the Hawaiki gallery features a number of original vessels, from Pacific Island dugouts to a twin-masted outrigger canoe. These are fittingly installed in a room beautifully decorated with traditional Maori woven wall panels.

Even more impressive are the displays about early settlement. The 300,000 European immigrants who came during the first wave of settlement in the 1840s faced three to six months at sea, travelling in cramped quarters with no daylight and only a pint of drinking water per day. The museum has re-created one such gloomy bunk cabin, peopled with lifesize dummies; moving floors give an instant sensation of being at sea.

The museum is just beside the passenger terminals at **Princes Wharf**. You may see some of the world's largest cruise ships berthed here, but this area is also the starting point for ferries sailing across the harbour and to the islands of the Hauraki Gulf (➤ 69).

Even seahorses can be seen at Kelly Tarlton's marine attraction

Exploring the Underwater World

Fronting the harbour about 6km (4mi) east of Viaduct Basin is 🔟 **Kelly Tarlton's Sea Life Aquarium**, reached on a free shuttle from Sky City. Kelly Tarlton was an avid diver and treasure hunter, and his idea of showing marine life is the reverse of the usual aquarium experience: here animals get most of the space while humans watch from a confined hide. There are two main sections: in the Antarctic Experience, you can visit a re-creation of Captain Scott's 1911

Insider Tip

The plexiglass tunnel at Kelly Tarlton's Sea Life Aquarium

South Pole hut then board a snowmobile to drive through a vast, authentic Antarctic landscape to see colonies of king and gentoo penguins. Afterwards, you walk past Stringray Bay to reach the plexiglass tunnel where sharks roam freely overhead.

TAKING A BREAK

The **café at the maritime museum** offers a range of reasonably priced drinks and snacks, and there are several bars and restaurants on Princes Wharf.

NZL-40 and *NZL*-41

✚ 222 B5 ✉ Booking booth next to maritime museum, Viaduct Basin ☎ (09) 359 5987, 0800 347 567 toll free; www.exploregroup.co.nz ⏰ Daily; up to five two-hour sailings in peak season. Match races three times a week 💲 NZ$60

Voyager New Zealand National Maritime Museum

✚ 222 B5 ✉ Corner of Quay and Hobson streets, Viaduct Basin ☎ (09) 373 0800, 0800 725 897 toll free; www.maritimemuseum.co.nz ⏰ Daily 9–5 💲 Museum. free; harbour tour: NZ$15

🐠 Kelly Tarlton's Sea Life Aquarium

✚ 222 off C4 ✉ 23 Tamaki Drive, Orakei, Auckland ☎ (09) 528 0603, 0800 805 050 toll free; www.kellytarltons.co.nz ⏰ Daily 9–5:30; last entry an hour before closing time 🍴 Refreshment Kiosk 🚌 746, 757, 767, 769 depart from bus terminal on Commerce Street. A free shuttle bus departs hourly from the Sky City foyer daily 9–4 and from 172 Quay Street 💲 NZ$36

INSIDER INFO

■ Several **historic vessels** are berthed at the maritime museum's marina, including a 1926 steam floating crane and the ***Ted Ashby***, a replica 19th-century scow that takes visitors on harbour cruises (Tue–Sun). AJ Hackett (► 25) runs **bungy jumps off the Auckland Harbour Bridge**, as well as the **Auckland Bridge Climb**, which offers great city views (tel: (09) 361 2000, 0800 286 4958 toll free; www.bungy.co.nz).

■ Opened in 1985, Kelly Tarlton's Antarctic Encounter and Underwater World was built into **disused sewage holding tanks**. The interesting story behind its construction is detailed in a photographic display there.

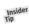

Insider Tip

⓭ Auckland War Memorial Museum

This superb museum houses one of the best collections of Maori treasures and ethnic crafts from the Pacific, and provides a compelling introduction to the country's history and culture. Built as a memorial to Aucklanders who died at war, the museum also chronicles New Zealand's involvement in global conflicts, from the 1800s to the present day.

Set in the Auckland Domain, one of the city's oldest volcanic cones, the Auckland War Memorial Museum Tamaki Paenga Hira is a landmark building with sweeping views across the waterfront. At the entrance a cenotaph is a reminder of the building's origins as a memorial to the country's war heroes. The museum's three architects, who had all served in World War I, chose a Greek neo-classical style to re-create the view of Greek temples they had seen from warships in the Mediterranean Sea.

Welcome to Maori Culture
Once you step inside, you will encounter a Maori warrior blowing a conch shell to draw people to the **exhibition of Maori treasures**. You could easily spend an hour in this part of the museum alone, and it's a good idea to allow two hours for your visit if you want to see other exhibitions.

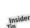
Insider Tip

The best way to start your visit, particularly if you're new to Maori culture, is by watching a 30-minute **cultural performance**, which includes several Maori action songs, traditional stick games, weaponry displays and a *haka*, the fierce Maori war dance.

A ferocious display of fighting spirit

The lavish decoration in the Maori meeting house

The **Maori treasures** are on display on the ground floor – the most impressive being the carved meeting house and the war canoe. Built around 1836 to transport people across Manukau Harbour, the canoe (known as T*e Toki a Tapiri* or "Tapiri's Battle Axe") is the **last of the great Maori war canoes**. One hundred warriors fit inside the 25m (82ft) hull, which was carved by hand from a single totara tree.

Inside the Meeting House

The **meeting house** is a magnificent example of **traditional Maori carving and weaving crafts**, both ancient methods of story telling. Each carved beam and woven panel depicts the stories of a tribe or an ancestor, and was crafted to transmit history from generation to generation. The house on display was a wedding gift, exchanged when one tribal chief's daughter married into another chief's tribe. The building was completed in 1875 and you can see that Maori had already started combining traditional carvings with modern materials such as corrugated iron, paint and milled timber. Inside you will find elaborate carvings of Hotonui, the ancestor after whom the house was named, as well as other, mythical figures.

The building follows the typical architectural plan for meeting houses, or *whare nui* (meaning "big house"), which represent a god-like guardian who watches over the people gathered within. At the apex of the roof is the guardian's head, the ridgepole is the backbone, the bargeboards are the arms, outstretched in a welcoming gesture, and, inside, the rafters represent the guardian's ribs.

Other Exhibits

Right next door to the large meeting house is the much smaller, but equally intricately carved **storage house**.

A House Steeped in Legend

The Maori's defensive settlements, known as *pa*, have existed in New Zealand since the 1300s. They consist of houses grouped around an open meeting space called a *marae*. At the centre of this clearing stands the "Whare Runanga", a highly decorated meeting house that embodies a venerated tribal ancestor.

❶ Tekoteko The roof ridge of the meeting house is topped by this standing figure of the revered ancestor.

❷ Roof Ridge The face of the ancestor can be seen in the form of a mask under the roof ridge. His outstretched right and left arms *(maihi)* are represented by the bargeboards on the roof's sloping edges.

❸ The Interior The interior of the house represents the ancestor's chest. The ridge beam acts as his spine.

❹ Rafters and Uprights The building's rafters and uprights symbolise the ancestor's ribs.

❺ Stories and Myths The artistic carvings on the interior walls display depictions of Maori mythology. A common character to look out for is Kupe, a seafarer who is often shown discovering New Zealand and fighting with a gigantic octopus.

Maori buildings aren't just museum pieces: the North Island boasts lots of richly decorated meeting houses that are still used for festivals, dancing, welcoming ceremonies and recitals of traditional song to this day.

A man plays a traditional shell trumpet as part of the national Waitangi Day celebrations

A traditional carved figure

Impressively proportioned: the museum's model of a Maori war canoe

Auckland & the Far North

These were erected on stilts to stop animals and water from damaging the precious food reserves inside. Take your time to explore the nearby collection of carved paddles, weapons and garments. There are also a number of objects used during rituals.

Upstairs, the emphasis moves away from Maori culture. The **first floor** has displays on **natural history** and two discovery centres, while the **second floor** focuses on war-related exhibits.

TAKING A BREAK
Try the **Columbus Café** in the atrium (daily 10–5).

➕ 222 near C2 ✉ The Domain, Auckland
☎ (09) 309 0443, 0800 256 7386 toll free, (09) 306 7067 recorded info; www.aucklandmuseum.com
🕐 Daily 10–5; closed 25 April (Anzac Day) morning.
Maori cultural performance: daily 11, noon, 1:30 (also 2:30, Jan–April)
🚌 Link bus (➤ 34)
💰 Cultural show: NZ$5; temporary exhibitions may cost extra;

A warrior in the War Memorial Museum brings the past to life

⑭ Hauraki Gulf

The balmy seas and enchanting islands of the Hauraki Gulf are only 30 minutes from downtown Auckland. More than 50 islands provide a refuge for both endangered wildlife and city-weary humans.

Rangitoto
Island as
seen from
One Tree Hill

The Hauraki Gulf is a protected marine area stretching from north of Auckland to the Coromandel peninsula (► 55). Several outer islands are nature reserves, off limits to people. However, the inner gulf islands are public reserves and visitors are free to explore. Ferry services leave Auckland's waterfront each day for Rangitoto and Waiheke, and there are sailings each week to other islands.

Rangitoto Island
Rangitoto guards the entrance to the Waitemata Harbour and is Auckland's largest and youngest volcanic cone. Its last eruption was only 600 years ago, and its **volcanic landscape** is clearly unfinished, almost alien, with eerie lava caves, rugged rock formations and primeval vegetation. The hardened lava hasn't had time to break down into soil, and the lower reaches of the island are covered in pohutukawa trees, growing straight from the fissured rock. There are no rivers, no lakes and no fresh water; any rainfall trickles straight through to underground reservoirs.

The strange landscapes alone are worth the visit, but the island's summit offers **spectacular views**. Guided tours cover the entire island on a canopied trailer towed by a tractor, which takes you to the start of a boardwalk, 900m from the summit.

Insider
Tip

Waiheke Island
Waiheke is a complete contrast: perfect for relaxing on sandy beaches. Covering 93km² (36mi²), it is the second largest of the gulf islands after Great Barrier Island, and it

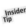

Auckland & the Far North

Waiheke's small port Matiatia

is also the most accessible (by ferry, car ferry or helicopter). In the past, it attracted mostly alternative lifestylers, but has since developed into a genteel suburb of Auckland. During the summer the island's 8,000 population swells to more than 30,000.

As you arrive at Waiheke's small port of **Matiatia**, buses, taxis, shuttles and trikes will be waiting to take you uphill to the island's main settlement of **Oneroa**, 2km (1mi) away. On the way to Oneroa is the **Artworks centre**, with several galleries, businesses, and the local visitor information centre. From there you can explore the beaches between the Oneroa and Onetangi bays and the southern coastline.

TAKING A BREAK

A Fullers **"coffee cruise"** provides a commentated tour around Auckland Harbour.

➕ 211 D/E2

Fullers Cruise Centre
➕ 211 B2 ✉ Ferry Building, 99 Quay Street, Auckland
☎ (09) 367 9111; www.fullers.co.nz
🕐 Office: daily 8–5:30;
phone reservation line: Mon–Fri 7:30–6, Sat–Sun 8–5

Waiheke Visitor Information Centre
➕ 211 D2 ✉ 2 Korora Road, Oneroa
☎ (09) 372 1234; www.waihekenz.com
🕐 Daily 9–5

INSIDER INFO

■ If you are planning to visit **Rangitoto Island**, bring sturdy footwear, sun protection and drinking water. **Tiritiri Matangi Island** is an open sanctuary where you can see endangered birds in their natural habitat. Up to seven days a week in peak season, ferries and small planes depart for **Great Barrier Island**, a mountainous island 90km (55mi) from Auckland. It's a popular destination for hiking, riding and water sports.

■ On the first floor of the **Auckland War Memorial Museum** (▶ 64), look for the footprints of an adult, child and dog made in the ash that fell during the last Rangitoto eruption and which have since hardened to a concrete.

At Your Leisure

15 Auckland Art Gallery

The reopened Auckland Art Gallery boasts the most comprehensive collection of New Zealand and international art in the country. Hosts temporary exhibitions and changing displays of the permanent collection, including works by prominent artists.

🏠 222 B3
✉ Corner of Wellesley and Lorne streets
☎ (09) 379 1349 (24-hour info line); www.aucklandartgallery.com
🕙 10–5; free tours daily 11:30am and 1:30pm
🍴 Café ($) 🚌 Link bus 🎫 Free; you only have to pay for special exhibitions.

16 One Tree Hill

This (along with Mount Eden) is the place to come for fantastic views of Auckland, but it also has an eventful history. Many of the volcanic cones around Auckland were once occupied by Maori, and One Tree Hill has remnants of a *pa*, or fortified village. The eponymous tree, however, is gone (► panel) and only the obelisk remains atop. On the fringe of the hill is the Stardome Observatory and Planetarium, which has a 360° digital dome theatre.

🏠 222 A2

Stardome Observatory and Planetarium
✉ Near gates to One Tree Hill Domain, 670 Manukau Road
☎ (09) 624 1246; www.stardome.org.nz
🕙 Mon 9–3:30, Tue–Fri 9:30am–4:30pm, Sat 12:30–5, Sun 11:30–9:30. Evening shows: Tue–Thu, Sun 8:30–9:30, Fri, Sat 6:30–11
🚌 302, 304, 305, 312 from mid-city
🎫 NZ$10

THE STORY OF ONE TREE HILL

The summit of One Tree Hill (also known by its Maori name Maunga-kiekie) was once marked by its single sacred totara tree. After settler vandals cut it down in 1852, Sir John Logan Campbell (a founder and mayor of Auckland) planted a pine to make amends. However, his choice of an exotic tree over a native totara proved to be controversial and provoked some local Maori to attack it with a chainsaw in the early 1990s. The tree has now been removed.

One Tree Hill offers stunning views over Auckland

Auckland & the Far North

Views of Auckland from Mount Eden

🔟 Mount Eden

Mount Eden (Maungawhau) is Auckland's highest volcanic scoria cone, and from its 196m (643ft) summit there are panoramic views of Auckland. Several quarries once produced dressed stone from here for the city's older buildings and the basalt kerbstones that line its streets. One quarry on the flanks of Mount Eden has since been rehabilitated as **Eden Garden**, known for its camellias and rhododendrons. July and August are the best times to see the flowers in bloom.

➕ 222 A2 ✉ 24 Omana Avenue. Road access to a car park near the summit off Mount Eden Road; pedestrian access from Clive Road and Owens Road (steep path). Access to Eden Garden is via Mountain Road to Omana Avenue
☎ (09) 638 8395; www.edengarden.co.nz
🕐 Garden: Sep–April 9–4:30; May–Aug 9–4
🍴 Café ($) daily 10–4
🚌 274, 275 from Commerce Street
💲 NZ$8; free for children under 12

🔟 Piha Beach

About an hour's drive from central Auckland, the city's western coastline is dramatic and rugged, with many iron-sand beaches. Piha Beach is one of the most popular black beaches and comes alive in summer with surf competitions, horse races and beach parties. Jutting several metres into the ocean is windswept **Lion Rock**, which has a short, steep track leading to its 101m (331ft) summit (a one-hour return trip). Beware: west coast beaches have powerful currents and you should always stay between the flags. Keep children under supervision and if in doubt, ask a lifeguard.

➕ 211 D2 ℹ www.piha.co.nz

🔟 Muriwai Beach

The colony of Australasian gannets was once confined to a small rock stack offshore, but has now spilled over to several cliffs along Muriwai Beach. An easy walking track skirts the cliffs, providing views of elegant seabirds as they nest on the rocks or dive for fish (binoculars are useful here). The first birds begin nesting in late July and their numbers peak by mid-November. Chicks fly when they are 15 weeks old and migrate to the east and south coasts of Australia. Several years later they return to Muriwai Beach to breed. The road to Muriwai Beach is signposted from Waimauku on SH16.

➕ 210 B3

🔟 Dolphins

The experience of seeing hundreds of dolphins swirling in the water with you is unforgettable, particularly as the water in the Bay of Islands is relatively warm, reaching 23°C (73°F) in January and February. Operators supply wetsuits, masks, snorkels and fins, and will generally take you on another free trip if you don't see any dolphins or whales. Visitor information centres in Auckland and Paihia list operators, but two reputable companies are detailed below.

➕ 210 C4

Swim with Dolphins

✉ Corner of Marsden and Williams roads, Paihia
☎ (09) 402 8234, 0800 365 744 toll free;
www.exploregroup.co.nz 🔷 Nature tours, snorkelling, swimming with dolphins

Fullers Great Sights

🞤 210 B4 ✉ The Maritime Building, Paihia
☎ (09) 402 7421, 0800 653 339 toll free;
www.dolphincruises.co.nz
🎫 Cruises, swimming with dolphins,
dolphin and whale watching

🄴 Ninety Mile Beach

If you want to go north as far as
Cape Reinga (see right) and Ninety
Mile Beach, take a morning flight
from Auckland to Kaitaia, and set
aside a day to drive to the country's
northern tip. Ninety Mile Beach is
the western portal through which
sands have been blown to create
the Aupouri peninsula, a skein of
land connecting Kaitaia with North
Cape and Cape Reinga, which were
once islands. The sand originates
from the volcanic eruptions of the
central North Island; the rock created was worn down and carried
north by the Waikato River, ocean
currents and the wind. Much of the
dune landscapes are now covered
by forests, but almost the entire
western coast is flanked by Ninety
Mile Beach (actually 90km/56mi
long). The beach is so hardened
that you can drive on it, but most
hire cars aren't insured for this.

Three roads lead from the main road
to the beach, sometimes negotiable
only by 4WD vehicles. Daily bus
tours and scenic flights are available
or simply take a beach walk.
🞤 210 A5

Information Far North
✉ Centennial Park, South Road, Kaitaia
☎ (09) 408 0879; www.visitfarnorthnz.co.nz
🕔 Daily 8:30–5

🄵 Cape Reinga

In Maori legend, Cape Reinga is
the departure point for spirits of the
dead, which travel from here to the
mythical homeland of Hawaiki. The
gnarled branches of an 800-year-old
pohutukawa tree, seen hanging off
the cliff-face at Cape Reinga, form
the entrance to the underworld.

The cape is often referred to as
New Zealand's northernmost point,
but that title is actually taken by
a cliff face at North Cape, 30km
(20mi) to the east. Nevertheless,
it's invigorating to walk on windswept Cape Reinga. It's the con-
vergence zone of the Tasman Sea
and the Pacific Ocean, and on a
stormy day 10m (30ft) waves swirl
around Columbia Bank below

Ninety Mile Beach – despite its name, the beach is actually only 56 miles long

Auckland & the Far North

Cape Reinga lighthouse. Tracks lead to the beaches on either side of Cape Reinga and to Cape Maria van Diemen.

✚ 210 A5

23 Te Paki Stream

Most of the northern sand dunes are now covered with forests, but where the wind blows unfettered, the sand has formed landscapes of rare elemental beauty, such as the giant, shifting dunelands that have built up at Te Paki stream. The turn-off to Te Paki stream is about 15km (9mi) from Cape Reinga. A picnic area is set aside at the road end, immediately below towering 30m (100ft) sand hills. Watch out for signs warning about areas of quicksand in the stream.

✚ 210 A5

24 Waipoua Forest & Tane Mahuta

Waipoua Forest is the largest re-maining tract of native kauri forest in Northland, which was once dominated by these giant trees. Most were felled for their timber during early settlement. However, pockets of kauri, such as Waipoua Forest, remain along the western coast.

It's not so much the height of kauri trees that is impressive as their girth and age. Tane Mahuta is the oldest kauri tree, a "mere"

52m (170ft) tall but with a girth of more than 13m (43ft) and an estimated age of 1,250 years. It stands in the northern reaches of Waipoua Forest (look for the road signs), and is only a short walk from SH12, which runs through the forest and along the west coast of Northland. About 2km (1mi) further south is another turn-off and car park; a track leads to The Four Sisters, a rare stand of four tall trees. Watch out for kauri trees whenever you turn a corner along SH12. No kauri was felled when the road was cut through the forest, so it has to wind its way around the giant trees.

✚ 210 B4

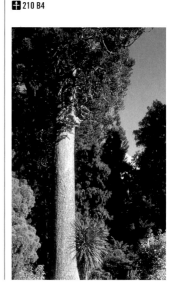

The native kauri are ancient giants; the oldest is estimated to be 1,250 years old

Where to...
Stay

Prices
Expect to pay for a double room per night:
$ under NZ$200 $$ NZ$200–$350 $$$ over NZ$350

AUCKLAND

The Great Ponsonby Art Hotel $$
This restored 1898 villa lies down a quiet street in the lively district of Ponsonby. Near by are Auckland Zoo, Eden Park and the waterfront. Bed-and-breakfast accommodation ranges from standard ensuite rooms with private balcony to luxury garden studios. The house is furnished with New Zealand Pacific artworks.
⊞ 222 off A4 ⊠ 30 Ponsonby Terrace
☎ (09) 376 5989; www.greatpons.co.nz

The Heritage $–$$$
Formerly an art deco department store, The Heritage is in a downtown location. It has 467 rooms and suites straddling two sites. The complex has a tennis court, ballroom, swimming pools, health clubs, restaurants, bar and shops. Suites have a bedroom, living and dining area, and full kitchen and there are options for guests with disabilities.
⊞ 222 A4 ⊠ 35 Hobson Street
☎ (09) 379 8553; www.heritagehotels.co.nz

The Langham Auckland $$–$$$
This five-star luxury hotel has convenient access by car but is also an easy walk to the Auckland Domain and War Memorial Museum. Its spa, Chuan Spa, is one of the most luxurious in the country. High tea is served daily (with or without champagne) in The Winery. Barolo restaurant takes its inspiration from the home of the Slow Food movement, Northern Italy's Piedmont region.

⊞ 222 B2 ⊠ 83 Symonds Street
☎ (09) 379 5132;
www.auckland.langhamhotels.co.nz

Sky City Hotel $–$$$
Part of the downtown Sky City complex, this hotel's 306 deluxe rooms and 38 suites all have super-king beds or double twins and many boast harbour views. There are also 17 restaurants and bars on site, two casinos, a heated rooftop pool, a sauna and a gym. The Sky City Grand Hotel is even more luxurious and home to the award-winning Dine by Peter Gordon restaurant.
⊞ 222 A3
⊠ Corner of Victoria and Federal streets
☎ (09) 363 6000, 0800 759 2489 toll free;
www.skycity.co.nz

WAIHEKE ISLAND

Vineyard Guesthouse $$–$$$
At the edge of Kennedy Point Vineyard on Waiheke Island (► 69), and with views across the Hauraki Gulf to Rangitoto Island, this beautifully furnished guesthouse offers a variety of accommodation. You can rent just one bedroom, or if you have a larger party the whole three-bedroom house. The vineyard itself produces quality red wines and a Sauvignon Blanc, as well as olive oil. Also available is a cosy two-bedroom beachside cottage on Great Barrier Island.
⊞ 211 D2 ⊠ Kennedy Point Vineyard,
44 Donald Bruce Road, Waiheke Island
☎ (09) 372 5600;
www.kennedypointvineyard.com

Auckland & the Far North

Copthorne Hotel and Resort Bay of Islands $–$$

This sprawling complex has an attractive waterfront location and landscaped gardens, and is conveniently set adjacent to the Waitangi National Reserve (➤ 53). The 180 rooms and suites are fairly standard, but the freeform rock swimming pools will appeal to children in particular. There is also a spa, massage studio and tennis courts, a restaurant and a bar, and next door is an 18-hole golf course (➤ 80). The resort offers very reasonable last-minute and off-season rates – see the website for details.

Insider Tip

➕ 210 C4 ✉ Tau Henare Drive, Paihia
☎ (09) 402 7411;
www.copthornebayofislands.co.nz

Ludbrook House $$

Ludbrook house is set on a 420ha (1,037-acre) sheep and cattle property, halfway between Paihia and the Kauri Coast. The Ludbrook family has been farming here since the mid-19th century. The homestead, built in the 1920s, has commanding views and is surrounded by mature gardens. Decorated in period style, it is a gallery for work by local artists. The four guest rooms are simply but comfortably furnished and have private bathrooms. Dinners are also provided.

➕ 210 C4 ✉ 7491 SH1, Uhaeawai, RD2, Kaikohe
☎ (09) 405 9846; www.ludbrook.co.nz

The Sanctuary $$$

This luxury bed and breakfast sits above an unmilled coastal rainforest surrounded by a native bush reserve with views to the Russell peninsula and beyond. Four spacious guest bedrooms on two floors ensure this lodge remains a hideaway, yet is only minutes from Paihia. Evening meals can also be booked and are served at a large table with fellow guests.

➕ 210 C4 ✉ SH 11, Port Opua, Bay of Islands
☎ (09) 402 6075;
www.sanctuarybayofislands.co.nz

The White House $$

This renovated villa was built during the first half of the nineteenth century, making it one of the oldest existing houses in New Zealand. Guests can choose between three comfortable, tastefully furnished *en suite* rooms. The breakfast buffet is included in the room price, but you'll have to pay extra for any *à la carte* dishes. Guests are free to use the fully equipped kitchen during the day, and you can cook any fish you catch on the grill outside. If you'd rather eat out, all of the local restaurants are easily accessible on foot.

➕ 210 C4 ✉ 7 Church Street, Russell
☎ (09) 403 7676;
www.thewhitehouserussell.co.nz

Kuaotunu Bay Lodge $$

This purpose-built lodge is set in 5ha (12 acres) of pasture and native bush overlooking Kuaotunu beach, with views of the Coromandel peninsula and nearby islands. Guest rooms have private bathrooms and French windows leading onto a private deck. Light evening meals are available by arrangement.

➕ 211 E2 ✉ SH25, RD2, Whitianga
☎ (07) 866 4396; www.kuaotunubay.co.nz

Villa Toscana $$–$$$

Giorgio and Margherita Allemano built a grand Tuscan villa in the hills above Whitianga, with spectacular views. The lower level is a lavish, self-contained, two-bedroom suite. Breakfast is provided and you can choose to dine with the Allemanos, who are lovers of gourmet Italian food. They also own a game-fishing boat, which guests can charter.

➕ 211 E2 ✉ Ohuka Park, Whitianga
☎ (07) 866 2293; www.villatoscana.co.nz

Where to…
Eat and Drink

Prices
Expect to pay per person for a meal, excluding drinks:
$ under NZ$45 $$ NZ$45–$60 $$$ over NZ$60

AUCKLAND

The Grove $$$
Crowned Auckland's best restaurant by *Metro* magazine, owner and award-winning sommelier Michael Dearth and his wife Annette hire some of the best chefs in New Zealand.

Wine matching to every course is The Grove's speciality. Try the perfect Hans Herzog with a starter of tuna sashimi and the velvety Mt Difficulty Pinot Noir with their superb pork belly and loin with petit pois dotted with edible flowers.

➕ 222 A/B4
✉ St Patrick's Square, Wyndham Street
☎ (09) 368 4129; www.thegroverestaurant.co.nz
🕒 Mon–Fri noon–late, Sat 6pm–late

Kermadec $$–$$$
Seafood is the theme of this first-floor complex in the Viaduct Basin. It has a casual brasserie and bar, which spills out onto a balcony. The upmarket restaurant next door carries the sea theme into its dramatic decor, with bright tapa-cloth sails slung from the ceiling and Japanese tatami rooms with a water wall and stone garden. As well as traditional Japanese *sashimi*, you can order seafood platters to share as well as delicious fusion dishes like seared tuna steak on soba noodles in shiitake and oyster mushroom broth.

➕ 222 B5 ✉ Viaduct Quay
☎ (09) 304 0454; www.kermadec.co.nz
🕒 Brasserie: daily 10–8;
restaurant: Mon–Fri noon–3, 6pm–late,
Sat–Sun 6pm–late

Prego $
One of the longest-standing eateries on Ponsonby Road's "munchy mile", this stylish Italian café serves good food (including pizzas and dishes from the grill) at reasonable prices. Dine alfresco in the enclosed front courtyard or inside the busy bistro-style restaurant itself.

➕ 222 off A3
✉ 226 Ponsonby Road
☎ (09) 376 3095; www.prego.co.nz
🕒 Daily noon–late; closed 25 and 26 Dec

WAIHEKE ISLAND

Mudbrick Vineyard and Restaurant $$$
Built in French provincial style from handmade earth bricks, Mudbrick Vineyard has spectacular views over the Hauraki Gulf. The upmarket restaurant offers an à la carte menu of French and rural vineyard dishes, like wafer-thin slices of seared venison fillet. Vegetables come from the vineyard's own gardens. Tours and tastings are also available.

Insider Tip

➕ 211 D2 ✉ 126 Church Bay Road, Oneroa
☎ (09) 372 9050; www.mudbrick.co.nz
🕒 Daily noon–3, 6–9

BAY OF ISLANDS

The Dining Room and Bistro, Duke of Marlborough Hotel $–$$
It's hard to think of a more romantic place than this old waterfront hotel in Russell. The site of so many dramatic goings-on in New Zealand history (► 53), it's now a peaceful spot, looking onto the sparkling

water and bobbing boats of the bay. The more formal Dining Room, which has a weatherproof veranda, is open for dinner only, while the Bistro serves lighter meals all day. Burgers, steaks and chicken are on offer as well as fresh local fish.

✚ 210 C4 ✉ 35 The Strand, Russell
☎ (09) 403 7829; www.theduke.co.nz
🕐 Dining Room: daily 6pm–10pm; bistro: daily 11–9

Marsden Estate $$

Named after Reverend Samuel Marsden, who planted New Zealand's first grapevines in Kerikeri in 1819, Marsden Estate is one of several vineyards that are bringing winemaking back to Northland. Guests can sit inside the informal restaurant itself or outdoors on a patio overlooking the vines. The menu ranges from antipasto platters to main courses such as chargrilled lamb. There is also a range of desserts from which to choose.

✚ 210 C4 ✉ Wiroa Road, Kerikeri
☎ (09) 407 9398; www.marsdenestate.co.nz
🕐 Aug–May daily 10–5, June–July 10–4

Only Seafood $

Seafood is an obvious choice in the Bay of Islands, an area famous for its game fishing. At Only Seafood, housed in a weatherboard building on the Paihia waterfront, you don't only get seafood – you also get a view. Oysters farmed locally at Orongo Bay are one of the specialities here. So is gamefish, served lightly seared with Asian seasonings, and hapuka.

✚ 210 C4 ✉ 40 Marsden Road, Paihia
☎ (09) 402 6066
🕐 Daily from 5pm; closed 25 Dec

The Wharf Restaurant and Bar $

This renowned waterfront restaurant is in the historic town of Russell. There are lovely views of the bay through wide glass windows, and in summer you can sit outside watching yachts swing on their moorings. Chef de Cuisine David Hull brings his experience in France and Australia by combining Mediterranean and Pacific Rim flavours with the local cuisine. Try the chargrilled gamefish with cannellini beans. Be sure to leave room for one of the tempting desserts – the bay espresso crème brûlée is particularly good. Reservations are recommended.

✚ 210 C4 ✉ 29 The Strand, Russell
☎ (09) 403 7771; www.thewharfrussell.co.nz
🕐 Oct–April daily 9–3, 5–late, May–Sep 5–late

COROMANDEL PENINSULA

Colenso Café $

This café and country shop on the main highway between Whitianga and Tairua is a delightful place to stop for lunch or a snack. Set in an old-fashioned herb garden, it has shady verandas where you can sit and relax among the flowers, and also tables indoors, where the rooms are crammed with goods made by local craftspeople. The blackboard menu includes home-baked lunch dishes, seasoned with herbs from the garden. There's also a selection of New Zealand wines, plus teas and coffees. Freshly squeezed citrus juice from the café's organic orchard is a speciality.

✚ 211 E2 ✉ Main Road, Whenuakite
☎ (07) 866 3725 🕐 10–5; closed Aug, 25 Dec

Wild Hogs Bar and Restaurant $$

A massive fireplace greets visitors to this rustic restaurant and bar on the waterfront overlooking Whitianga inlet, and the theme is carried on inside. The varied menu includes traditional pizzas from the wood-fired oven, baked flounder, rack of lamb and venison cutlet. There is also a selection of chef's specials, including pasta, curry and Coromandel oysters.

✚ 211 E2 ✉ 9 The Esplanade, Whitianga
☎ (07) 866 4828; www.wildhogs.com
🕐 Daily 11–2, 5–11

Where to...
Shop

AUCKLAND

Shopping Centres
Near the waterfront, the **Downtown Shopping Centre** (11–19 Customs Street, http://downtownsc.co.nz) has 70 speciality shops. **T Galleria**, in the Customhouse (corner of Customs and Albert streets; www.dfs.com) specializes in designer fashions.

Botany Town Centre has 150 shops (corner of Ti Rakau and Te Irirangi drives, Botany Downs; www.botanytowncentre.co.nz). **Newmarket** has upmarket fashion and high street stores. **Sylvia Park** is a shopping centre with 200 stores (286 Mt Wellington Hwy; www.sylviapark.org).

Factory outlets are found at **Dress Smart** (151 Arthur Street, Onehunga; www.dress-smart.co.nz/auckland).

Fashion
Head to Britomart Place to find such designers as **Kate Sylvester** (58 Tyler Street; www.katesylvester.com) and **Karen Walker** (The Pavilions, 18 Te Ara Tahuhu Walkway; www.karenwalker.com), or to Parnell for clothing by **Trelise Cooper** (536 Parnell Road, trelisecooper.com). Other chic stores in the suburb of Newmarket include **Zambesi** (38 Osborne Street; www.zambesi.co.nz) and **Workshop** (18 Morrow Street; www.workshop.co.nz).

Parnell
A cluster of heritage villas is now a village of boutiques, galleries and cafés. For crafts, browse at **The Elephant House** (237 Parnell Road; www.nzcrafts.co.nz).

Markets
La Cigale Market sells French products (cheese, charcuterie and bread), antiques and clothing on Saturdays from 8–1 (69 St Georges Bay Road, Parnell; www.lacigale.co.nz). The **Otara Market** in Newbury Street is also held on Saturday mornings. It's good for Pacific Island crafts (and bric-à-brac).

Food & Wine
The **New Zealand Winemakers Centre** (National Bank Centre, corner of Elliott and Victoria streets, tel: (09) 379 5858) offers wine tasting, retail, and tour advice. In Newmarket, gather a picnic at **Zarbo** deli-café (24 Morrow St.; www.zarbo.co.nz).

NORTHLAND

The Cabbage Tree has two shops in Paihia (Williams Road and Maritime Building; www.thecabbagetree.co.nz) selling crafts and leisure wear. Pick up a guide to Kerikeri's **Art and Craft Trail** from the Paihia visitor centre (The Wharf 101 Marsden Rd, tel: (09) 402 7345). **Living Nature** (1246 SH10, Kerikeri; www.livingnature.com) sells natural skincare goods. Buy cheese from **Mahoe Farm-house Cheese** (SH10, Oromahoe, http://mahoecheese.co.nz) or chocolates from **Makana Confections** (504 Kerikeri Road; www.makana.co.nz), and visit Kerikeri's Sunday farmer's market (9–noon, Books and More car park). At the **Ancient Kauri Kingdom** (229 SH1, RD1, Awanui; www.ancientkauri.co.nz), ancient logs are converted into furniture.

COROMANDEL PENINSULA

Pick up a Coromandel Craft Trail leaflet from an information centre. Choose from the cheeses at **Matatoki Farm** (12km (7.5mi) north of Thames; www.matatokicheese.co.nz) to enjoy with a picnic on your hike.

Where to...
Go Out

AUCKLAND

Information on events, clubs, cinema and theatre listings can be found on www.viewauckland.co.nz.

Nightspots
Karangahape Road ("K Road") is the centre of Auckland's club scene. Tune in to Radio95 bFM's gig guide for what's on. **Sky City Casino** (corner of Federal and Victoria streets; tel: 0800 759 2489 toll free) is open 24 hours.

Performing Arts
The **Aotea Centre** (Mayoral Drive; tel: (09) 309 2677) is Auckland's premier classical concert venue. The Auckland Theatre Company performs at several venues including the University's **Maidment Theatre** (8 Alfred Street; tel: (09) 308 2383).

Sports
Boat charters in Waitemata Harbour are offered by dozens of companies. There are popular **windsurfing** beaches at Bayswater, Mission Bay, Takapuna and Point Chevalier. The area boasts over twenty golf courses, including New Zealand's longest, the **Formosa Country Club** (110 Jack Lachlan Drive, Beachlands; tel: 0800 842 538 toll free).

Auckland has three stadiums, hosting rugby union, rugby league or test cricket. Call **Ticketek**; tel: 0800 842 538 toll free. Watch the tennis at the **ASB Bank Tennis Centre** (1 Tennis Lane, Parnell; tel: (09) 373 3623), or have a bet at **Ellerslie Race Course** (80 Ascot Avenue, Remuera; tel: (09) 524 4069).

Wine Trail
The Auckland visitor centre produces a brochure listing wineries in the region and can book tours (Viaduct Basin; tel: (09) 979 2333).

Festivals
Pasifika festival (March) showcases Pacific Islands arts, ➤ 46.

NORTHLAND

Sports
The Bay of Islands offers great game fishing; charter operators are found at Paihia Wharf. The region also has golf courses. Try the **Waitangi Golf Club** (tel: (09) 402 7713).

Wine Trail
Get a **wine trail map** from the information centre in Paihia (The Wharf, Marsden Road; tel: (09) 402 7345).

Festivals
The region's most famous celebration is **Waitangi Day** (➤ 46). The **Whangarei Jazz and Blues Festival** is held in October, while November heralds the **Taste Bay of Islands** wine and food festival and the **Bay of Islands A & P show** in Waimate North, and January the **Waipu Highland Games.**

COROMANDEL PENINSULA

Sports
Whangamata has a famous surfing beach, and charter operators offer water activities. Take a wilderness walk with **Kiwi Dundee Adventures** (tel: (07) 865 8809). Golf courses include **Mercury Bay Golf Club** (12 Golf Road, Whitianga; tel: (07) 866 5479).

Festivals
The crimson-flowered **pohutukawa tree** is celebrated in December. January brings the well-attended **Keltic Fair**.

Central Plateau

 Little Treats

Face to Face with Kiwi Chicks

Get close to shy Kiwi birds at the **Rainbow Springs Kiwi Wildlife Park** (▶ 89) near **Rotorua**.

I Scream for Ice Cream

Rush Munro's in **Hastings** (704 Heretaunga St West) has made the best ice cream in the land since 1926.

Picture Perfect

Enjoy views of the surrounding volcanic landscape at **Chateau Tongariro** (▶ 100).

Getting Your Bearings

The volcanic plateau in the central North Island is New Zealand's hotspot of angry natural forces – one of the world's most active geothermal areas. Towering geysers, hissing steam, boiling mud and evil smells are constant companions as you travel along the Thermal Explorer Highway from Rotorua to Taupo, exploring New Zealand's contribution to the Pacific Ring of Fire.

The Taupo Volcanic Zone stretches 250km (155mi), right through the central North Island. This band of thermal activity varies in width from 30km (20mi) to 80km (50mi), anchored by White Island in the north and the three Tongariro volcanoes in the south. These four active volcanoes enclose a huge field of dormant cones and vast craters formed by earlier eruptions.

In this area, the earth is constantly on the move, spewing fiery bad breath wherever toxic fumes find an escape route through the thin crust. Nature is at her rawest – her face pockmarked with festering boils and oozing craters – but also at her most impressive and beautiful.

The region's original inhabitants, Maori belonging to the Te Arawa tribe, learned to harness the region's tremendous natural energy, cooking their food in hot springs and relaxing in mineral-rich warm pools. They were also the country's first tour guides, back in the 1870s, as the area gained a reputation for its natural spectacles and began drawing British visitors, inspiring New Zealand's first commercial tourism ventures. But in 1886 Mount Tarawera erupted, destroying several villages and popular tourist attractions. The region recovered only slowly.

Rotorua finally rediscovered its heritage as a spa town and several of the original mock-Tudor buildings have been restored to their former glory, adding charm and contrast to the city. Today, many of the modern tourist guides are young Maori, proudly continuing their ancestors' tradition of hospitality.

The sun sets over the hills surrounding Te Mata Peak

A performance of a Maori ceremony

Central Plateau

Four Perfect Days

This itinerary includes four enjoyable days exploring the Central Plateau. You'll visit Rotorua, walk alongside Lake Tarawera, admire some great views and bathe in thermal water pools. For more information see the main entries (➤86–99).

Day 1

Morning

Check out the visitor information centre in downtown Rotorua to make bookings for Day 2's **㉖ *Hangi* and cultural performance** (➤92). Walk to the Government Gardens on the shores of Lake Rotorua and take your time to explore the **㉘ Rotorua Museum of Art and History** (above, ➤96), which has excellent exhibits about the eruption of **Mount Tarawera** (left). Have lunch in town (➤101), or drive 20km (12mi) on to Lake Tarawera.

Afternoon

Walk along the shore of Lake Tarawera or join a cruise on Lake Rotomahana past the former site of the Pink and White Terraces. Then drive back 1km (0.5mi) to visit the fascinating **㉕ Te Wairoa, the Buried Village** (➤90), which was devastated by the volcanic explosion. Return to Rotorua to relax in the hot pools at the **㉙ Polynesian Spa** (➤97).

Day 2

Morning

Spend another day in Rotorua, this time exploring **Whakarewarewa** (➤86), where most of the survivors from the Buried Village moved after the eruption. This thermal resort also offers excellent performances of Maori culture and is next to the **New Zealand Maori Arts and Crafts Institute**.

Afternoon
Return to Lake Rotorua's western shore and take a ride on the **30 Skyline Rotorua** (➤ 97) for sweeping views across Rotorua, the lake, Mount Tarawera and the steaming thermal areas in between. Spend the rest of the day exploring the **Agrodome** or **Rainbow Springs** animal park (➤ 89), and enjoy a traditional **26 *hangi* and cultural performance** (➤ 92) in the evening.

Day 3

Morning
Drive 19km (12mi) south along SH5 to the stunning **Waimangu Valley** ⭐**thermal area** (➤ 87), which was created by Mount Tarawera's eruption. Spend the morning exploring the startling landscapes and springs, and take lunch at the coffee shop.

Afternoon
Continue for another 10km (6mi) further south to visit the **Wai-O-Tapu** ⭐**thermal area** (➤ 887) to see its rainbow-coloured silica terraces and hot pools. Detour to Waikite (➤ 89) for a soak in the hot springs, then continue south towards Taupo (➤ 87). You can take a detour to **34 Huka Falls** (➤ 98) and enjoy a meal at the Huka Prawn Park (➤ 104).

Day 4

For your last day, stroll along the shores of **Lake Taupo** or explore any of the activities on offer. Then drive along the lake towards Turangi and Whakapapa in the magnificent **27 Tongariro National Park** (➤ 93). Take the chair lift up Mount Ruapehu for a view across the other two volcanoes, then take a short walk from the visitor centre in Whakapapa (➤ 94). Alternatively, drive 139km (86mi) from Taupo to **35 Napier and Hawke's Bay** (➤ 99) along SH5. Soak up the city's art deco architecture on a walk or visit some of the local wineries.

★4 Thermal Areas

Rotorua is the centre of a thermal wonderland of bubbling mud pools, kaleidoscopic silica terraces and spouting geysers. The odour of hydrogen sulphide pervades the city day and night, and has earned it the nickname Sulphur City.

Three of the most stunning spectacles are along the **Thermal Explorer Highway** (State Highway 5) between Rotorua and Taupo. Although they're all within 30km (20mi) of Rotorua, plan to spend at least two hours at Whakarewarewa Thermal Valley and a day at Waimangu Valley and the Wai-O-Tapu thermal area.

Insider Tip

Whakarewarewa Thermal Valley
Whakarewarewa Thermal Valley is closest to downtown Rotorua, at the southern end of the city, and is part of the **Te Puia complex**. Uniquely, this combines an extensive **geothermal park** with a centre of **Maori culture** and a kiwi house, where you can catch a rare glimpse of these nocturnal birds. Whakarewarewa village became the new home for those displaced by the 1886 eruption of Mount Tarawera (➤ 90). Villagers still use the hot pools for bathing and cooking.

Whakarewarewa's (Te Puia) main attraction is the **geyser flat**, a moonscape silica terrace of about 1ha (2.5 acres) pierced by seven active geysers. Two are very reliable: the **Prince of Wales Feathers** regularly spouts hot fountains about 12m (40ft) high and heralds the awakening of **Pohutu ("Big Splash") geyser**, at around 30m (100ft), New Zealand's highest. It erupts every hour or so, and

Vapours rising above the water in Wai-O-Tapu

Bubbling mud pools while you wait you can stroll through a bizarre landscape of burping mud puddles, bubbling hot pools and steaming vents.

Exhibits on Maori Culture

Most people come to see the geysers, but you shouldn't miss the **meeting house** (➤ 92, 97) or the **New Zealand Maori Arts and Crafts Institute** (Te Puia), established in 1963 to preserve Maori heritage and now a respected training school for carvers and weavers. You can watch Maori artisans instructing young craftspeople and browse the galleries for souvenirs. The ornately sculpted meeting house nearby is used for daily cultural concerts, which are included in the entrance fee. The grounds also boast an enclosure filled with kiwi birds!

Waimangu Valley

South of Whakarewarewa, 14km (9mi) along SH5, you'll see a sign for **Waimangu Valley**, about 6km (4mi) from the turn-off. This narrow valley was created by the eruption of Mount Tarawera, which tore a gash into the land around its base. The valley has since filled with regenerating bush, creating splendid landscapes. Before you enter the valley, browse through the photographs taken before and after Mount Tarawera exploded, and pick up a trail map.

Insider Tip

Just a few metres from the start of the walkway, the valley opens up for a panoramic view. From here the path winds its way past cool, algae-covered **Emerald Pool** to **Frying Pan Lake**. This is the world's largest hot spring,

Central Plateau

fed by boiling water and toxic fumes, and producing incredibly eerie sounds. Continue past smaller fizzing pools and a steaming rock face to a hot stream and a barren basin, whose rim is marked with a white cross. Here, in 1903, four people were killed by the **Waimangu Geyser**, the largest known hot fountain. For a short time in the early 20th century, the geyser used to spit scalding muddy water high into the air, but it is dormant at the moment.

A few minutes further into the valley, the constantly gurgling **Inferno Crater Lake** gives a performance that befits its name every month or so. Closer still to **Lake Rotomahana**, the magnificent **Marble and Warbrick terraces** channel hot water down a maze of scalloped sinter flats and cascading buttresses. The lake cruise is a very tranquil journey, past scarred and steaming cliffs and smaller geysers.

BUBBLING OVER

Wai-O-Tapu is home to the Lady Knox geyser, which erupts at 10:15am daily – with a little help. As the story goes, prisoners were brought here in the 1900s to wash their clothes in the hot pools. A warden noticed that the water started boiling as it became soapy, so he had the prisoners build a rock cairn over the pool to confine the water and drive up a fountain. Today, silica has coated the cairn and it acts as a natural geyser, but the eruption still has to be triggered with soap.

Wai-O-Tapu

From the Waimangu turn-off, it's another 13km (8mi) along SH5 to the awesome thermal wonders of 👫 **Wai-O-Tapu**. Here, the water flows over landscapes rich in silica. As it cools, the mineral forms sinter. This thermal area is most notable for the mineral-encrusted **Champagne Pool**, delicately tinged with all the colours of the spectrum, and the **Primrose Terraces**, which have formed over more than 900 years and are the largest in the southern hemisphere. There are also several large caves, whose overhanging ceilings are decorated with filigreed formations of crystallized sulphur.

Lady Knox Geyser blows her top on a daily basis

The mud pools of Hell's Gate

Both Waimangu Valley and
Wai-O-Tapu have excellent
coffee shops, which offer a
range of refreshments.

✚ 212 C3

**Whakarewarewa Thermal Valley
(Te Puia)**
✉ Hemo Road, Rotorua
☎ (07) 348 9047,
0800 837 842 toll free;
www.tepuia.com
🕐 Daily 8–5.
Guided tours: 9–5 on the hour.
Daytime Maori concerts:
daily 10:15, 12:15, 3:15
💰 NZ$50

Waimangu Valley
✉ 587 Waimangu Road, Rotorua
🕐 Daily 8:30–5 (last entry 3:45)
💰 NZ$35

**Wai-O-Tapu Thermal
Wonderland**
✉ 201 Wai-O-Tapu Loop Road,
off SH5, Rotorua
☎ (07) 366 6333;
www.geyserland.co.nz
🕐 Daily 8:30–5 (summer later)
💰 NZ$33

INSIDER INFO

- You'll need at least an hour to walk to the end of the Waimangu Valley at the shore of Lake Rotomahana, where you can join a cruise to view volcanic features inaccessible from the paths. Alternatively, a shuttle bus makes a regular loop around the valley's thermal sites to the lake.

Insider Tip

- Don't dress up – the odour of sulphur tends to stick to clothes for some time.
- Visit **Waikite**, a forested thermal valley with a small public pool fed by a hot stream. There are also private baths and a café. Turn into Waikite Valley Road at the Wai-O-Tapu Tavern on SH5 (tel: (07) 333 1861; www.hotpools.co.nz; open daily 10–9; café: noon–7:30).
- Te Puia's 🧒 **kiwi house** gives visitors the chance to view these rare nocturnal birds close up (through a glass wall). You can also admire kiwis at the **Rainbow Springs Kiwi Wildlife Park** (192 Fairy Springs Rd.; daily 8:30am–5pm).
- If you want to see more fumaroles and mud pools, **Hell's Gate** is about 15 minutes from Rotorua. Travel north on SH30 past Rotorua Airport, continuing right towards Whakatane. After about 4km (2.5mi) you will come to Tikitere and Hell's Gate, on the left (tel: (07) 345 3151; www.hellsgate.co.nz).

㉕ Mount Tarawera & Buried Village

Mount Tarawera is sacred to the Maori tribe that first settled this area. It isn't one of New Zealand's highest mountains, but its many jagged peaks and long, deep crater are reminders that it is one of the most volatile. One winter's night in 1886, the volcano exploded, burying the surrounding area under a layer of mud and obliterating its famous silica terraces.

The violence of the 1886 eruption is still evident even from a distance. One of the best places for a good view of Mount Tarawera is the **Landing Café at Lake Tarawera** (▶102). The mountain's summit is non-existent – instead it has a giant, gaping crater. When it blew, the mountain opened and ripped a 17km (11mi) fissure creating a new lake and the thermal Waimangu Valley (▶87), and ejecting enough material to blanket 16,000km² (6,000mi²) around it.

Tarawera's jagged and vast crater

Boat cruises are available on Lake Tarawera, and 4WD vehicles or helicopters can take you to Mount Tarawera's crater rim (at a price) to see the eruption's effect on the landscape. However, the most haunting sight of the mayhem that followed the eruption can be found at **Te Wairoa, the Buried Village**, about 1km (0.5mi) from Lake Tarawera.

Village Life

The village was the hub of tourism and home to several guides who took visitors to the famous **Pink and White Terraces** during the 1870s, the biggest tourist attraction of the time. Hot water once poured over these huge, silica terraces into nearby Lake Rotomahana, which was less than half its current size before the eruption.

A **small museum** at the entrance to the Buried Village provides an excellent introduction to the area. Photographs recount the development of Te Wairoa from a quiet settle-

THE PRICE OF WISDOM

An eerie atmosphere surrounds Tuhoto Ariki's house. He had warned villagers that they would be punished for their greed in encouraging tourism. When his predictions came true, villagers blamed him for the disaster and refused to dig him out. The sage was finally rescued four days later but died within a week.

ment to a thriving staging post. Eyewitness accounts describe the chaos and tragedy of the rescue effort and there is also the chilling story of the warnings that preceded it. According to several witnesses, shortly before the eruption a group of tourists was crossing Lake Tarawera with Guide Sophia, one of the most popular guides, when they saw a phantom Maori waka (canoe); the warriors paddling towards the mountain had the faces of dogs. The village sage, Tuhoto Ariki, interpreted the sight as a warning of imminent destruction. Soon after, the village was destroyed and more than 150 people were killed.

Revealing Artefacts

Excavations of Te Wairoa have revealed a number of small dwellings, accessible to visitors, and hundreds of artefacts, among them the blacksmith's tools, millstones from the village mill, the baker's large oven and full bottles from the tavern.

TAKING A BREAK

There are **tea rooms** at the entrance to the Buried Village, but if the weather's good, have a **picnic** under the tall aspen poplars that have grown from the original fence posts.

✚ 212 C3

Visitor Information Centre
✉ 1167 Fenton Street, Rotorua ☎ (07) 348 5179; www.rotoruanz.com
🕓 Nov–March daily 8–6; April–Oct 8–5:30

Te Wairoa – the Buried Village
✉ 1180 Tarawera Road, RD5, Rotorua ☎ (07) 362 8287; www.buriedvillage.co.nz
🕓 Nov–March daily 9–5; April–Oct 9–4:30 💲 NZ$32

Clearwater Cruises
✉ The Tarawera Landing, Lake Tarawera
☎ (07) 345 6688; www.clearwater.co.nz
🕓 Lake Tarawera Experience (3 hours): daily 9am 💲 Depending on tour

INSIDER INFO

- Join a **guided tour** through the museum and the excavation sites. Some of Guide Sophia's descendants now work as guides and their personal connection with the area brings the stories to life.
- Traditional Maori villages used to have communal storehouses to keep food for winter. During excavations of the storehouse at Te Wairoa, archaeologists discovered some rare **Maori stone carvings,** and two of these precious relics are now on display at the storehouse entrance.

㉖ Cultural Performances

After decades of assimilation, Maori language, culture and crafts are experiencing a renaissance among both Maori and Pakeha (New Zealanders descended from European settlers). Enjoying traditionally cooked food and a live performance are unmissable experiences.

The best way to experience Maori culture is to attend a performance at a venue such as Tamaki Maori Village (►97) or Te Puia (►87). Both sites include a traditional Maori village with a *whare nui* (large meeting house), smaller dwellings and storehouses, and combine a *hangi* with a performance of action songs and dances.

Hospitality is essential to Maori culture. You will receive a traditional welcome, when a warrior will perform mock attacks and lay out a small branch as a challenge. The elected "chief" of your group picks up the branch to signal a peaceful visit. The women will then call you onto the *marae* (area outside the meeting house), where hosts and guests exchange speeches and songs. Maori songs and dances are an integral part of oral history and are accompanied by actions to illustrate the story. A *hangi* is traditionally prepared in an earth oven by steaming vegetables and a range of meats together over hot rocks (►97).

Rituals, songs and dances form a traditional Maori welcome

➕ 212 C3

Tamaki Tours
✉ 1220 Hinemaru Street, Rotorua
☎ (07) 349 2999;
www.maoriculture.co.nz
🕐 Daily, booking required
💰 NZ$110 (includes a folklore show and traditional dinner)

INSIDER INFO

Insider Tip
■ Catch the **courtesy bus** to your venue rather than driving there yourself. The bus drivers often use the journey to explain the protocol of visiting a *marae*.

Insider Tip
■ Be prepared to **exchange songs** with your Maori hosts. It doesn't have to be anything elaborate – a popular song will do. It's better to sing something badly than to sing nothing at all!

㉗ Tongariro National Park

Few views are as striking as the first glimpse of the three volcanoes of the Tongariro National Park. Rising starkly from a surrounding plateau of tussocklands and near-desert, the peaks mark one of the country's most popular national parks.

A view across Lake Taupo

Tongariro was New Zealand's first national park, the vision of a Maori tribal chief who gave the mountains to the nation to ensure their protection (▶ 10). Volcanic forces and weather continue to mould this area, which is one of a handful of places worldwide with dual World Heritage status in recognition of its natural and cultural value. It's also a magnet for outdoor enthusiasts, who come to walk its tracks in summer and to ski the slopes of **Mount Ruapehu** (at 2,797m/9,174ft the North Island's highest mountain) in winter.

Calm Waters

The most scenic approach is from **Taupo**, at the northern end of **Lake Taupo**. The huddled peaks first come into view across the water as you drive along the lakefront. The lake's calm, deep blue water belies its violent creation from one of the world's biggest volcanic eruptions. The Taupo explosion in ad186 is believed to have darkened skies and caused blood-red sunsets as far away as Italy and China, and pumice now forms a thick layer over much of the North Island. The lake, which fills several of the craters carved by the eruption, is the country's largest and

Insider Tip

93

Central Plateau

is a trout-angler's paradise. Rainbow trout are hooked by the tonne each day and you are likely to spot lines of anglers sitting on the lake's banks as you drive south for about 50km (30mi) along its eastern shores.

The snow covered peaks of Mount Ngauruhoe, Tongariro and Ruapehu

Still Active
Even from a distance, it is clear that the volcanoes of Tongariro National Park are anything but dormant. **Mount Ngauruhoe**, an almost perfect cone with a clearly recognizable volcanic crater at its 2,291m (7,514ft) summit, smoulders and occasionally belches steam and gas into the sky. **Mount Tongariro**, at 1,967m (6,451ft) the lowest of the volcanic trio, is a maze of volcanic craters and spouts the cascading Ketetahi hot spring from one of its flanks. **Mount Ruapehu**, the only peak that is constantly snow-capped, erupts every few years and spews out clouds of steam and ash and several lahars (mud flows).

Introducing the Park
^{Insider Tip} The national park's main access is through the small settlement called **Whakapapa**, itself worth a visit, not least to see one of New Zealand's best known hotels, the **Chateau Tongariro** (➤ 100). The Department of Conservation, which administers all protected lands, runs a **visitor centre** at Whakapapa with excellent displays on the region's geology and history, as well as information about walks and weather forecasts. At the entrance, you are greeted by a bust of **Horonuku Te Heuheu Tukino IV** (➤ 14), the far-sighted paramount chief of the local Ngati Tuwharetoa people, who realized in 1887 that the only way to preserve an area of cultural significance was to give it to the nation. Just outside the centre, a commemorative rock is a reminder of the peaks' continuing importance for Maori.

To explore the park, you can take the ski field chair lift and on a clear day the views from the top terminal are stunning – just sit outside and take in the majestic atmosphere. Scenic plane and helicopter flights are available from a small airfield a few minutes from Whakapapa, and there are myriad short walks and nature trails starting from the village.

TAKING A BREAK

Take tea at the **Chateau Tongariro** (➤ 100) or eat at **Knoll Ridge Café** (open 7:30am–11pm), which, at about 2,000m (6,500ft) above sea level, is New Zealand's highest restaurant. Knoll Ridge Café closes in bad weather, but nearby **Lorenz's Bar and Café** (open 8:30am–4:30pm) at Top o' the Bruce always stays open.

The austere landscape around Mount Ruapehu

✚ 212 B2

Whakapapa Visitor Information Centre
✉ SH48, Whakapapa; mailing address: Private Bag, Mount Ruapehu 2650
☎ (07) 892 3729; www.doc.govt.nz
🕐 Nov–March 8–6; April–Oct 8–5

Mount Ruapehu
✉ Guided walks and chair lift from Top o' the Bruce, road end SH48, Whakapapa ski area ☎ (07) 892 4000; www.mtruapehu.com
🕐 Chair lift services to Whakapapa ski field (weather dependent): Mid Jan–Oct, mid Dec–Easter daily 8:30–4. Closed Sep–mid Dec, Easter–mid Jan

Mountain Air
☎ (07) 892 2812, 0800 922 812 toll free; www.mountainair.co.nz

Helistar Helicopters Limited
☎ (07) 374 8405, 0800 435 478 toll free; www.helistar.co.nz

INSIDER INFO

- Explore the **Whakapapa Visitor Information Centre** and its audiovisual displays on the national park's volcanoes, biodiversity and conservation.

- Be aware that out of the **skiing season** (approximately November to March), most of Whakapapa's amenities are likely to be closed.

- It is possible to **climb to the top of Mount Ruapehu**, but the track is not well marked and a return trip can take up to six hours, so it is only for experienced walkers with a guide who knows the area. The weather can change very quickly and clouds can close in around the peaks within a few minutes, so if you're not a confident hiker save your energy and stay close to the top station of the chair lift to enjoy the views.

- The 18.5km (11.5mi) **Tongariro Crossing** is one of the most popular day walks in New Zealand. The track makes its way over the saddle between mounts Ngauruhoe and Tongariro through volcanic landscapes of craters, steaming valleys, hot springs, and the tantalizingly named Emerald and Blue lakes. It takes about eight hours, and hikers should be prepared for changeable weather. Buy maps from the Whakapapa Visitor Centre.

At Your Leisure

Once a government-run spa, the Bath House is now home to the Rotorua Museum

28 Rotorua Museum of Art and History

Come here for more on Rotorua's thermal activity, the area's significance to local Maori tribes, and the town's past as a spa resort. The museum itself is housed in the Bath House, a Tudor-style building surrounded by the Government Gardens. The Bath House was the government's first major commitment to the region's tourist industry, which was thriving by the time the "Great South Seas Spa" opened in 1908. The rich and famous came to soak in the hot mineral waters that still bubble up near Lake Rotorua. They even took baths in tubs connected to electrical currents. The old treatment rooms and bathtubs have been restored and are now permanent exhibits at the museum. Another display features ancient carvings of the Te Arawa, the local Maori tribe. You can witness the violent eruption of Mount Tarawera (► 90) in a brief film, before exploring the museum's display on the tragedy. Next to the museum are the Blue Baths, designed during the 1930s for recreational rather than medicinal bathing and one of the first public pools to allow mixed bathing.

➕ 212 C3 ✉ Queens Drive, Government Gardens, Rotorua
☎ (07) 349 4350; www.rotoruamuseum.co.nz
🕐 Oct–March daily 9–8; April–Sep 9–5
🍴 Bath House Café ($) 💲 NZ$0

HAPPILY EVER AFTER

The love story of Hinemoa and Tutanekai is retold in the popular Maori song "Pokarekare Ana". Both lovers were of high birth in their respective subtribes, but as Tutanekai was an illegitimate son, Hinemoa's family was not in favour of a marriage. Hinemoa lived on the western shore of Lake Rotorua, while Tutanekai lived on the lake's Mokoia Island, where he liked to play his flute. The wind would carry the music to Hinemoa – until one night she couldn't resist and swam across to him. When the families heard of her feat, they celebrated the couple's union. You can see the lovers embracing at the main gates to the Whakarewarewa Thermal Valley.

29 Polynesian Spa

After a hard day's sightseeing, treat yourself to an evening soak in the hot mineral pools and elegant atmosphere of the Polynesian Spa. The facility has integrated elements of a spa house built on the same site during the 1930s. You can choose between warm, invigorating acidic pools, set in rocks at a sheltered part of Lake Rotorua's shoreline, and soothing pools that are fed by a boiling spring beside the complex. Follow up your soak with massages and mud baths – all with a view out to the lake.

➕ 212 C3 ✉ Hinemoa Street, Government Gardens, Rotorua

☎ (07) 348 1328; www.polynesianspa.co.nz

🕐 Daily 8am–11pm; therapies and treatments: 9–8

✋ Treatments: from NZ$100; pools: NZ25

30 31 Skyline Rotorua

For those with energy to spare, this family entertainment area combines a gondola ride with several luge tracks and bush walks. The gondola climbs the side of Mount Ngongotaha to almost 500m (1,500ft) above sea level, opening up panoramic views of Rotorua, the lake and the surrounding district. At the top you can choose different activities, including the Sky Swing and luge tracks, ranging from scenic to advanced. You can also walk downhill following easy footpaths.

➕ 209 D4

✉ Fairy Springs Road, Rotorua

☎ (07) 347 0027; www.skylineskyrides.co.nz

🕐 Daily 9am–late

🍴 Licensed restaurant ($$), Terraces Café ($)

✋ Moderate

31 Tamaki Maori Village

If you want to see how Maori people lived before Europeans arrived in New Zealand, visit this re-created village. It was built into a sheltered forest, complete with a market place, meeting house, sleeping houses, storehouses and a fortified entrance. Maori performers bring the village alive as they go about their daily business. A highlight is the cultural performance and *hangi* feast (➤ 92). Visitors receive a formal welcome and then enjoy a traditional concert and a dinner cooked in an earth oven.

➕ 212 C3

✉ 14km (9mi) south on SH5 towards Taupo. Tamaki Tours: 1220 Hinemaru Street, Rotorua

☎ (07) 349 2999; www.maoriculture.co.nz

🕐 Daily tours before the performance

🚌 Courtesy transport from and to accommodation, with introduction to Maori protocol

✋ NZ$110 (incl. bus transfer, around a 30-min drive from Rotorua)

32 White Island

The plume of smoke rising from White Island can be seen from the coastline of the Bay of Plenty. New Zealand's most active cone volcano is about 50km (30mi) offshore from the towns of Whakatane and Opotiki, and is accessible only by pre-booked boat or helicopter. The volcano had a sulphur mine within its crater in the late 19th and early 20th centuries, until an eruption in 1914 killed all 11 of the miners who were working there. The island's wide crater floor is littered with fumaroles, and hot water and steam constantly escape from these sulphur-encrusted vents. Trips are dependent on the weather and also demand a reasonable level of fitness.

➕ 213 D4

✉ 15 The Strand, Whakatane

☎ (07) 308 9588, 0800 733 529 toll free; www.whiteisland.co.nz

✋ White Island Tour: NZ$199

33 Waitomo Caves

Waitomo is a sleepy settlement famous for its limestone caves. The region is riddled with more than 50km (30mi) of cave passages, part of a karst limestone landscape that has been sculpted by water into blind valleys,

Central Plateau

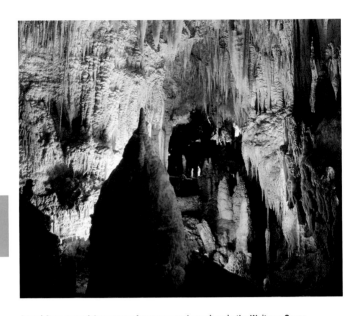

Aranui Cave, part of the warren of passages and openings in the Waitomo Caves

sinkholes, arches and fluted outcrops. About three hours' drive west of Rotorua, the village lies 8km (5mi) off SH3, between the towns of Te Kuiti and Otorohanga. Although the village is little more than a main road, over half a million visitors come to see the stalactites and stalagmites every year. The large selection of activities on offer means you can easily spend a whole day here: options **Insider Tip** range from three-hour blackwater rafting expeditions (navigating an underground river on a tyre inner tube) to all-day abseiling and climbing.

➕ 212 A3

Visitor Information Centre
✉ 21 Waitomo Caves Road
☎ (07) 878 7640, 0800 474 839 toll free;
www.waitomocaves.co.nz
🕐 Oct–24 Dec daily 8:45–5:30;
26 Dec–Feb 8:45–7:30; March–Sep 8:45–5
🚌 A shuttle bus runs daily return trips between Rotorua and Waitomo
(tel: (0508) 926 337 toll free).

34 Huka Falls

Just a few minutes north of Taupo, the Waikato, New Zealand's longest, and normally 100m (300ft) wide and 4m (13 foot) deep river, is forced through a narrow cleft only 15m (50ft) wide and 10m (30ft) deep. The blue water surges through the channel and bursts out in a foaming waterfall, plunging over an 11m (36ft) shelf. There is a footbridge across the channel and a walking track to the falls, but you can also take a jetboat or a cruise boat to view them from the water.

From Huka Falls it's a short drive to **Aratiatia Rapids**. The rapids and the beautiful narrow gorge here dried up after a dam was installed on the Waikato, but the dam is opened several times a day so that people can still see the majesty of the rapids.

➕ 212 BC2

Aratiatia Rapids
🕐 Rapids: Oct–March daily 10am, 12, 2pm, 4pm; April–Sep 10am, 12, 2pm 🎫 Free

Huka Falls River Cruise

✉ Departs from Aratiatia dam
☎ 0800 278 336 toll free;
www.hukafallscruise.co.nz
🕐 Daily 10:30, 12:30, 2:30
(plus 4:30 26 Dec–end Jan)
💲 NZ$37

Hukafalls Jet

✉ Wairakei Park, SH1, 6km (4mi) north of Taupo
☎ (07) 374 8572; www.hukafallsjet.com
🕐 Booking recommended 💲 NZ$109

🔢 Napier and Hawke's Bay

With a Mediterranean-like climate,
Hawke's Bay is New Zealand's
prime wine-growing and fruit-
producing area. Aside from the
wineries, its main appeal is the art
deco buildings in the city of Napier.

On 3 February 1931, a massive
7.9-rated earthquake struck Hawke's
Bay. Virtually every building in
Napier and Hastings collapsed, and
subsequent fires destroyed the city's
heart. Aftershocks continued for
10 days and more than 250 people
were killed. Napier unexpectedly
grew by 40km² (15.5mi²) as the
quake lifted a new piece of land
above sea level (in the area now
known as the Ahuriri harbour
district). The city was rebuilt in the
styles fashionable at the time, with
art deco foremost among them.
Today, Napier has one of the
highest concentrations of art deco
architecture in this part of the
globe. The best examples of this
pastel-coloured, geometric style are
on Emerson, Dalton and Tennyson
streets, all within the inner city and
close to Marine Parade. Take at
least half a day to stroll through
the city centre and along Marine
Parade with its trademark palms.
The annual Art Deco Weekend in
February draws hundreds of people
dressed in 1930s regalia.

Insider Tip

➕ 213 D1

Visitor Information Centre

✉ 100 Marine Parade, Napier
☎ (06) 834 1911, 0800 847 488 toll free;
www.hawksbaynz.com 🕐 Daily 9–5

Art Deco Shop

✉ Art Deco Centre, 163 Tennyson Street, Napier
☎ (06) 835 0022; www.artdeconapier.com
🕐 Daily 9–5

Napier has a fine selection of art deco buildings

Where to…
Stay

Prices
Expect to pay for a double room per night:
$ under NZ$200 $$ NZ$200–$350 $$$ over NZ$350

ROTORUA

Regent of Rotorua $
This former 1960s motel is now a chic boutique hotel within easy walking distance of the heart of the restaurant district. A new restaurant, cocktail bar and suites have been added. Enjoy the 30°C (86°F) geo-thermally heated pool or the indoor mineral pool, or sit beside the fire-place in winter with a glass of wine.

✚ 212 C3 ✉ 1191 Pukaki Street, Rotorua
☎ (07) 348 4079, 0508 734 368 toll free;
www.regentrotorua.co.nz

The Springs Fine Accommodation $$$
Colleen and Murray Ward have designed this luxury B&B to blend in with the 1930s bungalows in their quiet residential street. Plump sofas and *objets d'art* decorate the library, where guests are offered refreshments on arrival.

The four ensuite bedrooms have king-size beds, walk-in wardrobes and access to the tranquil private terrace. The hearty breakfasts in-clude pancakes, smoked salmon and scrambled eggs.

✚ 212 C3 ✉ 16 Devon Street, Rotorua
☎ (07) 348 9922; www.thesprings.co.nz

Treetops $$$
Set in 1,000ha (2,500 acres) of native bush, this luxury lodge is a secluded retreat. The main lodge has been built over a natural stream with hunting trophies standing ele-gantly over the enormous fireplace in the Great Room. There are four lodge rooms attached to the main building and eight villas in separate buildings, each with their own lake or bush views. Activities include trout fishing, hunting, horseback riding, clay shooting and hiking on some of the 70km (43mi) of trails that meander past lakes, glow-worm caves, streams and waterfalls.

✚ 212 C3
✉ 351 Kearoa Road, Horohoro, Rotorua
☎ (07) 333 2066; www.treetops.co.nz

TONGARIRO NATIONAL PARK

Chateau Tongariro $–$$$
Perched on the slopes of Mount Ruapehu, the Bayview Chateau was built in 1929 for skiers. The refurbished hotel retains an elegant atmosphere and there are spectacular views. The most appealing rooms look directly onto Ngauruhoe's volcanic cone, and there are also family units and a top-floor suite.

The hotel has seasonal packages for walkers and skiers, a golf course, gym and sauna, billiards table and tennis courts. There's a choice of dining, from à la carte in the elegant restaurant to casual in the café.

✚ 212 B2
✉ SH48, Mount Ruapehu, Tongariro National Park
☎ (07) 892 3809, 0800 242 832 toll free;
www.chateau.co.nz

Ruapehu Golf and Country Lodge $–$$$
This welcoming lodge overlooks the third tee of the Waimarino Golf Course just outside Ohakune, with views of either the greens or mountains. Vivienne Pitman has

Insider Tip

decorated the four bedrooms in French country style, and welcomes guests with pre-dinner drinks in the comfortable lounge. Her husband, a PGA professional, advises on golf – there are five courses within an hour's drive, plus a golf school. Non-golfers can enjoy hiking, canoeing or skiing.

➕ 212 B1
✉ Ohakune-Raetihi Road, Ohakune
☎ (06) 385 9594;
www.ruapehucountrylodge.co.nz

HAWKE'S BAY

Cobden Garden Homestay $–$$

This boutique bed-and-breakfast homestay has three king-size rooms, each with ensuite, in an 1880s Victorian villa. Run by fourth-generation New Zealanders, Phillip and Rayma Jenkins, you'll get to sample locally grown food and wine.

➕ 213 D1
✉ Cobden Crescent, Bluff Hill, Napier
☎ (06) 834 2090, 0800 426 233 toll free;
www.cobden.co.nz

Hawthorne House $$

This elegant Edwardian villa has four luxurious rooms. Located at the end of an avenue of 100-year-old plane trees in a beautiful garden setting, Hawthorne is a blend of calming period features and modern comforts. It has the benefit of being a short drive from both Hastings and Havelock North, and just a 20-minute drive from the city of Napier.

Upon arrival, a homemade afternoon tea is on offer. When the sun starts to set, join the owners for a pre-dinner glass of wine with accompanying canapés. In the morning, you can choose to take breakfast in the breakfast room, on your private verandah, or even on the old train platform overlooking the duck pond. The menu features local organic produce and free-range eggs from their own hens.

➕ 213 D1
✉ 1420 Railway Road South, Hastings
☎ (06) 878 0035;
www.hawthorne.co.nz

Where to...
Eat and Drink

Prices
Expect to pay per person for a meal, excluding drinks:
$ under NZ$45   **$$** NZ$45–$60   **$$$** over NZ$60

ROTORUA

Bistro 1284 $$$

The atmosphere is welcoming and the decor is simple but elegant, with dining on two levels. The menu offers modern New Zealand dishes. Try the ostrich carpaccio and goats' cheese followed by the boneless lamb shank wrapped in prosciutto. Home-churned ice cream is a speciality. There's a

largely New Zealand wine list, but you can also bring your own.

➕ 212 C3 ✉ 1284 Eruera Street
☎ (07) 346 1284; www.bistro1284.co.nz
🕐 Daily 6pm–late

Lime Caffeteria $–$$

Located at the lake end of Fenton Street, you can sit outside with a peep of the lake or cosy up indoors. This is a popular place with delicious breakfast and lunch menu, and wine by the glass. Try the signature creamy vanilla risotto topped with berries.

- 212 C3
- Corner of Fenton and Whakaue streets
- (07) 350 2033
- Daily 7:30am – 4:30pm

Tarawera Landing Café $–$$

An idyllic location overlooking Lake Tarawera makes this simple café worth a trip. Have a drink in the Garden Bar, or eat on the veranda (but mind the sandflies).

- 212 C3
- The Landing, Lake Tarawera
- (07) 362 8595; www.thelandinglaketarawera.co.nz
- May–Nov Wed, Sun 9:30–5:30, Thu–Sat 9:30am–late

The Pig and Whistle City Bar $

Housed in an imposing 1940s building that used to be the police station, this bar has a lot of fun exploiting the joke. Micro-brewed beers have names like Swine Lager. The bar menu ranges from burgers to fish and chips to seafood chowder and beef and chorizo hot-pot, and live bands play Thursday, Friday and Saturday nights.

- 212 C3
- Corner of Haupapa and Tutanekai streets
- (07) 347 3025; www.pigandwhistle.co.nz
- Daily 11:30–10
- Note that children are not welcome after 5:30pm on Fridays and 7:30pm on Saturdays

Replete Café $

A combined café, kitchenware shop and catering service, Replete is a local institution. The café serves breakfast, brunch and lunch, with good coffee. Dishes range from muesli to Thai beef salad. It's a casual place where you can browse through the magazines or pick up that vital kitchen gadget.

- 212 C2
- 45 Heu Heu Street
- (07) 378 0606; www.replete.co.nz
- Mon–Fri 8–5, Sat–Sun 8:30–4

Clearview Estate Winery $–$$

This vineyard, on the coast east of Hastings, has been winning awards for its wines for nearly 20 years. Its restaurant uses fresh herbs, olives, citrus fruits and avocados from the estate's gardens, along with other local produce, to create delicious brunch and lunch dishes. You can sit at long tables under the vines, in the shaded courtyard or by the seaside children's playground.

- 213 D1
- 194 Clifton Road, Te Awanga, RD2, Hastings
- (06) 875 0150; www.clearviewestate.co.nz
- Labour weekend–Easter daily 10–5; rest of year Thu–Mon 10–5

Shed 2 $–$$$

Shed 2 is a cleverly converted 19th-century wool store on the Ahuriri quayside. Head for the café and bar, with its harbourside tables during the day, or retreat to the restaurant at night, where the atmosphere is less casual. The café menu ranges from wood-fired pizza to Asian and Middle Eastern-inspired dishes, as well as seasonal offerings. Hawke's Bay produce features strongly on the wine list. Booking is necessary for the restaurant.

- 213 D1
- West Quay, Ahuriri, Napier
- (06) 835 2202
- Café and bar: daily 11:30–late; restaurant: daily 6pm–late

Wine Street $$$

This elegantly furnished dining room is in Napier's County Hotel, itself housed in the beautifully restored 1909 Edwardian-style Hawke's Bay County Council building. Despite the restaurant's formal decor, its menu consists of modern Pacific dishes. Chambers also offers a wide selection of excellent Hawke's Bay wines.

- 213 D1
- County Hotel, 12 Browning Street, Napier
- (06) 835 7800; www.countyhotel.co.nz
- Daily 7:30am–10am, 6pm–late

Where to…
Shop

In Rotorua, speciality shops are clustered around Tutanekai Street.

The **Outdoorsman Headquarters** (6 Tarawera Road; tel: (07) 345 9333) has outdoor clothes and equipment, while **Finns** (1281 Tutanekai Street; tel: (07) 348 7682), sells womenswear.

For menswear, try **Pollards** (1191 Tutanekai Street; tel: (07) 347 7139).

The government-owned **New Zealand Maori Arts and Crafts Institute (Te Puia)** at Whakarewarewa (tel: (07) 348 9047) preserves the arts of wood carving (*whakairo*) and weaving (*raranga*).

At the **Tribal Marketplace** in Tamaki Maori Village (tel: (07) 349 2999), artists make and sell wood-, bone- and greenstone-carvings, flax-weavings, foods, and tribal clothing.

The **Buried Village** (tel: (07) 362 8287) has Maori crafts not available elsewhere.

Downtown, at the **Jade Factory** (1280 Fenton Street; tel: (07) 349 3968), carvers produce jewellery, sculptures and bowls.

The gift shop at **Rotorua Museum** (tel: (07) 349 4350) is also a good place to find crafts, cards, posters, and books on local history.

The **Redwoods Gift Shop and Visitor Centre** (Long Mile Road; tel: (07) 350 0110), in Whakarewarewa Forest, sells giftware including items made by local woodturners.

In Taupo, crafts can be found along the **Lake Taupo Arts and Crafts Trail**.

The town also has a major independent wine merchant, **Scenic Cellars** (114 Spa Road; tel: (07) 378 5704).

Where to…
Go Out

ThermalAir, the weekly visitors' guide published in Rotorua on Fridays, lists concerts, exhibitions, and sporting fixtures.

Arts & Culture
Maori concert parties perform daily in Rotorua at the **Te Puia** complex (➤ 82), **Tamaki Maori Village** (➤ 86, 91), local *marae* and in many hotels.

To hear bands, check out **the Pig and Whistle** (corner of Haupapa and Tutanekai streets; tel: (07) 347 3025) on Friday and Saturday nights.

Rotorua also hosts several musical events, including **Opera in the Pa** in January at Rotowhio Marae. There are regular exhibitions at the Rotorua Museum of Art and History (➤ 90).

Adventure & Water Sports
You can swim in all the lakes in the Rotorua region except the Green Lake, which is sacred to Maori.

Whether you want to go jet boating, kayaking, white-water rafting, parasailing or water skiing, operators abound. From sky diving to aerial acrobatics and luging to off-road driving, the region can satisfy most thrill seekers. Zorbing is a local invention – you roll downhill in an inflated ball, either harnessed inside the Dry Zorb or loose in the Wet Zorb. Mountain biking is popular in Whakarewarewa Forest, and horse treks can be taken over farmland or forest trails. **Paradise Valley Ventures** (tel: (07) 348 3300) and **Peka Horse Trekking** (tel: (07) 346 1755) are reputable centres.

Fishing

Hamill's (1271 Fenton Street; tel: (07) 348 3147) stocks brochures to trout fishing in the area, and also sells licences and tackle.

Tourism Rotorua (1167 Fenton Street; tel: (07) 348 5179), has details of guides who can supply boats, rods and tackle.

Lake Cruises

Clearwater Cruises (tel: (07) 345 6688) offers three-hour luxury cruises, fishing trips and self-drive charters on Lake Tarawera.

On Lake Rotorua the paddle-boat *Lakeland Queen* (tel: (07) 348 0265, 0800 572 784 toll free) offers cruises.

The Ernest Kemp (tel: (07) 378 3444) is a replica steamboat giving trips on Lake Taupo, including an evening barbecue cruise in summer.

Walking

Well-maintained walking tracks explore native forest in the Rotorua lakes region and the volcanic terrain of Tongariro National Park. In addition to the 18.5km (11.5mi) **Tongariro Crossing** (▶95), shorter walks like the two-hour **Taranaki Falls Track** or **Silica Rapids Track** from Whakapapa Village also take in spectacular sights.

For maps contact the DOC **Whakapapa Visitor Centre** (tel: (07) 892 3729) or **Tourism Rotorua** (1167 Fenton Street, Rotorua; tel: (07) 348 5179).

Skiing

Two of New Zealand's largest ski areas are on the slopes of Mount Ruapehu: **Whakapapa** (tel: (07) 892 3738) and **Turoa** (tel: (06) 385 8456).

Golf

The Rotorua Golf Club (399 Fenton Street; tel: (07) 348 4051) promises unusual hazards – sulphur pits, boiling mud pools and steaming lakes.

Country Life

The show at the **Agrodome** (Western Road, Ngongotaha; tel: (07) 357 1050), near Rotorua, involves shearing and dog handling. Try your hand at milking a cow and feeding lambs, or take a tour of a working farm and orchard. The complex also includes a souvenir shop, café and adventure park.

At **Rainbow Springs** (Fairy Springs Road, Rotorua; tel: (07) 350 0440) you can feed trout, see kiwis in the kiwi house and take walks through native bush.

In Taupo, you can do a tour of the geothermal **Huka Prawn Park** (Huka Falls Road, Wairakei Park; tel: (07) 374 8474), then eat the prawns at the restaurant afterwards.

HAWKE'S BAY

Wine & Food Trails

New Zealand's oldest winery, **Mission Estate** (198 Church Road, Taradale; tel: (06) 845 9350) was established in Hawke's Bay by French missionaries in 1851. The region is now one of the country's leading producers, with nearly 40 wineries that are open to visitors.

Church Road Winery (150 Church Road, Taradale; tel: (06) 844 2053), for example, runs daily tours and has a winemaker's museum, restaurant and gift shop.

Get a wine trail leaflet from the **Napier Visitor Centre** (100 Marine Parade, Napier; tel: (06) 834 1911), or enquire about wine tours there.

The annual wine festival, **Harvest Hawke's Bay**, is held in February.

The **food trail** (tel: (06) 974 8931) includes wineries, orchards, cafés and restaurants.

Sileni Estates Epicurean Centre and Cellar (2016 Maraekakaho Road, RD1, Hastings; tel: (06) 879 8768) runs on-site winery tours, wine courses, a restaurant and a tapas bar.

Wellington & Around

 Little Treats

Camping in the Metropolis
Spend the night in a motorhome in the middle of the city at the **Waterfront Motorhome Park** near Civic Square (► 116).

Sand in the City
Head 400m (a quarter of a mile) eastwards down the promenade from Te Papa (► 110) to reach the beach at **Oriental Bay.**

Wines, Wines, Wines!
Martinborough Wine Centre has a large selection of varieties from this great wine-growing region (► 118).

Getting Your Bearings

By international standards Wellington is a small capital city, but its embassies and visitors endow it with a cosmopolitan atmosphere. A vibrant cultural scene is heightened by its attractive coastal location, buzzing cafés and good restaurants.

Defined by a magnificent harbour and hemmed in by steep forested hills, Wellington's downtown stretches across a narrow lip of flat land. Tall wooden houses cling to the hillsides, beyond the green belt of parks and reserves around the central core. The inner city is linked to the suburbs by steps, walkways and New Zealand's only public "cable car" (actually a funicular railway).

Wellington is only about a third of the size of Auckland, but in attitude, atmosphere and scenic appeal the two cities are equals. Their friendly rivalry for the title of New Zealand's best place to live keeps city planners on their toes. Redevelopment of Wellington's centre and waterfront has spruced up arts and performance venues and confirmed the city's reputation as New Zealand's cultural capital. This is epitomized by the national museum, Te Papa, whose mix of traditional and interactive exhibits draws more than a million visitors each year.

The capital's main function is the business of government, and the beautifully restored Parliament complex makes for a fascinating visit. Away from urban development, the North Island's southernmost city is just a hop from the vineyards of Martinborough and the bird life of Kapiti Island – all in all, it's worth the trip!

Getting Your Bearings

Wellington & Around

Four Perfect Days

This itinerary recommends four enjoyable days seeing the most important sights in and around Wellington. Follow our suggestions and you won't miss any of the highlights. For more information see the main entries (➤ 110–118).

Day 1

Morning
Pick up bus timetables and an events calendar at the **visitor information centre** (➤ 114) to check for any performances and exhibitions you may wish to see during your visit. Wellington is the site of New Zealand's government, so the best way to start your visit is to explore the refurbished **㊱ Parliament complex** (above, ➤ 112). From Parliament, head north to wander through the suburb of **㊲ Thorndon** (➤ 115) and have lunch there.

Afternoon
Stroll along **Tinakori Road** (➤ 115), one of the capital's oldest thoroughfares, and explore some of the charming galleries, boutiques and second-hand shops. At the northern end of the road, you'll find the **Katherine Mansfield Birthplace** (➤ 115) and its gardens.

Evening
Have dinner in town (➤ 121), then catch a performance at one of Wellington's many venues (➤ 124); choose from theatre, dance, opera, or classical, pop or jazz music.

Zealandia Karori Sanctuary
㊳

Thorndon
㊲

㊱ Parliament

Cable Car
㊴

Civic
㊵ Square

Te Papa ⑧

Day 2

42 Kapiti Island

Martinborough
43

41
Matiu/Somes Island & Days Bay

Morning

Spend the morning at **Te Papa national museum** (➤ 110), then walk to **40** **Civic Square** (➤ 114, the sculpture pictured right is suspended above the square). If you are travelling with children, explore the shows and activities at Capital E. You can also check out the art exhibitions at the City Gallery Wellington. Have lunch at the gallery's café or one of the many restaurants in the inner city.

Afternoon

Head back to the waterfront and stroll past the boat sheds here to the **41** **Matiu/Somes Island** (➤ 117) ferry terminal. Catch a boat to the island, or all the way to Days Bay, on the other side of Wellington's harbour, with one of the city's best swimming beaches.

Day 3

Morning

Ride the **39** **Cable Car** (➤ 116) from central Wellington up to the top terminal and take in the views over the city. At the nearby **Carter Observatory**, learn more about the southern hemisphere's night sky in a planetarium show. Walk downhill through the **Botanic Gardens** (Botanical Garden/Begonia House, right; ➤ 190).

Afternoon

After exiting the Botanic Gardens at **Bolton Street** (➤ 190), walk back down to the city. Alternatively, leave via Glenmore Street and catch bus 21 to **38** **Zealandia Ka-rori Sanctuary** (➤ 116), where you can join a guided tour.

Day 4

If you want to see rare birds, get up early and take a day trip to **42** **Kapiti Island** (➤ 117) (it's important to book in advance – usually one or two weeks before you go). It's also worth paying a visit to charming **43** **Martinborough** (➤ 118) in the Wairarapa wine-growing region.

⭐⑧Te Papa

Te Papa's full name is Museum of New Zealand – Te Papa Tongarewa; the Maori words mean "a treasure trove" in free translation. Bold, sometimes provocative and often imaginative, it houses national treasures of all kinds that chart the character of New Zealand.

The museum is New Zealand's most ambitious cultural project, built at a cost of NZ$317 million to tell the stories of the country's environment, arts, history and culture. Its intriguing mix of conventional museum exhibits with interactive virtual experiences can be overwhelming at first, but it's a hit with millions of visitors. You will need at least two hours to see the main galleries, but you could easily spend a whole day here.

The impressive entrance to Te Papa

Dr Cliff Whiting created the modern *marae*

The building itself covers the space of three rugby fields and contains enough steel to stretch from Wellington to Sydney. Set on the waterfront, it's a prominent and enticing landmark: two wings stretch from the glass facade of its entrance lobby as if welcoming visitors with an embrace.

Exploring the Museum

Insider Tip Start on **Level 4** with the undoubted highlight of the museum – a modern *marae* (Maori meeting place). The Maori master carver Dr Cliff Whiting has created a magnificent *whare nui* (meeting house), whose symbols encompass New Zealand's ethnic groups, conveying a sense of peace and unity between cultures. The inside walls are decorated with colourful carvings symbolizing historic events that set New Zealand apart. From the floor design to the wall decorations and a painted glass

Te Papa

door, every element in this hall tells a story. The popular **Golden Days** object theatre is also on Level 4. Instead of displaying photographs and artefacts, the gallery is set up as a walk-in theatre. The stage is a junk shop full of Kiwiana (everyday things that describe national identity).

The audience, seated in old armchairs and garden seats, watches a film portraying nationally significant moments as well as ordinary events: New Zealanders at work and play, but also images of larger events such as Kiwi soldiers returning home from war. As the film screens a particular event, items in the junk shop move or make noises. Though it's

Extremely elaborate wood carving in the Te Papa museum

most evocative for native New Zealanders, this is an opportunity for visitors from overseas to grasp something of the national pysche.

Move downwards through **temporary exhibitions** to more interactive exhibits on Level 2. The best, **Awesome Forces** and **Mountains to Sea**, cover natural history. The latter includes a realistic 🚻 "tree" large enough for children to climb to see birds and animals.

TAKING A BREAK

The **Te Papa Café** (Level 1) and the **Espresso** coffee shop (Level 4) are good places to stop and recharge your batteries.

➕ 223 F2 ⊠ Cable Street
☎ (04) 381 7000; www.tepapa.govt.nz
🕐 Fri–Wed 10–6, Thu 10–9
🎟 Free; Time Warp and short-term exhibitions: *c.* NZ$8

INSIDER INFO

- If you are overwhelmed or lost, ask the museum's hosts (in uniforms with Te Papa's fingerprint logo) for directions, or pick up the **Te Papa Explorer brochure** at the information desk on Level 2. It suggests tracks grouping permanent exhibitions in themes such as nature, arts, Maori or "Te Papa for kids". *Insider Tip*

- If you are short of time, join one of the *Insider* long guided tours of the main galleries (Nov–March daily 10:15, 11, 12, 1, 2, 3 (also 7pm Thu) April–Oct 10:15, 2 (also 7pm Thu); NZ$14). *Insider Tip*

- Children in particular will enjoy 🚻 **Our Space** (free), a multimedia experience. This includes a huge interactive video wall, an interactive floor map of New Zealand, and two virtual rides – **Deep Ride**, into the ocean depths; and **High Ride** (NZ$10).

- On Level 4 you'll find a **touchstone**, an enormous boulder of greenstone that has been polished on one side by the sheer number of hands touching it over time.

36 Parliament

It's the architecture of New Zealand's Parliament that grabs the attention. Of the three buildings in the complex at the northern end of Wellington's centre, the most distinctive is the modern Executive Wing – known as the Beehive. Beside it, the older, beautifully refurbished Parliament House and its library embody national heritage and pride.

The **Beehive** lives up to its name. Its dome rises from a broad base through layers of increasingly smaller circles of offices. A feature of Wellington since the 1970s, the building certainly stands out. It has its critics, but some people see it as a powerful example of modern architecture.

The rings of ministerial windows certainly suggest a hive of coordinated activity, but it is the imposing **Parliament House**, next to the Beehive, where politicians convene for debates. The current Parliament House was built in an Edwardian neoclassical style from granite and marble between 1911 and 1922. The original wooden General Assembly, which had been built when the city was declared the capital in 1865, was destroyed in a fire in 1907.

Loved and loathed, the Beehive stands alongside the neoclassical Parliament House

Protecting Parliament

Insider Tip If you want to see more than a live performance of politics, take a guided tour of the complex. Your first stop will be in the basement of Parliament House, where part of its foundations have been exposed to demonstrate its **earthquake protection**. Wellington straddles one of the South Pacific's most threatening fault lines, and masonry buildings with only minimal lateral movement, such as this one, can be at risk from collapse. So when the complex underwent a major facelift during a three-year refurbishment project in 1992, making the building earthquake-proof was a priority. The entire building now sits on 417 round rubber bearings, isolators that allow the building to sway

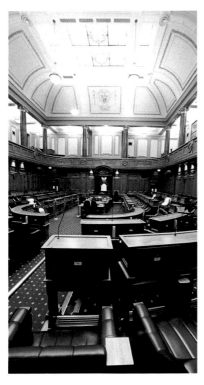

The debating chamber inside Parliament House

and roll should the earth move below. The same technology – invented by a Wellington engineer – protects the national museum Te Papa (► 110).

Tour Highlights

A highlight of the tour is the ornately decorated **Maori Affairs Select Committee Room**, where Members of Parliament meet to discuss proposed law changes relating to Maori issues and race relations. The walls are covered with woven panels and intricate carvings recalling Maori legends.

A stunning suspended three-dimensional **multimedia installation** graces the **Galleria**, a glass-covered open space, formerly an open courtyard in the original Parliament House, which was roofed over during the refurbishment. To match the Edwardian style of the original, later extensions to the building had to be faced in the same materials: some of the quarries that had supplied the marble 80 years earlier were reopened especially.

One of the most beautiful areas within the Parliament complex is the Victorian Gothic **Parliamentary Library**. Thanks to the knowledge and skill of 19th-century architects, who included in their designs an early version of fire-resistant doors, the library's collection survived two fires, including the 1907 disaster. For the most part, the library's resources are available only to students and political researchers but it's worth having a look at its halls and corridors, which are exquisitely decorated with plaster mouldings and stained-glass windows and doors.

Wellington & Around

The just around the corner, is available to the public.
By law, a copy of everything published in New Zealand
is sent here.

TAKING A BREAK

Word of Mouth café (100 Molesworth Street; tel: (04) 472
7202) is a hidden gem near Parliament for light meals.
The **Single File Café** in the foyer of the National Archives
(10 Mulgrave Street; tel: (04) 495 6216) make a welcome
change from cramped downtown bars. While at the Archives
take a look at the original Treaty of Waitangi (➤ 14 which
is on display.

Beautiful
architectural
details in the
Parliament
complex

✚ 223 E4

Visitor Information Centre
✉ Corner of Victoria and Wakefield
streets, Civic Square
☎ (04) 802 4860; www.wellingtonnz.com
🕑 Wed–Sun 8:30–5, Tue 9–5

Parliament Visitor Centre
✉ Ground-floor foyer of Parliament House,
left and below the main stairs leading up to
the entrance
☎ (04) 817 9503; www.parliament.govt.nz
🕑 Mon–Fri 10–4, Sat 10–3, Sun 11–3,
school holidays and Christmas period has
extra tours;
closed 1 and 2 Jan, 6 Feb, Good Friday,
25 and 26 Dec.
Tours leave on the hour and take about
an hour. Last tour Mon–Fri 4pm, Sat–Sun,
public holidays 3pm
🏛 Free

National Library
✉ 77 Thorndon Quay, Pipitea
☎ (04) 474 3000; www.natlib.govt.nz
🕑 Mon–Fri 9–5, Sat 9–1
🏛 Free

INSIDER INFO

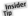

- Parliament usually sits on **Tuesdays**, **Wednesdays** and **Thursdays when in session**.
  The most heated and entertaining debates occur during question time (2pm–3pm).
  Check schedules with the visitor centre at Parliament.
- The **grounds** surrounding the Parliament complex are beautifully maintained and
  include several tranquil corners.
- Opposite the Beehive you'll find the **Old Government Building**, the second-largest
  wooden building in the world. You'll have to look twice to convince yourself that
  the building is not made of stone.

㊲ Thorndon

Thorndon is one of Wellington's oldest suburbs, first settled by Europeans in the 1840s and subsequently home to an arty set that included the likes of writer Katherine Mansfield and painter Rita Angus. Today, the area's lovely wooden villas – many of which retain their original features – are home to boutiques, galleries, B&Bs and lively cafés.

The historic district of **Thorndon** extends from the Parliament complex to Hobson Street and Tinakori Road, and can be explored on a three-hour self-guided walk – pick up a brochure from the information centre (► 114). A highlight is **Old St Paul's** at 34 Mulgrave Street, a church secluded in a small park, with a beautiful Gothic Revival interior in native timber: rimu, matai, totara and kauri. It was built in 1866 as a temporary cathedral, but maintained this role for a century until the Anglican Cathedral was erected.

Insider Tip

At the far end of Tinakori Road is the **Katherine Mansfield Birthplace**, the childhood home of the country's most distinguished author (1888–1923), known internationally for her short stories and letters. The house (built in 1888) and the surrounding suburbs feature in many of Mansfield's stories, and extracts from her work are displayed alongside photographs in the restored house. There's a **video portrait** of the writer and a **doll's house** has been built using details in her short story of the same name.

UPLIFTING EXPERIENCE
The earthquake that hit Wellington on 23 January 1855 measured 8.2 on the Richter scale and was the biggest ever recorded in New Zealand. It raised the beach at Thorndon by up to 1.5m (5ft) and caused a tsunami in the Cook Strait.

TAKING A BREAK
For lunch or a coffee, try one of the cafés along Tinakori Road, such as (No. 322; tel: (04) 471 2500).

➕ 223 D4–F5

Old St Paul's
➕ 223 F4 ✉ 34 Mulgrave Street
☎ (04) 473 6722; www.oldstpauls.co.nz
🕐 Daily 9:30–5 or by special arrangement; access subject to functions 🎟 Free

Katherine Mansfield Birthplace
➕ 223 F5 ✉ 25 Tinakori Road
☎ (04) 473 7268;
www.katherinemansfield.com
🕐 Tue–Sun 10–4
🚌 14 to Wilton stops at nearby Park Street
🎟 NZ$8

Katherine Mansfield's childhood home

At Your Leisure

38 Zealandia Karori Sanctuary

Just 2km (1mi) from downtown Wellington is one of New Zealand's most ambitious private conservation projects, established in 1995 when a group of Wellingtonians decided to reclaim a pocket of bush near the inner city and return it to its original state. First, the 225ha (556-acre) valley around the former Karori water reservoir was surrounded by a fence, to keep out predators. Then all pests inside the sanctuary were eradicated and, finally, endangered wildlife reintroduced. It's been a great success: the kiwi population produced chicks during the first season and other native birds are flocking here. A variety of guided walks, including a nocturnal tour (book in advance), allows visitors to appreciate the evolution of the sanctuary.

➕ 223 off D3
✉ 31 Waiapu Road, Karori
☎ (04) 920 9200; www.visitzealandia.org.nz
🕐 Daily 10–5 (night tours also available)
🚌 3, 17, 18, 21, 22, 23
💵 NZ$17; night tours: NZ$75

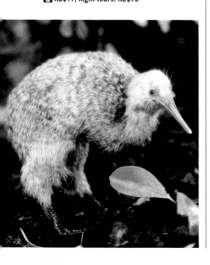

39 Cable Car

The bright red Cable Car is a Wellington icon and the fastest way of getting from downtown to the Botanic Garden (➤ 190), Victoria University or the suburb of Kelburn. The Cable Car opened in 1902, linking the new hill-hugging suburbs to the city centre, and was immediately popular.

In the 1970s the track was reconstructed and new Swiss-made cars introduced. Near the top terminal you'll find the **Cable Car Museum** and the **41 Carter Observatory**, which offers planetarium shows, telescope viewing and astronomy displays, though the view down over the city is also worth the ride.

➕ 223 D3   ✉ 280 Lampton Quay
☎ (04) 472 2199; www.wellingtoncablecar.co.nz
🕐 Every 10 minutes, Mon–Fri 7am–10pm, Sat 8:30am–10pm, Sun & public holidays 9–9
💵 NZ$4

Cable Car Museum

➕ 223 D3   ✉ Upland Road, Kelburn
☎ (04) 475 3578; www.cablecarmuseum.co.nz
🕐 Nov–April daily 9:30–5:30; May–Oct 10–5
💵 Free

Carter Observatory

➕ 205 A3   ✉ 40 Salamanca Road, Kelburn
☎ (04) 472 8167; www.carterobservatory.org
🕐 Nov–Feb Sun–Tue 10–5, Wed–Sat 10–late; March–Oct Mon–Thu 11–4, Fri–Sat 11–late
💵 NZ$18.50

40 Civic Square

Some of the capital's premier cultural centres surround the square: as you face the visitor information centre, to your left are the Michael Fowler Centre and the Edwardian Town Hall, both magnificent settings for concerts. Opposite these is the

The endemic kiwi is just one of the endangered species at Karori Sanctuary

Wellington's Civic Square is a cultural and social centre

Wellington public library and behind you is the City Gallery. Walk up to the gallery to Sea Bridge, which connects the square with the waterfront across Jervois Quay, and look back to see the visitor information centre and Wellington City Council building. Below the bridge is the entrance to 🎯 **Capital E**, a children's activity centre with a theatre, television and sound studios, and a playground. At the lagoon end of the bridge you can hire paddle boats; walk south along the waterfront towards Te Papa (➤ 110) for inline skates or north to Queens Wharf for kayaks.

➕ 223 E2

City Gallery Wellington
☎ (04) 801 3021; www.citygallery.org.nz
🕐 Daily 10–5
💲 Donation; charges for exhibitions

Capital E
☎ (04) 913 3740; www.capitale.org.nz
🕐 Mon–Fri 9–5, Sat–Sun 10–4;
phone for events schedule 💲 Approx. NZ$5

🔟 Matiu/Somes Island & Days Bay
Matiu/Somes Island is a former quarantine station now administered by the Department of Conservation, which has turned it into a wildlife sanctuary. Lying in Wellington Harbour 8km (5mi) from the city centre, it is a predator-free island and one of the few places where people can see tuatara, representatives of reptiles that appeared 200 million years ago, in the wild. Matiu/Somes Island has a network of footpaths and there are great views from the summit.

Departing from Queens Wharf, ferries continue on their 20-minute journey to Days Bay, on the eastern side of the harbour, or to Petone at its northern tip.

➕ 214 C1 ✉ Ferries from Queens Wharf, waterfront off Jervois Quay
☎ (04) 499 1282; www.eastbywest.co.nz
🕐 Up to 16 sailings daily to Days Bay; at least three daily trips to Matiu/Somes Island
💲 Approx. NZ$23

🔢 Kapiti Island
Kapiti Island is another pest-free wildlife reserve near the capital that sits 5km (3mi) offshore. The elongated 1,965ha (4,854-acre) isle dominates the coast off Paraparaumu, about 50km (30mi) north of Wellington. It is a sanctuary for kiwi, kaka and takahe, and

The Vynfield Estate is just one of the vineyards near Martinborough

the waters offshore are a feeding ground for birds and a nursery for fish. Kapiti Island is open to the public, but visitors are limited to 68 per day. You'll need to get a permit from the DOC's Wellington office and book the boat trip separately from the Kapiti Coast. There are a number of walking tracks, some leading to the summit of Tuteremoana (521m/1,709ft), but there are no shops or cafés so bring provisions with you.
✚ 214 C1

Kapiti Tours
🛈 www.kapititours.co.nz

Department of Conservation
✚ 223 E2
✉ 18 Manners Street, Wellington
☎ (04) 384 7770; www.doc.govt.nz
🕐 Mon–Fri 9–5, Sat 10–3:30

Kapiti Marine Charter
✚ 214 C2 ✉ Paraparaumu
☎ (04) 297 2585; www.kapitimarinecharter.co.nz
🕐 Departs Paraparaumu daily 9 or 9:30am, returning 3–4pm 💲 NZ$95

43 Martinborough
Martinborough is an ideal stopover for a vineyard visit. A popular weekend destination for Wellingtonians, it is an hour's drive from the city,

at the end of SH53. The main draw is the town's status as the centre of the Wairarapa vine-growing region, and most wineries give tours. November sees the Toast Martinborough Festival.
✚ 214 C1

Visitor Information Centre
✉ 18 Kitchener Street, Martinborough
☎ (06) 306 5010; www.wairarapanz.com
🕐 Mon–Fri 9–5, Sat–Sun and holidays 10–4

🎢 EXCITING ADVENTURES
- **Discovery Centres and StoryPlace** at Te Papa (➤ 110).
- **Capital E** on Civic Square (➤ 117).
- **Play area or rollerblading** on the waterfront.
- Seeing stars at the Planetarium in the **Carter Observatory** (➤ 116).

WALKING IN WELLINGTON
Wellington is hilly but compact and best explored on foot. Heritage trails take in suburbs such as Thorndon (➤ 115), historic streets and the waterfront, or you can try longer walks like the four-hour City to Sea route (➤ 190). Pick up a leaflet from the information centre.

Where to…
Stay

Prices
Expect to pay for a double room per night:
$ under NZ$200 $$ NZ$200–$350 $$$ over NZ$350

WELLINGTON

Amora Hotel Wellington $$–$$$
Just across the road from Te Papa (➤ 110) is this large luxury hotel, whose rooms all have views of Wellington's harbour. The rooms range from singles to doubles, twins and suites, all comfortable and stylishly decorated, and with the usual facilities expected of a modern hotel. Downstairs is a restaurant and bar (there are plenty of other excellent options near by if you fancy dining out), and there is also a gym. Check out the website for excellent-value deals.

➕ 223 E2
✉ 170 Wakefield Street
☎ (04) 473 3900;
www.wellington.amorahotels.com

Booklovers B&B $–$$
Host Jane Tolerton is a published writer who enjoys sharing her love of books with her guests. Every room in this bed and breakfast has shelves of books, including works by local author Katherine Mansfield (➤ 115). There are three guest rooms, each with a queen-size bed, ensuite bathroom, television and CD player. From here you can catch a bus or stroll down into the city – it is only a 15-minute walk from Te Papa – or explore the walking tracks on Mount Victoria.

➕ 223 off F1
✉ 123 Pirie Street, Mount Victoria
☎ (04) 384 2714;
www.booklovers.co.nz

Hotel InterContinental Wellington $$–$$$
Centrally situated, this striking, bronze-coloured building is a city landmark. It is close to Lambton Quay, Parliament, the waterfront and the Westpac Stadium. You're welcomed by a top-hatted doorman and the lobby gleams with marble. The 231 rooms include luxury suites, executive club level and standard rooms. There are restaurants and bars, and a health and fitness centre with a gym, spa, sauna and heated pool. It's worth checking for the less expensive weekend rates.

➕ 223 E3
✉ 2 Grey Street
☎ (04) 472 2722;
www.intercontinental.com/wellington

Museum Art Hotel $–$$$
The luxurious Hotel actually started life on the site of Te Papa (➤ 110), but the massive building was moved to its current site before the museum was built in 1993. Aside from being extremely handy for Te Papa and Wellington waterfront, the hotel has rooms, ranging from the standard option with queen-size bed, through to two-bedroom suites with harbour views. There are also seven suites specially designed to be wheelchair accessible. In addition, the hotel has a restaurant, bar and café, a heated lap pool and spa pool, and a gym, spa and sauna.

➕ 223 F1
✉ 90 Cable Street
☎ (04) 809 8900, 0800 994 335 toll free;
www.museumhotel.co.nz

Ohtel $$

This four-storey boutique hotel is located in the exclusive neighbourhood of Oriental Bay across the road from the sea and just a short walk from Te Papa. It was designed by architect and owner Alan Blundell, who wanted something very different, and a place to showcase his furniture collection. His designs are based on Danish Modern and 1960s retro. The focal point in each individually furnished room is the oversized bathroom with two-person bathtubs and large glass panels with New Zealand scenes behind them.

➕ 223 off F1
✉ 66 Oriental Parade
☎ (04) 803 0600; www.ohtel.com

Rydges $$

This sixteen-storey hotel by the Parliament buildings and the Westpac Stadium is an ideal base if you want to see a sports fixture and explore the city. Its luxurious leisure centre boasts a 17m (56ft) pool, a Jacuzzi and a sauna, and there's a bar and restaurant in the lobby. All of the modern rooms have kitchenettes and large bathtubs, and the hotel is adorned with artwork throughout.

➕ 223 E4
✉ 75 Featherston Street
☎ (04) 499 8686; www.rydges.com

Shepherds Arms Hotel $

Built in the 1870s and located in the historic Thorndon district (► 115), the Shepherds Arms is a good option in the heart of the city. There are 14 guest rooms, ranging from singles with a shared bathroom, to queen rooms and the King Suite, which has a four-poster king-size bed. Each room has the usual facilities, including Sky TV and a complimentary newspaper delivered each morning. Downstairs, the Speight's Ale House restaurant ($) serves hearty pub lunches and dinners.

➕ 223 D4
✉ 285 Tinakori Road, Thorndon
☎ (04) 472 1320, 0800 393 782 toll free; www.shepherds.co.nz

The Terrace Villas $$–$$$

Accommodation at The Terrace Villas is in eight 19th-century villas on The Terrace, close to the Cable Car and the Lambton Quay shopping district. The villas are divided into elegant apartments, ranging from studios to units with 3 large bedrooms. All have cable TV, laundry and kitchen facilities. Guests can park their cars for free.

➕ 223 E3   ✉ 202 The Terrace
☎ (04) 920 2020; www.terracevillas.co.nz

MARTINBOROUGH

The Old Manse $–$$

Sandra and John Hargrave have restored an old Presbyterian ministers' house that overlooks the local vineyards. There are six guest rooms, each of which has an ensuite bathroom. The lovely gardens around the house contain a petanque court and croquet lawn. In addition, there is a billiards table, Sky TV and a spa pool.

➕ 214 C1
✉ 19 Grey Street, Martinborough
☎ (06) 306 8599, 0800 399 229 toll free; www.oldmanse.co.nz

Tirohana Estate $$

This Martinborough winery, established 1988, has several accommodation options for visitors. Tirohana House, styled on a traditional French farmhouse, lies within the vineyard's grounds. It sleeps up to 12 in four suites and has all modern conveniences. In Martinborough itself is the Duckback Cottage, sleeping up to six. And last but not least is Greytown's 1905 Heritage Cottage, which sleeps up to eight.

➕ 214 C1
✉ Puruatanga Road, Martinborough
☎ (06) 306 9933; www.tirohanaestate.com

Where to...
Eat and Drink

Prices
Expect to pay per person for a meal, excluding drinks:
$ under NZ$45 $$ NZ$45–$60 $$$ over NZ$60

WELLINGTON

Caffe L'affare $
Enzo L'affare is credited with introducing Wellingtonians to espresso. A roaster roars at this relaxed café in a side street off Cambridge Terrace, and L'affare coffee appears on many restaurant menus. The café is a popular meeting place, serving snacks and all-day breakfast. There's even a 👫 children's play area.
➕ 223 F1
✉ 27 College Street, Wellington
☎ (04) 385 9748; www.caffelaffare.co.nz
🕐 Mon–Fri 7–4:30, Sat, Sun 8–4;
closed public holidays

Logan Brown $–$$$
Logan Brown has taken a grand 1920s Grecian banking chamber and turned it into a gracious restaurant in the French style, with a wine bar. It's a frequent winner of Wellington's best restaurant award. Its menu, which changes weekly, is contemporary with a seafood focus. Look for dishes like paua ravioli, and pan-roasted hapuku (fish) with tuatua (shellfish) fritters. The three-course bistro menu, **Insider Tip** available at lunchtime and pre-theatre, is excellent value. On some Fridays there's live jazz. Booking recommended.
➕ 223 E1 ✉ 192 Cuba Street, Wellington
☎ (04) 801 5114; www.loganbrown.co.nz
🕐 Mon–Fri noon–2, daily 5:30pm–late

Martin Bosley's $$$
Chef Martin Bosley has deservedly earned a reputation as one of the best in New Zealand, and his eponymous restaurant at the Royal Port Nicholson Yacht Club proves this point. The restaurant focuses on seafood, producing eye-catching dishes using local ingredients. For starters, select from the likes of a trio of fish tartars, then move on to the catch of the day, grilled, roasted or poached to perfection. If you can't choose a dessert, opt for the tasting plate so that you can sample several.
➕ 223 off F1
✉ 103 Oriental Parade, Wellington
☎ (04) 920 8302; www.martin-bosley.com
🕐 Lunch: Mon–Fri noon–2:30;
dinner: Tue–Sun 6–late

Matterhorn $$
Matterhorn is a Wellington institution: a restaurant, bar and café where the atmosphere is casual but the food top-notch. Bread baked freshly every day and butter churned on site are indicative of the chef's attention to detail. Dishes to try include an excellent butternut squash risotto for lunch, tasty crab ravioli for dinner, roast mushrooms on toast for brunch, or there is always a great-value roast on Sundays, which you can wash down with one of the 320-plus wines. It also attracts a trendy crowd for its live music on Thu–Sun nights.
➕ 223 E1
✉ 106 Cuba Street, Wellington
☎ (04) 384 3359; www.matterhorn.co.nz
🕐 Daily 10am–late

Wellington & Around

One Red Dog $

This lively restaurant in the centre of Wellington is just around the corner from Courtenay Place, hub of the city's nightlife district. Most people come here for the gourmet pizzas – the Shawshank has New Zealand flavours of lamb shank, caramelized onion and roasted pumpkin. Also on offer are anti-pasto starters and pasta and salad mains. The atmosphere is very relaxed, and it's also a great place to come if you have kids. You can find another branch on the waterfront at North Queens Wharf (tel: (04) 918 4723).

Insider Tip

✚ 223 F1 ✉ 9–11 Blair Street, Wellington
☎ (04) 384 9777; www.onereddog.co.nz
🕐 Daily 10am–late

Shed 5 $$$

Built in 1888 as a wool store on the wharf, Shed 5 is now an elegant restaurant and bar. The menu focuses on seafood and changes daily. It's also a pleasant place to have a coffee or a glass of wine, especially if you sit outside on the water's edge. It can get crowded and noisy inside, especially at lunchtime and in the early evening. Reservations are recommended.

✚ 223 F3 ✉ Queens Wharf, Wellington
☎ (04) 499 9069; www.shed5.co.nz
🕐 Mon–Fri noon–late, Sat–Sun 10am–late

Wagamama $

The popular Wagamama franchise is now on Wellington's watterfront, with views out across the harbour. Fans will find all their favourite Japanese noodle dishes on the menu, including seafood ramen noodle soup, ginger chicken fried udon noodles, and teriyaki salmon. The food is cooked fresh to order, and is great value if you are look-ing for an inexpensive yet tasty meal during a day's sightseeing.

✚ 223 E3 ✉ Meridien Building, 33 Customhouse Quay, Wellington
☎ (04) 473 7999; www.wagamama.co.nz
🕐 Daily 11:30am–late

The White House Restaurant $$$

Offering wonderful harbour views, this hotel offers first-rate food and service for more than 15 years. Dishes are made with seasonal ingredients. Starters include ravioli stuffed with local crab, while for your main course there is grilled salmon with wasabi mash. Save room for the excellent cheese platter

✚ 223 off F1
✉ 232 Oriental Parade, Wellington
☎ (04) 385 8555; www.whr.co.nz
🕐 Lunch: Fri noon–2; dinner: daily 6–late

Zibibbo $$

This restaurant in an old police station has been serving up Mediterranean cooking for nearly 15 years. The menu focuses on Spanish and Italian cuisine. Their pizzas are cooked in a wood-fired oven, and vegetarians are catered for, too. A top tip: if you go for a drink at Zibibbo's bar between 5pm and 7:30pm, they'll give you some complementary tapas!

✚ 223 F1
✉ 25–29 Taranaki Street, Wellington
☎ (04) 385 6650; www.zibibbo.co.nz
🕐 Lunch: Mon–Fri noon–2;
dinner: Mon–Sat from 5:30

MARTINBOROUGH

Saluté $$

Modern Middle Eastern and Mediterranean cuisine can be enjoyed in the casual dining room or in the shaded courtyard. At weekends, brunch is served until 3pm. The lunch selections are fairly light, with dishes such as spinach and feta soufflé and freshly baked bread filled with falafels. Dinner is more substantial, although you can still order mezze dishes such as spiced lamb and pork dumplings, fried halloumi and chickpea-battered mussels.

✚ 214 C1
✉ 83 Main Street, Greytown
☎ (06) 304 9825; www.salute.net.nz
🕐 Wed–Sat noon–late, Sun noon–3:30

Where to...
Shop

Shopping Centres
Wellington is a compact city, with most shopping districts close together. There are several centres on Lambton Quay, including **Capital on the Quay** (No. 226–262; tel: (04) 474 9865), with 25 shops and eateries. Or visit the country's oldest department store, **Kirkcaldie and Stains** (No. 165–177; tel: (04) 472 5899), founded in 1863.

Fashion
The Old Bank Arcade (233–237 Lambton Quay; tel: (04) 922 0600) houses some top NZ designers. For avant-garde labels, try **Zambesi** (107 Customhouse Quay; tel: (04) 472 3638) and **Spacesuit** (164 Cuba Street; tel: (04) 382 8786). Also along Cuba Street you can find **Frutti** (No. 176; tel: (04) 384 6965) and **Mandatory** (No. 108; tel: (04) 384 6107) for men. Get a **Fashion Map** from the Wellington Visitor Centre (corner of Victoria and Wakefield streets; tel: (04) 802 4860).

Arts & Crafts
For fine and applied art, try **Emerge Gallery** (corner of Wakefield and Chaffers streets; tel: (04) 385 2766) and **Avid** (48 Victoria Street; tel: (04) 472 7703). For souvenirs, try **Sommerfields** (296 Lambton Quay; tel: (04) 499 4847). You'll find some more unusual items in the museum stores at **Te Papa** (▶ 108–109) and the **Museum of Wellington City and Sea** (Bond Store, Queens Wharf; tel: (04) 472 8904).

Food & Drink
The **Dixon Street Deli** (45–47 Dixon Street; tel: (04) 384 2436) bakes its own bread and pastries and has a selection of cheeses and other deli items. Other downtown delis include **Caffe' Italiano** (229 Cuba Street; tel: (04) 385 2703), which sells coffee machines as well as food, and **Truffle** (22 Garrett Street; tel: (04) 385 2802), the largest importer of truffle-based products in New Zealand.

For sweet treats, check out **Butlers Chocolate Café** (103 Willis Street; tel: (04) 472 7630), **Ciocco Chocolaterie and Espresso Bar** (11 Tory Street; tel: (04) 382 8907), and **Tempt** (Old Bank Arcade, Lambton Quay; tel: 0800 868 367 toll free), with its delectable cakes.

To buy delicious fresh produce, visit the **City Market** (Chaffers Dock, Waterfront; tel: (04) 801 8380) or **Harbourside Market** (Waitangi Park, Cable Street; tel: (04) 495 7895). Both are held on Sunday mornings.

Children
The Baby's Room in Old Bank Arcade on Lambton Quay (tel: (04) 386 1171) is a specialist baby boutique. **Kids' Store** on Level 2 at Te Papa (▶ 110), stocks toys that are both educational and fun. Teenagers, meanwhile, should check out **Real Groovy** (250 Cuba Street; tel: (04) 385 2020) for music, DVDs, games, posters and T-shirts.

Sports & Outdoor Gear
For outdoor supplies try **Bivouac Outdoor** (39 Mercer Street; tel: (04) 473 2587) or **Kathmandu** (57 Willis Street; tel: (04) 472 0113). For water and winter sports, head to **Rip Curl** (82 Willis Street; tel: (04) 473 2298) or **Surf n Snow** (45 Cuba Street; tel: (04) 473 3371).

The **Lindale Centre** (SH1, Paraparaumu; tel: (04) 297 0916) boasts a number of farm shops selling a range of foods, including honey, ice cream and a selection of cheeses from the region.

Where to...
Go Out

For what's on, see the Thursday and Saturday editions of the **Dominion Post**. **Cuba Street** and **Courtenay Place** are the nightlife centres – bars, clubs, cinemas, theatres and cafés stay open until late.

Performing Arts

Wellington calls itself the cultural capital of New Zealand. The large, modern **Michael Fowler Centre**, Wakefield Street, is home to the New Zealand Symphony Orchestra (tel: (04) 801 3890). The **town hall**, next door, hosts more intimate concerts. The New Zealand String Quartet, Chamber Music New Zealand and the Wellington Sinfonia also give regular concerts. The Royal New Zealand Ballet (tel: (04) 381 9000) is based at the **Westpac St James Theatre** (77–83 Courtenay Place, tel: (04) 381 9000), also the venue for musical shows and the NBR New Zealand Opera (tel: (04) 384 4434).

For professional theatre, try **Downstage** (corner of Courtenay Place and Cambridge Terrace, tel: (04) 801 6946) or **Circa** (1 Taranaki Street, tel: (04) 801 7992). Alternative performers appear at **Bats** (80 Cuba Street, tel: (04) 802 4175). Get an **Arts Map** from the visitor information centre (corner of Victoria and Wakefield streets, tel: (04) 802 4860).

Nightlife

Live music venues include the trendy **Matterhorn** (▶ 121), as well as the **Bodega bar** (101 Ghuznee Street, tel: (04) 384 8212), that showcases up-and-coming New Zealand bands. For live jazz, try **Blondini's Jazz Lounge and Café** on the first floor of the Embassy Theatre (see below), or on Wednesday nights **Sandwiches** bar and restaurant (corner of Majoribanks Street and Kent Terrace, tel: (04) 385 7698). The latter also hosts national and international club DJs on Friday and Saturday nights, and has soul/funk/disco nights on Thursdays.

Cinemas

The 1924 **Embassy Theatre** in Courtenay Place (10 Kent Terrace, tel: (04) 384 7657) has been refurbished in grand style. Near by are the **Paramount Theatre** (25 Courtenay Place, tel: (04) 384 4080), Wellington's longest established cinema, and the Rialto (corner of Cable and Jervois streets, tel: (04) 385 1864).

Sports

Wellington's Westpac Stadium (Waterloo Quay, tel: (04) 473 3881) is the capital's main venue for major sporting events, including international soccer, cricket and rugby tournaments.

Festivals

The **New Zealand International Arts Festival** is held in March in even-numbered years, and overlaps with the annual **Wellington Fringe Festival**. A **Jazz Festival** is held in November. The **Montana World of Wearable Art Show** and the presentation of the coveted Wearable Art Award take place in September.

The region celebrates its annual **Toast Martinborough** festival in November, when the finest wines are served to the sounds of live music. For wine tasting throughout the year, join a tour with **Martinborough Wine Tours** (tel: (06) 306 8032) or pick up a vineyard map from the visitor information centre (▶ 114).

Top of the South Island

 Little Treats

Last Chance for Dinner!
The Park Café at the south entrance to **Abel Tasman National Park** (▶ 130) is a culinary haven in the middle of nowhere.

Market Forces
Artisans gather to sell their wares on Montgomery Place in **Nelson** every Saturday (▶ 136).

Mussels Galore
Take a Greenshell Mussel Cruise (tel: 0800 99 08 00) from **Havelock** to learn everything there is to know about this crustacean.

Getting Your Bearings

The Top of the South Island is a microcosm of New Zealand, where all the natural features for which the country is renowned can be found in a relatively small area. Here, you can ski down alpine peaks, soak in natural hot springs, sip wine among the vines, kayak past golden beaches, hike through forests and see marine mammals – all in the space of a few days.

The region was fairly heavily populated by Maori in early times, and the first ever encounter between Europeans and the *tangata whenua* (native people) took place in Golden Bay in 1642 when Dutch explorer Abel Tasman anchored here. Unfortunately, the meeting was not a happy one, ending with the deaths of four of the Dutch sailors. Some 130 years later, Captain James Cook also sailed along this coast, spending time in Ship Cove in the Marlborough Sounds, mapping the region and naming many of its features. Following on Cook's heels in the 1820s came whalers, who set up stations in the Marlborough Sounds and at Kaikoura, and then the New Zealand Company, which bought land off local Maori in the early 1840s to establish the city of Nelson.

Today, European immigrants and holidaymakers are still attracted to the region in large numbers, drawn to its sunny climate, beautiful scenery and vibrant arts and crafts scene. Visitors stepping off the ferry in Picton can choose either to spend some time locally, exploring the Marlborough Sounds and nearby vineyards around Blenheim; travel west to historic Nelson and the beaches of the Abel Tasman National Park and Golden Bay; or go whale watching off Kaikoura and relax in the hot pools of Hanmer Springs. Whether your interests lie in such active pursuits as skiing and kayaking, the Top of the South will not disappoint.

Tourists board a water taxi to explore the coastline of Abel Tasman National Park

Queen Charlotte Sound, Marlborough Sounds

Getting Your Bearings

TOP 10

Don't Miss

At Your Leisure

Four Perfect Days

The top of New Zealand's South Island isn't just a place for boat tours – follow our suggested four-day route to see all of the area's highlights. For more information see the main entries (➤ 130–137).

Day 1

Morning
Join a half-day cruise in the **44 Marlborough Sounds** (above, ➤ 134), either to Motuara Island to go birdwatching or to historic Ship Cove, keeping an eye out for dolphins along the way.

Afternoon and Evening
On your return to Picton, have lunch in a local café and take a look at the *Edwin Fox* exhibition. Drive to nearby **45 Blenheim** (28km/17mi) and join a guided tour of the surrounding **vineyards**, or pick up a map from the visitor centre and create your own itinerary.

Book dinner at one of the excellent **winery restaurants**, such as Twelve Trees (Allan Scott) or Herzog's (➤ 140).

Day 2

Morning
Drive the 112km (70mi) to **46 Nelson** (➤ 136), stopping off in the city for a coffee or early lunch at one of the many cafés there (➤ 141). If you are visiting on a Saturday, be sure to check out the funky craft stalls in the **Montgomery Square Market.**

Afternoon and Evening

Continue 50km (31mi) west along the coast to the town of Motueka to join a half-day guided **kayak tour** of the beautiful coves and golden beaches of the ★**Abel Tasman National Park** (▶130). Alternatively, catch a water taxi to Awaroa Lodge (▶138), where you can go for a walk, kayak or relax on the beach before staying the night.

If you're not staying in the park, head back to Nelson. Dine on fine seafood – at the **Boat Shed Café** (▶141), for example.

Day 3

Morning

Pick up a picnic in Nelson before driving 117km (73mi) inland to Lake Rotoiti in the heart of the **48 Nelson Lakes National Park** (▶137). Enjoy your lunch on the lakeshore, surrounded by bush-covered mountains, then go for a nature walk or rent a boat for a paddle on the calm waters.

Afternoon and Evening

From Lake Rotoiti, continue 233km (145mi) through the spectacular mountain scenery surrounding Murchison, Springs Junction and the Lewis Pass to **49 Hanmer Springs** (▶137). Stretch your limbs on arrival – literally – by making a bungy jump, or hiring a mountain bike and cycling along the forest tracks around the town.

Soak away the dust of the day in the alpine resort's hot pools, before enjoying a meal in one of the restaurants here (▶141).

Day 4

Morning

After an early morning dip in Hanmer's rejuvenating springs, head off for ★**Kaikoura** (124km/77mi) via the scenic SH70 Waiau road, to join a pre-booked **whale-watching tour** (▶132). Don't forget your camera!

Afternoon and Evening

See more of the marine wildlife by **swimming with dolphins** or from above on a **whale-spotting plane tour**, or join a **cultural tour** to learn more about the history of the local Maori.

Before dinner, take a drive out to the **seal colony** to watch the sun set, then literally *kai koura* ("eat crayfish") at one of the restaurants back in town (▶140).

⭐ Abel Tasman National Park

New Zealand's smallest national park is also one of its most popular, drawing local and international visitors alike to its golden beaches, bush-covered hills, turquoise waters and granite outcrops.

The area was originally used seasonally by Maori, who came to gather food here and cultivate *kumara* (sweet potato). Inhabitants at a *pa* (fort) at **Taupo Point** were the first Maori to come into contact with Europeans when they were involved in a skirmish in 1642 with Dutch explorer Abel Tasman, after whom the park is named. The 22,530ha (55,647-acre) park was founded in 1942, largely through the efforts of a single local conservationist, Perrine Moncrieff, who had become concerned about logging in the area.

Best Foot Forward

Today, the park attracts large numbers of visitors in summer, not least because of its easy access and lovely beaches. Hikers can tackle the 51km (32mi) **Abel Tasman Coastal Track** over three to five days, or those with less time can use the park's water-taxi service to get dropped off and walk short sections instead. The track is relatively easy, passing over forested headlands from bay to golden bay. The Department of Conservation (DOC) manages the park huts and campsites that are found at regular intervals along the way (advance booking required). In addition, there is a 27km (18mi) inland track that, like the coastal route, starts at Marahau and ends at Wainui, as well as shorter walks at Totaranui.

Insider Tip

Kayak Tours

An increasingly popular way of exploring the stunning bays is from the sea by **kayak**. You can spend three days kayak-

The park's coastal track covers 51km (32mi)

ing, swimming and camping on beaches as you go. Aside from the seals, you may also come across pods of dolphins or even an orca. Groups of two or more confident paddlers can also hire kayaks to explore independently. If you want to take things easier, there are **boat charter** options and **guided cruises**, or you can even fly direct to the luxurious Awaroa Lodge (➤ 138).

TAKING A BREAK

Awaroa Lodge (➤ 138) has an excellent restaurant, or if you join a kayak or boat tour food is usually provided as part of the package.

✚ 217 D5

Department of Conservation Visitor Centre
✉ Corner of King Edward and High streets, Motueka
☎ (03) 528 1810; www.doc.govt.nz ⊙ Mon–Fri 8–4:30
ℹ Hut passes can also be booked at the visitor information centre in Nelson (➤ 136)

Abel Tasman Aqua Taxi
✉ Marahau, RD2, Motueka
☎ (03) 527 8083, 0800 278 282 toll free; www.aquataxi.co.nz
⊙ Daily service (weather dependent)
💵 From NZ$40

Sea Kayak Company
✉ 506 High Street, Motueka
☎ (03) 528 7251, 0508 252 925 toll free; www.seakayaknz.co.nz
⊙ Daily (weather dependent)
💵 From NZ$85

Catamaran Sailing and Launch Charters
✉ 46 Martin Street, Monaco, Nelson
☎ (03) 547 6666; www.sailingcharters.co.nz
⊙ Daily 💵 From NZ$170

Abel Tasman Seal Swim
✉ Kayak Abel Tasman Base, Main Road, Marahau, RD2, Motueka
☎ (03) 527 8022; www.sealswim.com
⊙ Nov–May daily 9:15, 11:15 💵 Approx. NZ$170

INSIDER INFO

- The best time to visit the park is in February or March, after the school holidays have finished but while the weather is still warm and sunny. *Insider Tip*
- **Taupo Point**, on Wainui Bay in the northwest of the park, has an information board describing the *pa* (fort) that existed here when Abel Tasman arrived in 1642. The beautiful beach adjoining the headland is popular with nudists and rarely busy.
- If you have time, join a **seal swim** tour to Tonga Island. The seals may look ungainly on land, but their grace underwater is incredible to observe as you snorkel above them. *Insider Tip*

Kaikoura

The sperm whales that come to feed in the nutrient-rich waters off Kaikoura attracted whalers in the early 19th century, who hunted them down for their precious oil. Today, the whales are still the town's main drawcard, but visitors now come to shoot photos rather than harpoons.

Kaikoura is a small town on the northeast coast of the South Island, uninspiring in itself but backed by the stunning and precipitous Kaikoura Range, and with offshore waters that teem with a diverse range of marine wildlife. Early Maori named it after the abundant crayfish found here (*kai koura* means "eat crayfish").

From Hunting to Tourism

Fyffe House is the earliest building in Kaikoura and was built by George Fyffe, whose cousin Robert established the first whaling station here in 1842. Whale vertebrae were used as piles in the construction of the house, which is now open to visitors; in 2008, storms uncovered whale bones from the station's heyday on the beach in front.

The main industry of Kaikoura today is **whale watching** rather than whale hunting, which pulls in thousands of visitors year-round. Tour boats head 2km (1mi) out to sea, where underwater canyons that plummet to depths of 1,500m (5,000ft) and more come close to shore. Here, an upwelling of nutrients and minerals attracts all manner of sea creatures, including sperm whales, orca, pilot whales, humpbacks, dolphins, seals and sharks, as well as seabirds.

Wildlife Watching

The **sperm whales** are present year-round and are located with the aid of hydrophones and sharp eyes. Once a whale is spotted, the boat motors to within a respectful distance and the incredible leviathan can be observed resting at the surface for 10 minutes or so, before its vast tail rises up as it dives into the deep canyons to resume feeding. You may also see **bottlenose dolphins** or even rare **Hector's dolphins** (▶ Insider Info). Back on land, you can visit the **seal colony** at the end of the peninsula beyond Fyffe House and walk along the cliffs there (see box), join a **Maori cultural tour** to learn more about the area's first inhabitants, or take to the sky for **aerial views** of the whales and the stunning coastline.

HECTOR'S DOLPHINS

Hector's dolphins are endemic to New Zealand and are the rarest marine dolphins in the world, numbering fewer than 8,000 individuals. They are also the smallest dolphin species at just 1.4m (4.6ft) from nose to tail, and are instantly recognizable by their rounded dorsal fin.

TAKING A BREAK

On your way to the seal colony, stop off at the open-air **Kaikoura Seafood BBQ** (tel: 027 376 3619).

A tour boat catches a glimpse of a sperm whale

🞤 217 E3

Visitor Information Centre
✉ West End ☎ (03) 319 5641; www.kaikoura.co.nz
🕐 Mon–Fri 9–5, Sat–Sun 9–4

Fyffe House
✉ 62 Avoca Street ☎ (03) 319 5835; www.historic.org.nz
🕐 Oct–April daily 10–6; May–Sep Thu–Mon 10–4 💰 NZ$7

Maori Tours
✉ 10 Churchill Street ☎ (03) 319 5567; www.maoritours.co.nz
🕐 Half-day tours daily 9, 1:30 💰 From NZ$125

Whale Watch Kaikoura
✉ Whaleway Station ☎ (03) 319 6767; www.whalewatch.co.nz
🕐 Daily 7:15, 10, 12:45 💰 Approx. NZ$145

Wings Over Whales
✉ Kaikoura Airport, PO Box 55, Kaikoura
☎ (03) 319 6580; www.whales.co.nz
🕐 30-min tours daily 💰 Approx. NZ$145

Dolphin Encounter
✉ 96 The Esplanade ☎ (03) 319 6777; www.dolphin.co.nz
🕐 Nov–April daily 5:30am, 8:30am, 12:30pm; May–Oct 8:30am, 12:30pm
💰 Approx. NZ$170

INSIDER INFO

- The best time to go on a **whale-watching tour** is early in the morning, before the wind gets up and the sea is likely to be calmer.
- A rewarding walk follows part of the **Kaikoura Peninsula Walkway** from the seal colony at Point Kean to Whalers Bay (25 minutes). The path leads up onto the cliffs, giving great views down to the seals basking below.
- Just when you thought you'd seen it all: large pods of dusky dolphins frequent Kaikoura's inland waters year-round. For the rare chance to see these acrobatic mammals up close, join a **dolphin swim** tour.

Insider Tip

⓸ Marlborough Sounds

For many visitors, the Marlborough Sounds are their first sight of the South Island. The tranquil waterways are ideal for a relaxing stop-off, where you can potter about in boats, wander along the Queen Charlotte Track or fish for snapper.

Many travellers strike out further afield as soon as they get off the inter-island ferry from Wellington, but Marlborough Sounds are worth an exploration in their own right. Here, at the South Island's northeastern tip, the rise in sea-level after the last ice age created a labyrinth of islands, peninsulas and coves.

The Seaward Kaikoura Range on the south coast of the Marlborough Sounds

Cook Strait

The ferry crossing of Cook Strait is itself a rewarding and scenic journey. There are two inter-island services available from Wellington: Tranz Rail's **Interislander ferries** and **Bluebridge ferries**, both of which carry cars and foot passengers. They leave daily at varying frequencies (see opposite). Each ferry company takes a similar amount of time to get to Picton: around 3½ hrs, of which 60 mins is spent on often rough, open sea.

For the longest part of the journey the ferry travels through the narrow passages of the Marlborough Sounds, passing dramatic scenery. The sea calms down once you pass the tight entrance to **Tory Channel,** which stretches between a narrow tongue of the South Island mainland and Arapawa Island. It was here that 18th-century explorer Captain Cook first spotted the strait now named after him, and also here that the Polynesian explorer Kupe finally caught up with the giant octopus that led him to discover New Zealand (➤ panel).

KUPE AND THE OCTOPUS

A Maori legend tells of the Polynesian explorer Kupe, who was being pestered by a giant octopus that was eating his harvest of fish. Kupe decided to kill it, but the creature fled and Kupe had to chase it across the ocean to the southern Pacific, where he discovered New Zealand. He finally caught the octopus at Arapawa Island in the Marlborough Sounds.

Exploring Queen Charlotte Sound

Once the boat passes the island, the channel opens into **Queen Charlotte Sound**, at whose head is the small port of **Picton**, where passengers can transfer to buses or trains. The town makes a good base from which to explore the sounds. Picton's wharf, a short walk from the ferry terminal, is the departure point for cruise boats and water taxis. Cruise options range from short journeys around the inner Queen Charlotte Sound to full-day trips to the neighbouring **Kenepuru** or **Pelorus sounds.**

Another popular stop for visitors is **Ship Cove**, almost at the seaward end of Queen Charlotte Sound, which Captain Cook visited repeatedly on his voyages. It was here that he claimed the country on behalf of Britain, as well as letting loose the first sheep in New Zealand. The cove is also the starting point of the 67km (42mi) **Queen Charlotte Track**; you can hike the length of it (allow four days) staying in huts overnight, or get dropped off by water taxi and walk just a section.

TAKING A BREAK

For a good cup of coffee in Picton, try **Le Café** at noon–14 London Quay (tel: (03) 573 5588).

➕ 217 F5

Visitor Information Centre
✉ The Foreshore ☎ (03) 520 3113; www.destinationmarlborough.com
🕐 Nov–March Mon–Fri 8:30–6, Sat–Sun 8:30–5;
April–Oct Mon–Fri 9–4, Sat–Sun 10–3

Interislander
✉ Booking agents throughout the country ☎ (04) 498 3302;
www.interislander.co.nz 🕐 Sailings up to 10 times daily 💲 Range of fares

Bluebridge
➕ 205 C4 ✉ 50 Waterloo Quay, Wellington ☎ (04) 471 6188, 0800 844 844;
www.bluebridge.co.nz 🕐 Sailings 4 times daily 💲 Range of fares

INSIDER INFO

■ You can fly from Wellington to Picton, Nelson or Blenheim and get a **bird's-eye view** of the landscapes of the Marlborough Sounds (➤ 37).

■ Some of the smaller islands of the sounds have been cleared of predators and turned into **sanctuaries for endangered native species**. Access is restricted to most islands but you can visit **Motura Island** on a guided tour.

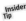
Insider Tip

■ On Picton's foreshore is the last remaining ship of the British East India Company, *Edwin Fox* (www.nzmaritime.co.nz/edwinfox.htm).

At Your Leisure

45 Blenheim

Set on the wide plains of the Wairau River valley, Blenheim has risen to prominence as the centre of the Marlborough wine industry, known for its Sauvignon Blanc. You can join a guided tour of the wineries in the area, stopping off for tastings and food among the vines, or pick up a map from the visitor information centre to create your own itinerary. Just outside town is the **Omaka Aviation Heritage Centre**, with a large collection of rare World War I planes that form the centrepiece of realistic dioramas created by special effects experts from film director Peter Jackson's Weta Workshop.

➕ 217 E4

Visitor Information Centre
✉ Railway Station, Blenheim ☎ (03) 577 8080; www.destinationmarlborough.com
🕐 Mon–Fri 8:30–5, Sat–Sun 9–3

Marlborough Travel
✉ PO Box 1000, Blenheim
☎ (03) 577 9997, 0800 990 800 toll free; www.marlboroughtravel.co.nz
🕐 Guided wine tours daily 🎫 From NZ$100

Omaka Aviation Heritage Centre
✉ 79 Aerodrome Road, Blenheim
☎ (03) 579 1305; www.omaka.org.nz
🕐 Daily 10–5; closed 25 and 26 Dec, 1 Jan
🎫 NZ$25

46 Nelson

Nelson is one of the oldest settlements in New Zealand, established by the New Zealand Company back in 1841. This heritage can be seen in the row of cottages in South Street behind the cathedral and in other mid-19th-century homes such as **Broadgreen House** in the suburb of Stoke, and is covered more fully in the excellent **Nelson Provincial Museum**.

Today, Nelson has a lively arts and crafts scene – visit the Saturday morning market in **Montgomery Square** for fun, funky pieces to take home, or browse the exhibitions at the **Suter Art Gallery**.

The city also makes a great base from which to explore Abel Tasman National Park (➤ 130) and Nelson Lakes National Park (➤ 137).

➕ 217 D 4

Visitor Information Centre
✉ Millers Acre Centre, corner of Trafalgar and Halifax streets, Nelson
☎ (03) 548 2304; www.nelsonnz.com
🕐 Nov–March daily 8:30–6; April–Oct Mon–Fri 8:30–5, Sat–Sun 9–4

Broadgreen House
✉ 276 Nayland Road, Stoke ☎ (03) 547 0403
🕐 Daily 10:30–4:30 🎫 NZ$4

Nelson has a number of arts and crafts outlets

The clear, fresh water of Waikoropupu Springs in Golden Bay

Nelson Provincial Museum
✉ Corner of Trafalgar and Hardy streets, Nelson
☎ (03) 548 9588; www.museumnp.org.nz
🕐 Mon–Fri 10–5, Sat, Sun and public holidays 10–4:30 💵 Donation

Suter Art Gallery
✉ 208 Bridge Street, Nelson
☎ (03) 548 4699; www.thesuter.org.nz
🕐 Daily 10:30–4:30 💵 Donation

47 Golden Bay
A winding drive 100km (60mi) northwest of Nelson over the Takaka Hill takes you to sleepy Golden Bay. At Waikoropupu Springs just outside the main town of Takaka, the clearest fresh water bubbles out of the ground at a rate of 14,000 litres (3,000 gallons) per second. The springs are sacred to Maori, so swimming in them is forbidden, but a viewing platform allows visitors to see underwater and a walking trail winds around the site.

The bay itself is dotted with shallow swimming beaches from the western end of Abel Tasman National Park (► 130) right round to the 30km-long (19mi) Farewell Spit, the site of several whale strandings. On the outside of the spit is the wild and dramatic Wharariki Beach, reached via a 20-minute walk over ancient dunes.

Golden Bay is also the start (or end) of the 82km (51mi) Heaphy Track, which traverses the remote Kahurangi National Park before emerging on the West Coast.
➕ 217 D5

Visitor Information Centre
✉ Willow Street, Takaka ☎ (03) 525 9136; www.nelsonnz.com 🕐 Nov–April daily 9–5; rest of year Mon–Fri 9–5, Sat–Sun 9–4

48 Nelson Lakes National Park
Centred on the small settlement of St Arnaud, the Nelson Lakes National Park is a 102,000ha (252,000-acre) wilderness of mountain peaks, glacial lakes and alpine vegetation. It is popular in summer for hiking, boating and trout fishing, and in winter for ski-ing on the small Rainbow Ski Area.

The short walk through the **Lake Rotoiti Nature Recovery Project** is ideal if you're not stopping – look for bellbirds, fantails and kaka along the way.
➕ 216/217 C/D3

Department of Conservation Visitor Centre
✉ View Road, St Arnaud
☎ (03) 521 1806; www.starnaud.co.nz
🕐 26 Dec–6 Feb daily 8–6; 7 Feb–Easter 8–5; rest of year 8–4:30

Rainbow Ski Area
✉ PO Box 76, St Arnaud
☎ (03) 521 1861; www.skirainbow.co.nz
🕐 Mid July–mid Oct daily 9–4

49 Hanmer Springs
At the thermal reserve in this alpine resort, natural hot springs feed a sequence of pools and have attracted visitors since 1859. As well as the spa, aqua therapy centre and beauty treatments, there are numerous outdoor activities.
➕ 217 D2

Hanmer Springs Thermal Pool and Spa
✉ Amuri Avenue, Hanmer Springs
☎ (03) 315 0000; www.hanmersprings.co.nz
🕐 Daily 10–9
💵 From NZ$20

Where to…
Stay

Prices
Expect to pay for a double room per night:
$ under NZ$200   **$$** NZ$200–$350   **$$$** over NZ$350

MARLBOROUGH SOUNDS

Punga Cove Resort $–$$$

Punga Cove is a remote and beautiful spot. Tucked in a sandy cove in the Marlborough Sounds, on a hillside covered in *punga* (native tree ferns), the resort is accessible (just) by road, but most easily by boat. Accommodation ranges from luxury suites to cabins for backpackers on the Queen Charlotte Track (➤ 135). There's a restaurant with a million-dollar view of the cove and Queen Charlotte Sound, and also a shop, pool and sauna. Activities include walking, kayaking and fishing.

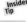 Insider Tip

✚ 217 F5
✉ Punga Cove, Endeavour Inlet
☎ (03) 579 8561; www.pungacove.co.nz

ABEL TASMAN NATIONAL PARK

Awaroa Lodge $$–$$$

This relaxed luxury beachside lodge, 50km (30mi) to the north-west in Abel Tasman National Park, is accessible only by air, boat or on foot. Accommodation ranges from superior suites to family rooms, all well designed. There is an excellent restaurant that uses local seafood as well as organic produce grown on site. Activities include beachcombing along Awaroa beach, hiking the Abel Tasman Track, sea kayaking and sailing.

✚ 217 D5
✉ Awaroa Bay
☎ (03) 528 8758; www.awaroalodge.co.nz

KAIKOURA

Hapuku Lodge $$$

Some 12km (7mi) north of Kaikoura is this unusual luxury lodge. Here, treehouses stand perched above a grove of kanuka trees, with views of mountains in one direction and out to sea in the other. Two of the treehouses have an additional "lower branch" room that is connected to the upper level via an internal staircase, perfect for families. There are also six guest rooms in the main lodge and an open-plan apartment that sleeps up to six. Included in the price is a buffet Continental breakfast, and in the evening guests can enjoy delicious food made with fresh local ingredients.

✚ 217 E3
✉ SH1 at Station Road, RD1
☎ (03) 319 6559, 0800 524 568 toll free; www.hapukulodge.com

Nikau Lodge $$

Built from native timbers in 1925, Nikau Lodge today offers stylish bed-and-breakfast accommodation. There are seven guest rooms, five with a queen-size bed, one with a king that can be converted into two singles, and one with just a single. All have ensuite bathrooms, and the rooms upstairs have the bonus of spectacular mountain views. At the end of your day, soak in the garden hot tub before wandering down into town for dinner, a five-minute walk away.

Insider Tip

✚ 217 E3 ✉ 53 Deal Street, Kaikoura
☎ (03) 319 6973; www.nikaulodge.com

BLENHEIM

Blue Ridge Estate $$

Situated very close to some of Marlborough's leading vineyards, this bed and breakfast has three guest rooms. All have direct access to the garden, with a private seating area, and the views look out over the estate's 8ha (20 acres) of grape vines to the Richmond Range. The property is not suitable for children.

✚ 217 E4
✉ 50 O'Dwyers Road, Rapaura, RD3
☎ (03) 570 2198; www.blueridge.co.nz

Hotel d'Urville $$–$$$

The heritage Public Trust Building provides a grand location for this boutique hotel. Much of the hotel is in the old bank vaults, and the 11 themed rooms have lofty ceilings, wooden floors and exotic furniture. The original central vault has been converted into a guest lounge with books and complimentary aperitifs. The restaurant and bar serve local food and wine.

✚ 217 E4 ✉ 52 Queen Street
☎ (03) 577 9945; www.durville.com

NELSON

South Street Cottages $$–$$$

South Street, behind Nelson Cathedral, is distinguished by its diminutive 1860s cottages. Three of these cottages have been turned into self-contained holiday accommodation. Each has two bedrooms, one with a double bed and the other with a queen, as well as a fully equipped kitchen and garden courtyard. Also available is a nearby two-bedroom apartment, South Haven, and Haven Light, a one-bedroom waterfront villa on Wakefield Quay, designed around a pohutukawa tree and with fabulous views of the water.

✚ 217 D4 ✉ South Street
☎ (03) 540 2769;
www.cottageaccommodation.co.nz

Te Puna Wai Lodge $$

This early Victorian villa nestles in the hills above Nelson Port. The house has been lovingly refurbished, and rooms have adjoining bathrooms and antique furnishings. The three rooms can be booked separately or together. Upstairs is a self-contained suite with fabulous sea views, while downstairs is a double room and a one-bedroom apartment with a kitchen.

✚ 217 D4 ✉ 24 Richardson Street
☎ (03) 548 7621; www.tepunawai.co.nz

HANMER SPRINGS

Cheltenham House $$

Just around the corner from the hot pools is a 1930s heritage home with four spacious suites inside, two cottages in the garden, and a modern four-bedroom, three-bathroom villa that takes a maximum of eight guests. Each suite features antique furniture and king-size or twin beds. The cottages have queen-size beds and private bathrooms. This luxury bed and breakfast includes complimentary wines in the evening.

Insider Tip

✚ 217 D2 ✉ 13 Cheltenham Street
☎ (03) 315 7545; www.cheltenham.co.nz

The Heritage Hanmer Springs $$

Part of the Heritage hotel chain, the Heritage Hanmer Springs is a restored early 20th-century Spanish-style lodge that, like its sister establishments in Auckland and Queenstown, provides luxury accommodation. The standard rooms all have queen-size beds, while those opening onto the gardens also have an outside patio. The lodge has also six self-contained villas in its grounds. There is a bar and restaurant, outdoor pool and tennis courts, and it is just a short downhill walk to the town's thermal pools.

Insider Tip

✚ 217 D2 ✉ 1 Conical Hill Road
☎ (03) 315 0060, 0800 368 888 toll free;
www.heritagehotels.co.nz

Where to...
Eat and Drink

Prices
Expect to pay per person for a meal, excluding drinks:
$ under NZ$45 $$ NZ$45–$60 $$$ over NZ$60

MARLBOROUGH SOUNDS

The Mussel Pot $

The Mussel Pot is more than enough reason to stop in Havelock. The set-up is casual, with wooden tables and benches inside and on the patio. On offer are "steamers" (whole steamed mussels) and "flats" (grilled half-mussels), both of which come with a choice of sauces and plenty of bread.

✚ 217 E4 ✉ 73 Main Street, Havelock
☎ (03) 574 2824; www.themusselpot.co.nz
🕐 Nov–March daily 11:30–3:15, 5:30–10;
April–Oct 11:30–2:30, 5–10

KAIKOURA

The Store at Kekerengu $–$$

Halfway between Blenheim and Kaikoura on State Highway 1 is this café-cum-crafts shop-cum-post office. The building fits well in the landscape, with bare wooden beams, a double-sided fireplace and a bleached outside deck. It's a great place to stop for a light snack to break up your journey, or you can fill up on more substantial dishes such as crayfish and blue cod. In summer, sit outside and watch the surf, or in winter warm yourself by the open fire. Local Marlborough wines feature big on the drinks list.

✚ 217 E3 ✉ SH1, Kekerengu
☎ (03) 575 8600
🕐 Nov–April daily 7:30–7:30; May–Oct 8–6

White Morph $$$

Adjacent to the motor inn of the same name on Kaikoura's Esplanade, and with views out to sea, is the town's only fine dining establishment. Like many other local restaurants it specializes in fresh seafood, including the crayfish after which the town is named. Seafood starters include bouillabaisse Pacifica, and for mains there is a platter containing a selection of *kai moana* (seafood). The restaurant has won several awards.

✚ 217 E3
✉ 94 The Esplanade, Kaikoura
☎ (03) 319 5676;
www.whitemorphrestaurant.co.nz
🕐 Nov–April daily 5:30–8:30;
May–Oct 5:30–9:30

BLENHEIM

Herzog's $$$

A gourmet destination re-created by Hans and Therese Herzog in the style of their celebrated Swiss restaurant. The decor is opulent, with antiques, formal flower arrangements and the tables set with fine china. There's a five-course menu focused on seasonal produce, fish and game. With more than 550 labels, the wine cellar is one of the most extensive in New Zealand. The vineyard also has a bistro.

✚ 217 E4 ✉ 81 Jeffries Road, Blenheim
☎ (03) 572 8770; www.herzog.co.nz
🕐 Mid Oct–mid May Tue–Sun 6:30pm–late;
bistro: mid Oct–mid May Tue–Sun noon–5;
Mid Dec–March Tue–Sun noon–5

Twelve Trees Restaurant $$

The restaurant at Allan Scott's striking rammed-earth winery is a popular place for lunch. Eat out on the sheltered garden terrace, or inside under the vaulted ceiling, where you can admire the artworks. The menu is simple and fresh, ranging from pear, blue cheese and kumara or bread and dips to local mussels, salmon and fresh salads. Allan Scott is a pioneer of viticulture in Marlborough and the producer of fine wines, so it's a good place to try them, too.

Insider Tip

🔡 217 E4 ✉ Allan Scott Wines and Estates, Jackson's Road, RD3, Blenheim
☎ (03) 572 7123; www.allanscott.com/restaurant
🕐 Daily 9–5 (lunch 11:30–3:30)

NELSON

The Boat Shed Café $$–$$$

A converted boat shed, with water lapping its foundations, this restaurant not surprisingly specializes in seafood. Choose from Nelson scallops and Tasman Bay crabs to salmon. Crabs and crayfish come straight from the restaurant's holding tanks. Either dine inside or enjoy the views from the deck.

🔡 217 D4
✉ 350 Wakefield Quay, Nelson
☎ (03) 546 9783; www.boatshedcafé.co.nz
🕐 Mon–Fri 11–late, Sat, Sun 10–late

The Honest Lawyer $–$$

Styled on an English country pub, and built of locally quarried stone, the Honest Lawyer sits on a peninsula about 10 minutes' drive from Nelson. Open fireplace and bric-a-brac set the scene inside. Outside, a beer garden overlooks the estuary. The pub has 13 beers on tap, a good wine list and hearty pub food. You can also have breakfast, snacks and cream teas. There's accommodation on site with 10 rooms and three cottages.

🔡 217 D4
✉ 1 Point Road, Monaco, Nelson
☎ (03) 547 8850; www.honestlawyer.co.nz
🕐 Daily 7am–midnight (food until 9:30pm)

Morrison Street Café $$

A regular winner of Nelson's best café award, the Morrison Street Café is the perfect place to reboot your system with a coffee and cake. Alternatively enjoy a hearty weekend brunch, or relax over lunch in the courtyard.

🔡 217 D4
✉ 244 Hardy Street, Nelson
☎ (03) 548 8110; www.morrisonstreetcafé.co.nz
🕐 Mon–Fri 7:30–4, Sat 8:30–4, Sun and public holidays 9–4

GOLDEN BAY

Mussel Inn $

This micro brewery has become something of a local institution. Quench your thirst on a Captain Cooker manuka beer, Apple Roughy cider or Lemming Aid (lemonade), all made on the premises, while you relax in front of the open fire. Meals are simple but tasty and include fish, pies and the signature mussel chowder. The inn has won awards for its environmental stance and has an anti-mobile phone policy.

Insider Tip

🔡 217 D5
✉ Onekaka, RD2, Takaka
☎ (03) 525 9241; www.musselinn.co.nz
🕐 Daily 11am–late; closed mid July–mid Sep

HANMER SPRINGS

Malabar $$

Chef Sudip Masra has brought a whole new range of flavours to Hanmer Springs from his native India, combining spices from the subcontinent with seasonings from elsewhere in Asia to create exciting fusion dishes. You can start with a Thai hot-and-sour tom yum soup, before moving on to spice-encrusted rack of lamb or an Indian thali tray.

🔡 217 D2 ✉ Alpine Pacific Centre, 5 Conical Hill Road, Hanmer Springs
☎ (03) 315 7745
🕐 Daily noon–3, 6–late; takeaway service also available

Where to…
Shop

MARLBOROUGH

The **Marlborough Art and Craft Trail** has more than 25 craftspeople (Railway Station, Sinclair Street; www.marlboroughbb.co.nz/marlborough-art-craft.html). **Matua Valley** (New Renwick Road; www.matua.co.nz) sells wines, olive oil and souvenirs. **Sherrington Grange** (Mahau Sound, Picton) sells local cheese and honey. **Traditional Country Preserves** (12 Hilton Place; www.countrypreserves.co.nz) makes preserves and sells crafts. **Prenzel Distillery** (28 Sheffield Street; http://prenzel.com) makes liqueurs and fruit brandies. **Leighvander Cottage** (The Village, RD1, Wairau Valley; http://www.leighvandercottage.co.nz) has lavender-related products. On Sundays (9–noon) **Marlborough Farmers' Market** has good local produce (A & P Showgrounds, corner of Alabama and Maxwell roads; marlboroughfarmersmarket.co.nz; Oct–June).

NELSON

At Nelson's **Saturday Market** (Montgomery Square; www.nelsonmarket.co.nz) there's everything from dog outfits to organic produce. You can watch glassblowers at **Höglund Art Glass** (52 Lansdowne Road, Richmond; www.hoglundartglass.com; 10–5). The nearby **Grape Escape Complex** (corner of McShanes Road and SH60, Richmond; www.thegrapeescapecafé.co.nz) includes the **Escape Gallery**, with local crafts, a café and chocolate shop. Get crafty yourself and choose world-class beads from the **Bead Gallery** (153 Hardy Street, Nelson; http://beads.co.nz).

Where to…
Go Out

MARLBOROUGH

Visit some of the 45 wineries in the region using the **Marlborough Wine Trail map** from the Blenheim Visitor Centre (Railway Station, Sinclair Street; tel: (03) 577 8080; https://marlboroughnz.com).

Festivals
Marlborough Wine Festival is the culmination of a festival week in February.

Hunter's Garden Marlborough is held in November.

NELSON

The Suter (28 Halifax Street E; www.thesuter.org.nz) is the region's art museum, with galleries, a café and a theatre. Enjoy jazz at **The Vic Mac's Brewbar** (281 Trafalgar Street; www.vicbrewbar.co.nz).

A number of wineries are open to visitors. Pick up a copy of the **Wineart guide map** from the visitor information centre (77 Trafalgar Street; tel: (03) 548 2304; www.nelsonnz.com). This is a major hop-growing region: sample a brew at the organic **Founders** brewery (Founders Historic Park, 87 Atawhai Drive; http://foundersbrewery.co.nz).

Festivals
Nelson's annual **Arts Festival** is held in October. The **Adam New Zealand Chamber Music Festival** takes place in odd-numbered years. **The Nelson Summer Festival** is held from Christmas–Feb and includes a range of events. The Ecofest in August celebrates regional produce and the issue of sustainability.

Christchurch & the Southern Alps

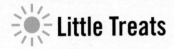 **Little Treats**

A Date with the Dolphins

Take a **boat trip** near Akaroa (➤ 153) to come face-to-face with dolphins.

Hot Pools by a Glacial Lake

The hot waters of **Tekapo Springs** (daily 10am–9pm) are a perfect place for a dip when it's cool at **Lake Tekapo** (➤ 159)!

Serious Souvenirs

You'll find a good selection of high-quality crafts at **Punakaiki Crafts** (➤ 160) near Pancake Rocks.

Getting Your Bearings

If you thought the scenery of the North Island was magnificent and the people too nice to be true, prepare to be surprised. In the South Island, the mountains soar even higher, the forests are more vigorous and the landscapes will astonish you.

Christchurch is the South Island's largest city and a gateway to all other destinations in the south. The city was planned as an antipodean outpost of the Church of England and is currently busy recuperating from the dreadful earthquake of February 2011. The Canterbury Plains around the city are New Zealand's largest stretch of flat land and one of its most important agricultural areas. Some of the country's biggest farms use the land here for anything from traditional sheep and dairy farming to boutique vineyards and olive groves.

The plains were built up over millions of years from silt carried by rivers from the Southern Alps, the South Island's mountainous backbone, which separates the drier eastern regions from the humid and lush West Coast.

Most of New Zealand's national parks are on the South Island, so whichever way you go from Christchurch you'll find spectacular land- or seascapes and see some amazing wildlife. If you travel north to Kaikoura by water, you'll share the ocean with hundreds of dolphins and whales. Head south to Aoraki/Mount Cook, and you'll get to walk through a wonderland of snow-capped peaks. Finally, go west through Arthur's Pass to the rugged West Coast and you could be taking a stroll on a glacier within minutes of leaving the beach.

CHRISTCHURCH EARTHQUAKE

At 12:51 on 22 February 2011, Christchurch was hit by a terrible earthquake, killing 185 people and laying waste to the city centre, the residential quarter to the east, and the little harbour town of Lyttelton nearby. Most of the city's prestigious buildings were destroyed and many houses became uninhabitable. Downtown Christchurch was closed off to allow the damaged structures to be torn down and rebuilt. It didn't become accessible again until August 2013 – a milestone in bringing tourism back to the area. A few salvageable historic buildings have been restored and reinforced with steel for extra protection, and a number of hotels have opened their doors for business once again.

Getting Your Bearings

Christchurch & the Southern Alps

Five Perfect Days

This five-day trip round Christchurch and the Southern Alps shows you the delights of the South Island's largest metropolis and the allure of the mountains nearby. For more information see the main entries (➤ 148–160).

Day 1

Morning
Start your exploration of ⑤⓪ Christchurch (➤ 151) by taking a walk round the city centre, an area which is set to change a great deal over the next few years. Take a stroll over **Cathedral Square** to see the new **Cardboard Cathedral** (➤ 151) before continuing down the freshly-renovated Regent Street (➤ 151). You could also hop on a tram to visit the Arts Centre (currently being rebuilt).

Afternoon
Visit the **Canterbury Museum** (➤ 152) before ambling through the **Botanic Gardens** and the magnificent **Hagley Park** (➤ 152). Enjoy the wildlife and experience a Maori cultural evening at the ⑤④ **Willowbank Wildlife Reserve** (➤ 158), or take the Christchurch **Gondola** (➤ 159) up the Port Hills (➤ 159) to watch the sun set behind the Southern Alps.

Day 2

Explore ⑤① **Banks Peninsula** (➤ 153) and its French settlement, Akaroa. On your way, stop at the Hilltop Tavern, about 60km (35mi) from Christchurch, for the first view of the peninsula. Take SH75, the coastal route to Akaroa and join a harbour cruise to see some **Hector's dolphins**. Have lunch and browse the craft shops in Akaroa. Return to the hilltop via the summit road.

Day 3

Morning
Leave Christchurch early to drive to ⑤②**Aoraki/Mount Cook** (above, ➤ 156), via ⑤⑦**Lake Tekapo** (➤ 159) – the main roads are SH1 and SH8. Explore the area and the glaciers that flow into the valley and join a walk or boat trip on the glacier lake.

Afternoon
Take a scenic flight over New Zealand's tallest mountain range and, weather permitting, land on ⑤⑧**Tasman Glacier** (➤ 160) for a short walk. In the late afternoon, walk into the **Hooker Valley** along the glacial moraine, and across two swing bridges, for some of the best sunset views of Aoraki/Mount Cook.

Day 4

Morning
Drive back to Christchurch and travel to the ★**West Coast** (➤ 148) through ⑥⓪**Arthur's Pass** (➤ 160). Either take the **TranzAlpine Express** (➤ 30), or drive along SH73, if you want to stop for short walks in the **Southern Alps**. Explore the limestone formations at ⑤⑨**Castle Hill** and **Cave Stream** (➤ 160) on the way.

Afternoon
Have lunch in **Greymouth**, then head south along SH6 and visit greenstone-carving and glass-blowing workshops in **Hokitika** (➤ 149).

Day 5

Continue exploring the rainforests, lakes and beaches of the West Coast south of Hokitika. Walk to the face of either **Franz Josef** or **Fox glaciers** (➤ 149), and join a walking tour or a helicopter excursion to the top of Fox Glacier. Alternatively, walk to **Lake Matheson** (➤ 193) for some of the best views of the Aoraki/Mount Cook range.

This is page 148.

⭐The West Coast

On a calm and sunny day, the West Coast is a wonderland of snowy peaks, glistening lakes and lush rainforests. But "The Coast" – as New Zealanders refer to the narrow strip of land between the Tasman Sea and the South Island's mountainous spine – also experiences some ferocious weather, bringing more than 5,000mm (200in) of rain a year and sometimes whipping the surf into a mighty ocean.

Westland could be called Wetland. The area's rainfall is surpassed only by Fiordland (▶ 170), New Zealand's largest national park, with which south Westland shares the honour of World Heritage status. You can often see clouds looming over the western side of the mountains as soon as you reach **Arthur's Pass** (▶ 160). They rarely reach the golden hills on the eastern side of the Main Divide, dissolving instead into rain as they reach the wall of mountains. The rain however is what gives the coast its exuberant freshness and vigour in the form of the region's forests, pastures, lakes and imposing glaciers.

TRAMPING
Fox Glacier is a short drive from the mirroring waters of **Lake Matheson** and the un-tamed beauty of **Gillespies Beach** (▶ 187–189).

Greymouth's Fortunes

Travelling from Christchurch, you meet the coast at **Greymouth**, a port on the River Grey and the region's largest town, with about 10,000 inhabitants. Founded on gold and continued on coal, it now survives on timber, fishing and tourism. Although not exciting, it is a handy base for exploring the area. Follow SH6 south towards Hokitika, and about 10km (6mi) south of Greymouth you will see the turn-off 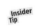 to 🔲**Shantytown**, a re-creation of an 1880 gold-rush town, where you can still pan for gold – great for children.

Perfect reflections on the waters of Lake Matheson

Hokitika and the Landscape Beyond

In **Hokitika**, about 40km (25mi) south of Greymouth, the memorial clock tower marks the town centre and there's a scattering of arts and crafts studios along Tancred and Revell streets. Several stone- and bone-carvers and glass-blowers have opened their workshops to the public and you can watch your souvenirs evolve in their hands. This is also where the annual Wildfoods Festival (▶ 16) takes place.

Insider Tip

South of Hokitika the scenery becomes grander and the population sparser. The mountain ranges rise gradually as you approach the **Aoraki/Mount Cook massif,** with New Zealand's highest peaks, Aoraki/ Mount Cook (▶ 147–148)

The ever-moving Franz Josef Glacier

and Mount Tasman. The road moves away from the ocean to wind through pastureland, past glacier-carved lakes and along wind-battered rainforests. Trees along this coastal seam have a distinct eastward lean, their branches reaching for the mountains.

The Southern Alps' Glaciers

After about 150km (90mi) you'll reach the Southern Alps' glacier region, an impressive vista of ragged mountains with large snowfields and ice walls. There are more than 60 glaciers in the Westland National Park alone, and about 3,000 throughout the Southern Alps, but most are inaccessible to anybody but mountaineers. **Franz Josef** and **Fox glaciers**, however, stretch their icy tongues so far down the ranges they could almost lick the sea.

If you have never seen a glacier up close it is worth walking for a few minutes to get a good view of the frozen pinnacles, crevasses and ice falls. Pick up information about guided walks and scenic flights at the information centres at Franz Josef or at Fox village, 25km (16mi) further south. These are both tiny resort towns with just a main street lined with eateries and tour-operators' shops. The car park for the Franz Josef Glacier is 5km (3mi) inland from the main road, and the first lookout is a 20-minute return walk. At the larger Fox Glacier, you'll find a car park 4km (2.5mi) from the main road and similar options, from short walks to a one-hour excursion to the glacier's terminal face.

Christchurch & the Southern Alps

■ TAKING A BREAK

The **Lake Mahinapua Hotel** (tel: (03) 755 8500) is just south of Hokitika, on SH6 opposite the turn-off to Lake Mahinapua. It's a typical colonial building, plain inside, but the pub is a great place to drink with the locals and enjoy some salty West Coast repartee.

✚ 216 A3

Greymouth Visitor Information Centre
✚ 216 B2
✉ Corner of Herbert and Mackay streets
☎ (03) 768 5101; www.greydistrict.co.nz
🕑 Nov–March Mon–Fri 8:30–6, Sat 9–5, Sun and public holidays 10–5; April–Oct Mon–Fri 8:30–5:30, Sat 9–5, Sun and public holidays 10–4

Shantytown
✚ 216 B2
✉ Rutherglen Road, Greymouth
☎ (03) 762 6634, 0800 742 689 toll free; www.shantytown.co.nz
🍴 Everybody's Tearooms ($)
🕑 Daily 8:30–5 💲 NZ$32

Franz Josef Visitor Centre
✚ 218 C4 ✉ Main Road, Franz Josef
☎ (03) 752 0796; www.doc.govt.nz
🕑 Nov–March daily 8:30–6; April–Oct 8:30–5

Franz Josef Glacier Guides (Glacier Walking Tour)
✚ 218 C4
✉ Main Road, Franz Josef ☎ (03) 752 0763, 0800 484 337 toll free; www.franzjosefglacier.com 🕑 Daily, weather-dependent

Guiding Fox Glacier (Glacier Walking Tour)
✚ 218 C4
✉ Main Road, Fox Glacier ☎ (03) 751 0825, 0800 111 600 toll free; www.foxguides.co.nz
🕑 Daily, weather-dependent

White Heron Sanctuary Tours
✚ 216 A1
✉ SH6 (PO Box 19), Whataroa
☎ (03) 753 4120, 0800 523 456 toll free; www.whiteherontours.co.nz
🕑 Heron tours daily during breeding season late Oct–early March; nature tours and jet boating year-round
💲 From NZ$12

INSIDER INFO

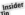
Insider Tip

- Consider joining **a guided walk** or **helicopter flight to the glacier surface**. No mountain experience is required and you will be equipped with a pair of boots, instep crampons and an alpenstock. If you are planning a **glacier excursion**, or even just approaching one, bring warm clothing and stay behind the safety barriers.

- The road between Hokitika and the glaciers passes several **glacial lakes**. Lake Mahinapua, the first glacial lake on the route south from Hokitika (from SH6, turn right to Ruatapu), is fringed by tall stands of kahikatea. About 40km (25mi) further south, SH6 runs along the shores of Lake Ianthe, which offers picnic spots and a small campsite. Further south, about 10km (6mi) before Franz Josef Glacier, is Lake Mapourika.

- Visit the **breeding area of the *kotuku***, the majestic white herons, which nest in New Zealand only at Okarito Lagoon. The breeding area is accessible only for guided tours as the birds are protected. The best time to visit is between November and February, when the birds are on their nests. You can organize a guide at White Heron Sanctuary Tours at the address above.

⑩ Christchurch

Despite the 2011 earthquake, Christchurch still looks like a lost corner of old England. Willows line the Avon River as it meanders through the heart of the city, green spaces abound, and many streets carry the names of English cathedral cities. There isn't much left of the town's neo-Gothic architecture, however, and the famous Christchurch Cathedral stands in ruins.

If you are arriving by air, you will see this city of gardens snuggling up against the Port Hills and spilling out onto the Canterbury Plains. Farming has always been Canterbury's economic backbone and Christchurch is hemmed in by a patchwork of field.

Go punting in the Botanic Gardens

Exploring Christchurch

Start your visit at the lively **Cathedral Square**, now home to the ruin of the once majestic Christchurch Cathedral. Walk from Cathedral Square down **Worcester Street** to **Latimer Square**, where you'll spot the unusual **Cardboard Cathedral** rising up at the corner of Madras Street. As the name suggests, the structure is made of cardboard – a temporary solution dreamt up after the earthquake by Japanese star architect, Shigeru Ban. It's totally unique and definitely worth a look. Head down **Gloucester Street** to the carefully renovated **New Regent Street**, which now looks just as beautiful as it did back in the 1930s when the Spanish Mission architectural style was all the rage. Little shops, restaurants and cafés line the quiet, pedestrianised street, making it ideal for a coffee break or an early lunchtime snack. You might also spot the **Wizard**, a real character and an icon of the city, standing in the street philosophising loudly about God, the universe and – his favourite subject – women.

Christchurch & the Southern Alps

Clamber aboard one of the street's historic **trams** and hop off when you reach the **Arts Centre**. Just across Rolleston Avenue is the **Canterbury Museum** (with displays on natural history and the Antarctic), and the entrance to **Christchurch Botanic Gardens** and **Hagley Park**. This 165ha (407-acre) park, the city's largest, boasts a golf course among its facilities. The native plants in the vast botanic gardens were gleaned from all over the country. They look particularly lovely in the evening light.

TAKING A BREAK

There are lots of nice, quiet spots to discover along the little river Avon: Grab a piece of cake at the **Boatshed Café** or rent a boat from the **Antigua Boatsheds**.

🔂 219 F4 (see panel ➤ 144)

i-SITE Visitor Centre
🖂 Rolleston Avenue, next to the Canterbury Museum ☎ (03) 379 9629; www.christchurchnz.com
🕒 Daily 8:30–6

Cardboard Cathedral
🖂 Corner of Latimer Square and Madras Street
ℹ️ www.cardboardcathedral.org.nz

Christchurch Cathedral
🖂 Cathedral Square
ℹ️ www.christchurchcathedral.co.nz

Antigua Boatsheds
🖂 2 Cambridge Terrace
☎ (03) 366 6768
ℹ️ They also rent out bicycles

Christchurch Art Gallery
🖂 Worcester Boulevard
ℹ️ www.christchurchartgallery.org.nz

🕒 Currently still closed due to earthquake damage.

Christchurch Arts Centre
🖂 2 Worcester Boulevard
🕒 www.artscentre.org.nz
🕒 Closed for the forseeable future.

Canterbury Museum
🖂 Rolleston Avenue, at Botanic Garden entrance
ℹ️ www.cantmus.govt.nz
🕒 Oct–March 9–5:30; April–Sep 9–5
💲 Donation; exhibitions priced separately

Christchurch Botanic Gardens
🖂 Rolleston Avenue
ℹ️ www.ccc.govt.nz
🕒 Gardens: 7am–one hour before sunset; conservatories: 10:15–4; information centre: Mon–Fri 9–4, Sat–Sun 10:15–4 💲 Free

INSIDER INFO

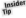
Insider Tip

- **Trams** travel regularly along a 2.5km (1.5mi) loop that takes in all inner-city attractions. Passes (valid for two consecutive days) are available from the conductor and you can hop on and off as you please.
- The region's **dry northwesterly winds** are similar to Europe's föhn and can cause headaches for some people.
- Experience a city being reborn from the rubble: take a **guided cycle tour** and witness first-hand how Christchurch is recovering from the catastrophic effects of the earthquake. Christchurch Rebuild Bike Tour: daily 10am and 2pm, tel: 0800 733 257 (toll free), www.chchbiketours.co.nz.

🖲 Banks Peninsula

Banks Peninsula was once an island and, although it has been connected to the mainland for thousands of years, it has retained an independent spirit and a distinctive landscape, with many secluded bays and golden beaches.

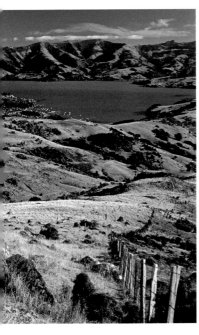

The volcanic beginnings of Banks Peninsula can be seen in the landscape

The biggest settlement, **Akaroa**, has a distinct Gallic flavour, with street names such as Rue Jolie and Rue Lavaud, the L'Aube hill as a backdrop and a romantic atmosphere reminiscent of a fishing village on the Côte d'Azur. French whaling captain Jean Langlois fell in love with the peninsula when he landed here in 1838 and promptly negotiated a land sale with the resident Maori chiefs. When he returned with French settlers two years later, British officials had claimed sovereignty under the Treaty of Waitangi (▶ 14). The French stayed, nevertheless, and left an indelible mark on the town.

It's fun just to walk Akaroa's narrow picturesque streets, to sample local food and wine or to enjoy some of the water activities available. In summer, a **catamaran cruise** of the Akaroa harbour is particularly special because large pods of Hector's dolphin, come into the sheltered waters to calve and will often swim alongside the boat.

Take a Road Trip

Although there is public transport to Akaroa, it is worth driving the 85km (53mi) from Christchurch so that you can stop for sweeping views over the peninsula and to explore some of the hidden bays. Take State Highway 75 through Taitapu to **Little River**, about halfway between Christchurch and Akaroa. This sleepy township near the head of **Lake Forsyth** is worth a brief stop for a coffee, before the road narrows and starts winding up to the hilltop. The views from the summit are stunning, sweeping across the entire Akaroa harbour and the small Onawe peninsula. Remnants of the once lush native forests still nestle in the humid gullies.

Christchurch & the Southern Alps

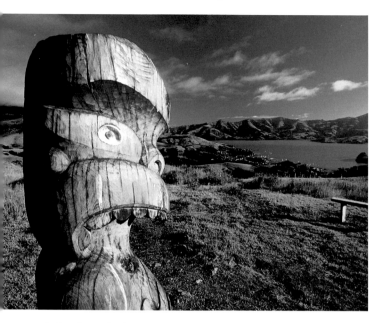

Volcanic Beginnings

From this viewpoint it becomes obvious that Banks
Peninsula was born from a violent volcanic eruption. The
land flows down in all directions to the sea, which has
sculpted the coastline into rocky cliffs and sandy beaches
and filled the crater to create long, narrow Akaroa harbour.
The cogwheel-shaped volcanic cone was originally an
island, until the land bridge was formed by shingle and
debris, washed down from the Southern Alps and onto
the Canterbury Plains, about 20,000 years ago. In 1769,
Captain James Cook mistakenly named it Banks Island
because the isthmus connecting the peninsula to the
mainland was so low; the truth was discovered by
Europeans only in 1809, when another explorer, Captain
Chase, tried to sail through the gap.

**A Maori statue
guards the
shores of
Akaroa**

The Summit and Coastal Routes

At the hilltop, the road forks: SH75 on the right is the coastal
route – the faster way of getting to Akaroa – and the other
route is the Summit Road, which skirts the peninsula's
spine with turn-offs to several smaller bays. As you drop
down to the coast on SH75, the first bay you'll find is
Barry's Bay, where, on alternate days from October to May,
you can watch cheese being produced by the cheese-
maker there, and sample and buy the finished product
(tel: (03) 304 5809).

On the way back to Christchurch, take the **Summit Road**
and explore **Le Bons Bay**, a safe and sheltered beach with
a scattering of holiday homes, or secluded **Okains Bay**,

with its small museum that houses an impressive collection of ancient Maori treasures. Take the turn-off to **Birdlings Flat**, about 8km (5mi) from Little River. You may find semi-precious stones among the pebbles on the long and untamed beach, and it's a beautiful place to watch the sun set over the ocean.

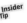

Insider Tip

TAKING A BREAK

Turn left into the Grehan Valley as you enter Akaroa to get to **Tree Crop Farm** (Grehan Valley Road; tel: (03) 304 7158), a quirky place with extensive wild gardens. The entry charge includes a coffee or berry juice. The farm also offers romantic accommodation in a historic 1850s cottage or in huts in the grounds.

Grassy hilltops provide excellent grazing

✚ 219 F4

Visitor Information Centre
✉ Post Shop Building, 80 rue Lavaud, Akaroa
☎ (03) 304 8600; www.akaroa.com
◉ Oct–March daily 9–5, April–Sep Mon–Fri 9–5, Sat–Sun 9–4

Akaroa Harbour Cruises
✉ Main Wharf, Akaroa
☎ (03) 304 7641; www.canterburycat.co.nz
◉ Mid Oct–mid April daily 11, 1:30, mid Dec–mid March 11, 1:30, 3:40 ▥ NZ$72

Hinewai Reserve
✉ Long Bay Road, RD3, Akaroa ☎ (03) 304 8501
◉ Casual walks: 24 hours
▥ Free; donations to Maurice White Native Forest Trust
ℹ Bring sturdy footwear for track walking.
Lodge available overnight by arrangement

Akaroa Museum
✉ 71 rue Lavaud, Akaroa ☎ (03) 304 1013
◉ Mid Oct–Easter daily 10:30–4:30, rest of year 10:30–4 ▥ NZ$8

INSIDER INFO

- The Summit Road is narrow and windy, so **drive with care**. Some roads in the area may be difficult to negotiate after rain.

- Pick up a copy of *Akaroa: An Historic Walk* (inexpensive) from Akaroa Information Centre on Rue Lavaud. It gives details of more than 40 historic buildings.

- **Hinewai Reserve** is a 1,050ha (2,594-acre) conservation project southeast of Akaroa with good walking tracks through remnants of native forest. A series of 31 other small reserves is scattered over the peninsula; some are easy to explore on foot. Ask for a map at the visitor information centre.

- Three historic buildings, including Langlois-Eteveneaux House, which was partly made in France, make up some of the **Akaroa Museum** complex.

52 Aoraki/Mount Cook

New Zealand's highest mountain rises from the icy landscape of Aoraki/Mount Cook National Park. The pyramid of Aoraki – "cloud-piercer" – dominates all the land around it.

More than one-third of the park's 700km² (270mi²) is covered in permanent snow or ice. Of New Zealand's 27 peaks over 3,000m (10,000ft), 19 are huddled together in this area and Aoraki/Mount Cook, which towers above other peaks at 3,724m (12,218ft), is the centrepiece of this sparkling landscape.

Mount Cook is a difficult mountain to climb, being exposed to ferociously rapid weather changes along the Main Divide, the mountainous chain that separates the eastern and western coasts of the South Island. It is even a difficult mountain to see: as its Maori name suggests, it often has its head in the clouds. Most visitors get only a drive-by glimpse of the giant as they travel from Christchurch to Queenstown, but if you enjoy walks, it's worth exploring the area around Mount Cook Village.

Take to the Skies

Beautiful: the Mount Cook lily

For a good view of the mountains, take a **ski plane** from Mount Cook Airport, near Mount Cook Village, or a **helicopter** from Glentanner Park, about 15 minutes from the village. You can choose different routes through the national park but all will give you stunning views of the massive plateau from which Aoraki rises, with the Tasman Glacier (► 160), the largest ice flow in the southern hemisphere outside Antarctica, along its side. Whichever way you go up, you can **land on a glacier** and go for a short walk in the snow. Once the engines are turned off, the silence can be quite eerie.

Explorations by Water

If you want to go **boating on a glacial lake**, join a guided sea-kayaking tour or take a trip in a small, motorized inflatable to explore the lake at the mouth of the **Mueller Glacier**. The glacier flows into the **Hooker**

FEELING PEAKY

The first people to ascend the formidable peak were locals Jack Clarke, Tom Fyfe and George Graham, who reached the summit on 25 Dec, 1894, but several famous climbers, including Sir Edmund Hillary (► 28), have since sharpened their skills on Aoraki/Mount Cook.

A glacial lake in Mount Cook National Park

Valley at Mount Cook Village and forms a small lake, eventually narrowing into a river. The water is a milky azure from the "glacial flour" or dust ground off the mountains as the frozen river flows over them. As the glacier slowly melts, large chunks of ice also break off (you can explore some of these) and you may also see some avalanches crashing down from the surrounding peaks.

TAKING A BREAK

The **Sir Edmund Hillary Alpine Centre** at The Hermitage Hotel has a self-service café/bar.

✚ 218 B/C4

Park Visitor Centre
✉ 1 Larch Grove, Mount Cook Village
☎ (03) 435 1186; www.doc.govt.nz,
www.mtcook.com
🕐 Oct–April daily 8:30–5;
May–Sep 8:30–4:30

Mount Cook Ski Planes
✉ Mount Cook Airport,
Mount Cook Village
☎ (03) 430 8034;
www.mtcookskiplanes.com

Glacier Sea Kayaking
✉ Trips depart from the Old
Mountaineers' Café and Bar,
next door to the visitor centre

ℹ Book at the Park Visitor Centre,
YHA or Hermitage Hotel
☎ (03) 435 1890; www.mtcook.com

Helicopter Line
✉ Glentanner Park,
Mount Cook Village
☎ (03) 435 1801;
www.helicopter.co.nz

Tasman Valley Tours
ℹ 2.5-hour trip to the flats above
Tasman Glacier; information or
bookings at the Park Visitor Centre,
Hermitage Hotel or YHA
☎ (03) 435 1601;
www.mountcooktours.co.nz

INSIDER INFO

■ Mount Cook Village is an excellent base for short walks: pick up a brochure at the Park Visitor Centre. Be sure to **check the weather before you set out**, as it can change quickly.

■ There are no banking facilities and few shops in the national park, so **bring food and cash**.

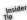
Insider Tip

■ **The Hermitage Hotel** (► 161) is home to the Sir Edmund Hillary Alpine Centre, with a 3D movie on Aoraki/Mount Cook, a planetarium, a museum dedicated to the region and to Sir Ed (► 24), and a café and bar.

At Your Leisure

53 Nga Hau E Wha – National *Marae*

This *marae* (➤ 92) is the South Island's largest Maori cultural centre. The name Nga Hau E Wha stands for the four directions of the wind, signifying that the *marae* welcomes visitors from all corners of the world. Tours of two carved buildings – the *whare nui* (meeting

and the impact introduced species have had on the indigenous wildlife. Highlights include the Alpine Walk-Through Aviary with its resident kea (alpine parrots), and the Nocturnal House, home to the kiwi. The park also takes part in the Department of Conservation's Kiwi Recovery Programme, hatching and rearing kiwi eggs to boost populations in

house) and *whare wananga* (house of learning) – are available, as are cultural evenings and *hangi*.

🚩 219 F4 ✉ 250 Pages Road, Christchurch
☎ (03) 388 7685 🚌 5, from Cathedral Square
🕐 Booking essential; tours require numbers of 20 or more to run, ℹ Visitor information: http://maatawaka.org.nz

54 🛉🛉 Willowbank Wildlife Reserve

On the edge of Christchurch city near the airport is the **Willowbank Wildlife Reserve**, which explains the natural history of New Zealand

the wild. Evenings are one of the best times to visit, when you can join a guided tour to see Willowbank's nocturnal inhabitants waking up for the night or join in the Ko Tane Maori cultural performance.

Insider Tip

🚩 219 F4 ✉ 60 Hussey Road, Christchurch
☎ (03) 359 6226; www.willowbank.co.nz
🕐 Daily 9:30am–7pm; guided evening nature tours; Ko Tane shows: 5:30pm
🚌 11 💲 From NZ$28

55 Sumner

It's worth spending a whole day in this little seaside suburb to the east of Christchurch – explore its gastronomy, stroll down the promenade that stretches across to Scarborough, and relax on the sheltered beach next to the hollowed-out Cave Rock. The Port Hills, part of an extinct twin volcano that once erupted to form the natural harbour at Lyttelton, provide a picturesque backdrop. The earthquake has a lot to answer for here: the street running from Sumner to Lyttelton remains closed, and parts of the hillsides behind the suburb –

A sculpture at Nga Hau E Wha, the large Maori Cultural Centre in Christchurch

once a popular residential area with fantastic Pacific views – are no longer fit for habitation. Nevertheless, the views remain intact: drive up to Panorama Road via Clifton Terrace or follow the winding lanes in Scarborough (not suitable for big motorhomes)!

🚩 219 F4; www.christchurchnz.com

56 Lyttelton

South of Christchurch lies the pleasant harbour town of Lyttelton with its large natural bay. The earthquake was particularly merciless here,

ravaging numerous historic buildings from the pioneer period. One victim was the fortress-like Timeball Station from 1876, where a 'time ball' was once dropped at 1pm every day to let sailors check their clocks and accurately determine their position. Today, Lyttelton is a popular destination for dining out and shopping at the farmers' market on London Street in the centre of town (on Saturdays). If the skies are clear, make a detour to the **Christchurch Gondola** on your way to Lyttelton – the panoramas from up on the **Port Hills** are absolutely fantastic. Instead of taking the tunnel to the town, you could also head up Dyers Pass Road from Cashmere via the **Sign of the Kiwi** to enjoy some magnificent views of the Canterbury Plains and the harbour.

🚩 219 F4

Visitor Information Centre
✉ 65 London Street, Lyttelton Harbour
☎ (03) 328 9093; www.lytteltonharbour.info
🕐 Daily 9–5

Christchurch Gondola
✉ 10 Bridle Path Road, Heathcote Valley
☎ (03) 384 0310; www.gondola.co.nz
🕐 Daily 10–5 💰 Approx. NZ$25

57 Lake Tekapo

Lake Tekapo, between Christchurch and Aoraki/Mount Cook, is a lovely place for a break. The town has sweeping views over the glacier-fed lake; its turquoise colour is thanks to minerals and dust deposited by the icy rivers from the Southern Alps.

The pretty little Church of the Good Shepherd beside the lake was built in the 1930s and is a memorial to the pioneer farmers of the Mackenzie Country.

🚩 218 C4; www.christchurchnz.com

58 Tasman Glacier

The Tasman Glacier is the largest ice flow in the southern hemisphere outside Antarctica: it stretches for 27km (17mi), and is 3km (2mi)

Christchurch & the Southern Alps

Snow-capped Mount Rollerton, the highest peak in Arthur's Pass National Park

wide and 600m (1,968ft) deep. Unusually, its last few kilometres are almost flat, and are covered with debris from its higher sections. The unsealed Tasman Valley Road ends at a car park about 8km (5mi) from Mount Cook Village, from where it is a 20-minute walk to a lookout point over the glacier's terminus. Guided tours are available – enquire at the visitor information centre at the village.

✚ 218 C4

59 Castle Hill & Cave Stream

If you are driving to Arthur's Pass on SH73, take a break after about 110km (70mi) to explore Castle Hill and Cave Stream. Limestone formations run through the length of the east coast of the South Island and in several places form bizarre-looking outcrops. Castle Hill features vast gardens of sculpted limestone, weathered into amazing shapes, including gargoyles and scallops. At Cave Stream, a small river has diverted underground and carved out a 362m (1,188ft) tunnel. The cave is easily accessible, but you must go in a group with an experienced guide (tours are often organized by nearby accommodation). Don't walk into the cave during or after heavy rain.

✚ 216 B4
✉ Signposted on SH73
☎ www.doc.govt.nz

60 Arthur's Pass

Just 90 minutes' drive from Christchurch, Arthur's Pass National Park is a 1,145km² (442mi²) wilderness straddling the Southern Alps, which form a rugged spine along the length of South Island and separate the dry eastern coast from the temperate forests of the West Coast. It is a popular weekend destination for Christchurch residents, with skiing, hiking or mountaineering being popular pursuits. The main centre, Arthur's Pass village, is a good place to have a break if you are on your way to the West Coast (▶ 158), either along SH73 or aboard the TranzAlpine train (▶ 30).

✚ 207 D4

Department of Conservation Visitor Centre
✉ SH73, Arthur's Pass
☎ (03) 318 9211; www.doc.govt.nz
🕐 Nov–March daily 8–5; rest of year 8:30–4:30
ℹ Information on park walks, maps and route guides; information panels on the history of the area and the natural history of the park; up-to-date online weather information

61 Punakaiki

Pancake rocks are the main feature of this small settlement, about 40km (25mi) north of Greymouth. Stratified limestone stacks jut from the beach. A 10-minute wheelchair-accessible track leads to geological forms weathered into curious shapes. Down the road, the 30-minute Truman Track leads through a coastal forest to reach the coastline. At low tide, walk down the beach past a succession of reefs, caves and waterfalls.

✚ 207 D5 ☎ www.punakaiki.co.nz

Where to…
Stay

Prices
Expect to pay for a double room per night:
$ under NZ$200 $$ NZ$200–$350 $$$ over NZ$350

See panel ➤ 144.

Ibis Christchurch $
This Accor Group hotel with 155 rooms is located between Cathedral Square and Cashel Mall (➤ 163), the city's new shopping centre. Guests staying in the building's upper floors can see out across what remains of downtown Christchurch following the earthquake. The interiors are modern and functional.
➕ 219 F4 ✉ 107 Hereford Street
☎ (03) 367 8666; www.accorhotels.com

The Château on the Park $
This unashamedly romantic hotel is set in a residential suburb beside Hagley Park (➤ 145). The swimming pool is surrounded by lavender bushes, there's a suit of armour in the lobby, and you have to cross a moat to get to the bar. A regular shuttle bus ferries guests into town. Choose one of the rooms or opt for the suite when booking.
➕ 219 F4 ✉ 189 Deans Avenue, Riccarton
☎ (03) 348 8999; www.chateau-park.co.nz

The George Hotel $$$
The small luxury hotel on the banks of the Avon has 53 deluxe rooms and suites with views over Hagley Park. The Residence wing is set in a traditional English-style garden. The emphasis is on understated elegance and good service. The fine-dining Pescatore (➤ 156), which specializes in seafood, has been named one of New Zealand's top 10 restaurants, and the hotel's brasserie 50 Bistro is renowned for its breakfasts.
➕ 219 F4 ✉ 50 Park Terrace
☎ (03) 379 4560; www.thegeorge.com

Maison de la Mer $–$$
This elegant house in the centre of Akaroa has been beautifully restored in French country style and offers three luxurious suites, all with harbour and beach views. Upstairs are the Fleur de Lys suite, with a private sunroom, and the Provence suite, with a spa bath. The self-contained Boathouse has its own kitchen and deck. Breakfasts are included.
➕ 219 F4 ✉ 1 rue Benoit, Akaroa
☎ (03) 304 8907; www.maisondelamer.co.nz

The Hermitage Hotel $–$$$
The spectacularly situated Hermitage is one of New Zealand's most famous hotels. The original hotel was destroyed in a flood in 1913; the second burned down in 1957. The present hotel consists of a stone alpine lodge, a new luxury wing, and a modern lodge, motel and chalets. For a spectacular view of Aoraki/Mount Cook, book one of the luxurious rooms in the Aoraki Wing or, in summer, a table at the Panorama Restaurant. There's a choice of restaurants and bars, a gift shop, sauna and tennis courts.
➕ 218 B/C4 ✉ Terrace Road, Mount Cook Village ☎ (03) 435 1809, 0800 686 800 toll free; www.hermitage.co.nz

Where to...
Eat and Drink

Prices
Expect to pay per person for a meal, excluding drinks:
$ under NZ$45 $$ NZ$45–$60 $$$ over NZ$60

CHRISTCHURCH

See panel ➤ 144.

Cook'n with Gas $$
Housed in a historic villa from the 1860s, this Christchurch restaurant certainly isn't short on atmosphere. The food is classical with an un-mistakable French influence: the selection includes salmon, lamb and steaks cooked to perfection. Don't be surprised when they add an extra two dollars to your bill – it's an obligatory donation to the Christchurch City Mission.
✚ 219 F4 ✉ 23 Worcester Boulevard
☎ (03) 377 9166; www.cooknwithgas.co.nz
🕐 Mon–Sat from 5pm

Pescatore $$$
This restaurant within The George Hotel has panoramic views over Hagley Park. It is formal dining in a minimalist interior and is con-sidered one of New Zealand's best dining experiences. Executive Chef Andrew Brown has created season-al menus, which are matched with top vintages from Pescatore's wine list, honoured by *Wine Spectator* magazine as being one of the world's best restaurant lists.
✚ 219 F4 ✉ 50 On Park
☎ (03) 371 0257;
www.thegeorge.com/pescatore
🕐 Tue–Sat 6pm–late

Yamagen $$$
Yamagen offers the best of Japanese dining using the finest New Zealand produce. Their creations are pre-sented traditionally or with the flair of teppan-yaki cooking. The chefs can cook up to 10 dishes at a time on the teppan grills. The restaurant was part of the Crowne Plaza hotel before it was ruined by the quake. It reopened a few metres away in early 2014.
✚ A219 F4
✉ 53 Victoria Street, Christchurch
☎ (03) 365 7799
🕐 Sat–Thu 6pm–late, Fri noon–2:30, 6pm–late

BANKS PENINSULA

French Farm Winery and Restaurant $
Make a detour just to visit this striking building in its beautiful rural setting. Wines from the little vineyards in the valley are made on site and feature on the wine list. The à la carte menu includes salads with Akaroa salmon, local cheeses and platters to share.
✚ 219 F4
✉ 12 Winery Road, Akaroa
☎ (03) 304 5784; www.frenchfarm.co.nz
🕐 Daily 10–4, Fri, Sat until 10

WEST COAST

Café de Paris $–$$
French chef Pierre Esquilat and his Kiwi wife Joy run this little bit of *Rive Gauche* on the West Coast. An airy café during the day, serv-ing coffee and pastries and light lunches, it offers an à la carte menu in the evening. Look for French cuisine classics.
✚ 2216 A2 ✉ 19 Tancred Street, Hokitika
☎ (03) 755 8933; www.cafédeparis.net.nz
🕐 Daily 7:30am–late

Where to...
Shop

See panel ➤ 144.

City Centre

The devastating earthquake of 2011 almost brought the retail sector to a standstill here until the advent of **ReSTART/Cashel Mall** – an unconventional shopping centre made of piled up shipping containers near Cathedral Square that's attracting customers back downtown.

Head to the pedestrian zone to see shop window displays filled with outdoor equipment (**Kathmandu**), books (**Scorpio Books**) and souvenirs (e.g. **Simply NZ** or the **toi toi Design Store**), and check out **Untouched World** if you're on the hunt for high-quality eco fashion for men and women. Take a break at the inviting cafés and snack stands between the containers and watch the street artists at work. There's even a market held at the weekends (Fri, Sat, Sun, 9am-4pm).

The earthquake didn't do much damage to the defiant, 3-storey concrete edifice of **Ballantynes** (corner of Cashel St/Colombo St), a traditional department store that's a real local institution. They sell cosmetics, fashion, tableware and furniture... in fact, anything they don't stock isn't worth having!

New Regent Street has been freshly renovated in the Spanish Mission architectural style. It's already home to such attractive little shops as **Beadz Unlimited** (Nr. 7), who make meaningful jewellery from pieces of earthquake rubble. **Youngs Jewellers** (Nr 3.) is one of the oldest jewellery stores in the city.

Victoria Street is slowly regaining its reputation as a lively shopping strip for all things elegant and outlandish – **Frogmore** (Nr. 70), a popular accessories store, has already made a comeback. **South City** (555 Colombo Street), a shopping centre on the southern edge of downtown Christchurch, squeezes 46 stores under one roof. There's lots of space to park outside. **Colombo Street** will also be used for commercial purposes in the future.

Suburbs

Merivale, a shopping destination to the north of the city centre, is still as chic and expensive as ever. Fashion boutiques, antiques shops and designer stores (e.g. **Quinns**, 195 Papanui Road) crowd along and around **Merivale Mall**. You'll also find some shops for more day-to-day needs, such as **Traiteur** (corner of Aikmans and Papanui roads; tel: (03) 355 7750), a European-style butchers.

With around 200 shops, the two-storey **Westfield Shopping Centre** (129 Riccarton Road) in the district of Riccarton is a retail paradise for every budget, whatever the weather. **The Palms** (corner of Marshland/New Brighton Road, tel: 03 3 85 30 67) in Shirley is also a popular (and less gargantuan) alternative.

The **Riccarton Rotary Market**, held on Sunday from 9am to 2pm at Riccarton Park Racecourse (Racecourse Road; tel: (03) 339 0011), has more than 300 stalls selling crafts, food, clothing, jewellery and bric-a-brac. **Dress Smart Hornby** (409 Main South Road, Hornby; tel: (03) 349 5750) has more than 50 stores, each with 30–70 per cent off normal prices.

You'll find the headquarters of **Untouched World** (➤ above) near the airport. It's a striking complex with a retail store, a restaurant, a garden and a wine bar.

Where to...
Go Out

CHRISTCHURCH

See panel ➤ 144.

The **Court Theatre** (Bernard Street), a renowned cabaret stage, is located in the suburb of Addington. It hosts a constantly changing programme of events. As most of the city's event venues didn't survive the earthquake, **Christchurch Casino** (30 Victoria Street) is increasingly being used for artistic performances – check out the live music offerings in the Mashina Lounge. As well as gambling (Mon-Fri from 11am, Sat, Sun from noon until late at night), the casino boasts further bars and a restaurant.

Dux Live (363 Lincoln Road, Addington) predominantly features rock and pop acts from the New Zealand and international scenes. The managers also run **Dux Dine** (28 Riccarton Road, Riccarton), a vegetarian restaurant that was opened as a successor to Dux de Lux, a famous quake-damaged eatery (formerly at the Arts Centre).

Party animals are beginning to head back to the small, heavily-scarred harbour town of Lyttelton. Visit **Wunderbar** (19 London Street) for regular live bands and club nights. Head to the bar or out onto the terrace for fantastic views of the harbour.

Christchurch's arts and cultural scene is having to improvise following the earthquake, and temporary indoor and outdoor performance spaces are popping up all over town (e.g. in **Hagley Park**). Get hold of *The Press* newspaper or visit www.visitchristchurch.info/whats-on for the latest listings.

The **Masters Hollywood Theatre** (28 Marriner Street) in Sumner is the most authentic cinema around – it managed to survive the earthquake almost entirely unscathed.

Sports

Major rugby fixtures and test cricket are played at **AMI Stadium** (30 Stevens Street; vbase.co.nz/venues/ami-stadium), as are the home games of the **Canterbury Crusaders** (Super 14 rugby union). Book tickets through **Ticket Direct** (tel: 0800 224 224; www.ticketdirect.co.nz).

For horse racing, go to **Riccarton Park Racecourse** (Racecourse Road; www.riccartonpark.co.nz), or catch the harness racing at **Addington Raceway** (Jack Hinton Drive; www.addington.co.nz).

The Estuary at Ferrymead is good for windsurfing and parasailing, while Sumner has surf and swimming beaches. Canterbury rivers offer salmon fishing, jet boating and rafting. In the city, there's boating on the Avon.

Mount Hutt is the largest commercial ski field, or try the club fields in the **Craigieburn ranges**, where the facilities are basic but you can stay overnight.

Golfers should try the city course in **Hagley Park** (hagleygc.org.nz) or the 36-hole twin course at **Harewood** (371 McLeans Island Road; www.harewoodgolf.co.nz)

Wine and Beer Trails

Canterbury and Waipara (an hour's drive north of Christchurch) are distinctive wine-growing regions. Contact the visitor centre for a wine trail map, or join a half- or full-day guided tour with **Canterbury Wine Tours** (www.canterburywines.co.nz).

Festivals

The arts, literature, jazz, comedy, buskers, flowers, wine and food, summertime – Christchurch has festivals for all of them, and more.

The Wild South

 Little Treats

A Route with a View
The route from **Wanaka** (➤ 182) to Queenstown over the Crown Range offers some magnificent views.

A Tee under your Pillow
Die-hard golfers sleep near the course at the luxurious **Millbrook Resort** (➤ 188).

Wine and Cheese
Try the sheep's and goat's cheese from the cheesery at the **Gibbston Valley Winery** (➤ 186).

Getting Your Bearings

The southern regions of the South Island are often bypassed by visitors – yet they feature some of the wildest and most scenic places on Earth. Many of the more remote areas may have remained unexplored to this day, had it not been for a stampede of fortune seekers, attracted by the lure of gold.

Like moths heading for the flame, miners swarmed to the southern parts of New Zealand in the mid-19th century, abandoning the exhausted gold fields of California and New South Wales. Their picks and shovels shaped the landscape from Queenstown to Dunedin. Here, you can challenge your body and mind amid stunning scenery – and then relax and enjoy the deserved rewards of fine food and wine.

Queenstown is also a gateway to Fiordland, New Zealand's largest national park and a World Heritage area of majestic mountains and seascapes. Towering peaks, icy lakes and sheer-sided fjords, carved by glaciers and separated by narrow, densely forested valleys, combine to create a landscape of unmatched grandeur.

The central part of the southern South Island is where the gold-miners' heritage is best preserved by a dry and sunny climate. Here, modern pioneers have successfully established the world's southernmost vineyards and orchards. On the southeastern coast, Dunedin combines Scottish charm with scenic appeal and easy access to rare wildlife.

Milford Sound's famous Mitre Peak

The Wild South

Five Perfect Days

Plan to spend five days exploring the wild south of New Zealand. Follow our itinerary to make sure you don't miss any of the highlights. For more information see the main entries (➤ 170–181).

Day 1

Start the morning by exploring the buzzing downtown of ★**Queenstown** (➤ 173). Then walk along the shores of beautiful **Lake Wakatipu** (➤ 174) and join a cruise on the vintage steamship **TSS *Earnslaw*** (➤ 174). Have lunch at a café in town. After lunch, drive to **64 Shotover River** (➤ 182) to see the magnificent canyon or to test your nerves with a bungy jump. Try **66 white-water rafting**, jet boating (below), or **67 river surfing** (➤ 183). Alternatively, visit the old gold-mining town of **68 Arrowtown** (➤ 182) or the family attractions in **68 Wanaka** (➤ 182).

In the evening catch the **Skyline gondola** (➤ 174) for night-time views of the lake and city. Have dinner at one of the restaurants downtown or visit the nearby **Gibbston Valley Winery** (➤ 186).

Day 2

If you want to experience the scenic road to **Milford** (➤ 170), fly or drive to Te Anau and drive from there to the fjord. Otherwise, fly directly to Milford and spend the day exploring ★**Fiordland** and the majestic **Milford Sound** (➤ 170). Join a cruise to see the Fiordland crested penguins and resident dolphins, and to get close to Mitre Peak and the 146m (479ft) **Stirling Falls** (➤ 171). Other activities at Milford Sound include kayaking excursions and a trip to an under-water observatory to view Fiordland's awe-inspiring marine life. Return to Te Anau in the evening.

Day 3

Drive through ruggedly scenic **62 Central Otago** (➤ 179) and visit orchards or vineyards to taste the produce of New Zealand's fruit bowl. Stop in small rural places such as **Cromwell**, **Clyde** and **69 Alexandra** (➤ 184) for meal breaks and to explore the area's gold-rush history. Continue driving to the wildlife capital, ★**Dunedin** (➤ 175).

Day 4

Explore the southern city's Victorian architecture and Scottish heritage. Spend the morning investigating the Octagon, St Paul's Cathedral and the Dunedin Public Art Gallery. Take the train journey along the **71 Taieri Gorge** (➤ 184) in the afternoon.

Day 5

Explore the untamed beauty of the ★**Otago Peninsula** (➤ 175), with its seaside towns and wildlife. Visit **70 Larnach Castle** (➤ 184) and the royal albatross colony at **Taiaroa Head** (➤ 177). On the way back, join a tour to see yellow-eyed penguins, or walk to Sandfly Bay to watch the birds return from the ocean and waddle up to their nests. Take a break at the pretty town of **Portobello** (➤ 177).

★Fiordland

Fiordland is pure wilderness. The best way to discover the raw beauty of New Zealand's largest national park is to explore Milford Sound. Brooding and serene, it's the most northern of Fiordland's 14 glacier-carved fjords and the only one accessible by road. Although Milford Sound and its landmark Mitre Peak are often photographed, the mountains, rainforests and waterfalls still leave visitors in awe.

The South Island's southwestern tip is New Zealand's least explored part, and is one of the greatest wildernesses of the southern hemisphere. Together with the Westland/ Tai Poutini (➤ 148), Mount Aspiring and Aoraki/Mount Cook (➤ 156) national parks, Fiordland makes up the World Heritage Area called **Te Wahipounamu** – "the place of greenstone". The scenery is the result of over 500 million years of sculpting, with the landscape relentlessly ground, split, pressurized and washed down by the elements.

A Natural Wonderland – Milford Sound

Te Wahipounamu covers 10 per cent of New Zealand's total area and most of its wilderness is difficult, sometimes almost impossible, to reach. **Milford Sound's** dramatic splendour provides a window to this natural wonderland. You can reach Milford by air, road or on foot. The sound is the end point of the Milford Track, a four-day walk established by 19th-century pioneers who discovered

Virgin forest clings to the sheer mountain slopes in Milford Sound

New Zealand's highest waterfall, the **Sutherland Falls**, and who were the first to cross overland to Milford. The track is extremely popular, so numbers are strictly limited and accommodation is only in huts along the route (no camping is permitted). You will have to organize the walk well ahead, particularly during the summer months.

The road to Milford (➤ 200) is a spectacular alpine drive, with many points of interest and short nature walks along the 120km (74mi) from Te Anau. The well-constructed road is open to campervans and trailers, but can be winding. Warning: lots of buses head that way. The route is sometimes also closed due to avalanche danger or high winds, so check with the **Fiordland Visitor Information Centre** in Te Anau in advance.

Visitors can begin to grasp the vastness of the Fiordland on boat trips

All Aboard
After the remoteness of the journey, the bustle of Milford's main bus terminal and car park may come as a bit of a shock. Milford's small wharf is the departure point for all cruises, which vary from **one-hour boat trips** to **overnight voyages** (➤ 172). The exact route depends on weather conditions, but generally each trip will take you to Milford Sound's mouth and a short distance out onto the Tasman Sea. On the way, the boats pass below towering **Mitre Peak** (1,692m/5,550ft) and cruise close to lush rainforests that cling to the sound's sheer rock walls. Chances are that bottlenose dolphins will join the boat within a short distance of the wharf; sightings of seals and Fiordland crested penguins are also common. Weather permitting, the ship will be steered under the magnificent **Stirling Falls**, which drop sheer into the sea.

A Rich Ecosystem
Thanks to a top layer of fresh water, courtesy of the phenomenal 6,000mm (235in) of annual rainfall, Milford Sound is a special ecosystem below the surface, as well as above. The relatively warm top layer allows rare marine organisms, such as black coral, to grow at shallower depths than elsewhere, and you can get a glimpse of them at the **Milford Deep** in **Harrison's Cove**, accessible by cruise. Here, you descend 10m (30ft) to the viewing room, whose large windows give outstanding **close-ups of the marine life** at a depth that would otherwise be inaccessible.

The Wild South

Milford
Sound's
Mitre Peak

TAKING A BREAK

Walk to Bowen Falls, about 10 minutes from the wharf, to have a **picnic at Cemetery Point**. The area was named after its mounds of debris brought from the falls, which resemble graves. However, there are actually three real graves there, containing fatalities from the old whaling and sealing days.

➕ 220 B4

Fiordland i-site Visitor Information
➕ 220 B3 ✉ Lakefront Drive, Te Anau
☎ (03) 249 8900; www.fiordlandnz.com
🕐 Daily 9–5:30

Real Journeys
➕ 220 B3 ✉ Lakefront Drive, Te Anau
☎ (03) 249 7416, 0800 656 501 toll free; www.realjourneys.co.nz
🕐 Daily ℹ️ Bus tours, flights and cruises of Milford and Doubtful sounds and Lake Manapouri depart from Milford Sound, Te Anau and Queenstown; booking essential
💵 Bus tours from NZ$230; Milford Sound cruises from NZ$70

Milford Sound Red Boat Cruises
➕ 220 C4 ✉ Milford Wharf, Milford Sound
☎ (03) 441 1137, 0800 264 536 toll free; www.redboats.co.nz
🕐 Daily 💵 NZ$770

Mitre Peak Cruises
➕ 220 C4 ✉ Visitor Terminal, Milford Sound
☎ (03) 249 8110; 0800 744 633 toll free; www.mitrepeak.com
🕐 Daily 💵 NZ$70

INSIDER INFO

- Milford Sound changes its mood as quickly as the weather, so **bring rain gear and sun protection**. Don't forget an **insect repellent**, as sandflies can be a nuisance throughout Fiordland.
- Consider a **coach-cruise-fly combination** to get the best out of a short visit. There are a number of operators who offer trips from Te Anau or Queenstown.
- **Overnight cruises** will give you an idea of Milford Sound after daytime visitors have gone – and you might hear an unforgettable dawn chorus.
- **Doubtful Sound**, further south, will appeal to those looking for an experience with fewer companions. Doubtful is not as easily accessible and can only be reached by crossing **Lake Manapouri** by boat and taking a bus over Wilmot Pass, but its unspoiled and remote wilderness makes up for the effort.

★ Queenstown

For a few crazy years after the discovery of gold here in 1862, Queenstown's fortunes were extracted from the Shotover River. But, with its rugged beauty and wild waters, the river has become Queenstown's modern gold mine, and the gold rush has given way to the adrenalin rush.

High-Adrenaline: bungy jumping in Queenstown

Queenstown is a magnet for thrill seekers. Every year it welcomes a million international visitors, most coming to part with their money so that they can swoop down a river in a raft, whizz off in a jetboat, or take a gut-wrenching freefall or hair-raising helicopter ride. With ubiquitous tour operators promising adventure activities ranging from bungy jumping to snowboarding, the alpine resort buzzes all year round (➤ 188). Queenstown is only the size of a sprawling village, but it has a cosmopolitan atmosphere and rivals the capital Wellington with its variety of downtown cafés and restaurants.

Skippers Canyon

There's a proud gold-mining heritage too. Of all the Wakatipu diggings, the most reliable was **Skippers Canyon**, a beautiful gorge cut by the Shotover into soft schist about 27km (17mi) from Queenstown. The area around Skippers was still being dredged for gold in 1992, but now only the school building and cemetery remain. The last gold digger, Joe Scheib, established **Skippers Park** (➤ 182), and his family continues to gather gold-rush relics and explain the history of gold mining in the area at Winky's Museum.

Picture Perfect Boat Trips

Queenstown's enviable position on the shores of **Lake Wakatipu,** framed by the majestic Southern Alps, means that some of New Zealand's most picturesque scenery is within reach. So, if you are looking for something less energetic, take a cruise on the vintage steamship **TSS Earnslaw**. The ship has been ploughing Lake Wakatipu since 1912, transporting goods for run holders (farmers) and conveying passengers. You can explore the engine room and fireboxes, browse old photographs or just enjoy the stunning scenery. The *Earnslaw* makes daily excursions to a high country farm at Walter Peak, where you can join a farm tour, have a barbecue lunch or go for a horse trek. **Insider Tip** A gondola ride up **Bob's Peak** is a perfect finale to an action- and scenery-filled day. Evening light colours the view across the city, Lake Wakatipu and Coronet Peak, and the Remarkables to the Cecil and Walter peaks.

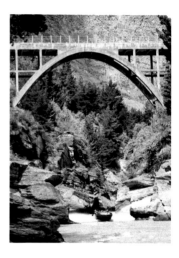

A tour boat powers through Shotover Gorge passing beneath Edith Cavell Bridge

TAKING A BREAK

After a day out, try some wholesome foods, check your email and hang out with the cool crowd at the funky **Vudu Café** (23 Beach Street; tel: (03) 442 5357; www.vudu.co.nz).

➕ 221 D4

Queenstown Visitor Information Centre
✉ Clocktower Building, corner of Shotover and Camp streets
☎ (03) 442 4100; www.queenstown-vacation.com
🕐 Dec–March daily 7:30–6:30; April–Nov 7:30–6

TSS *Earnslaw*
✉ Steamer Wharf, end of Shotover Street
☎ (03) 249 7416, 0800 656 501 toll free; www.realjourneys.co.nz
🕐 Oct–mid-April 10, 12, 2, 4, 6, 8, May–Sep 12, 2, 4; Duration: approx. 90 mins.
💲 From NZ$55

Skyline Gondola
✉ Brecon Street
☎ (03) 441 0101; www.skyline.co.nz 🕐 Daily 9–late 💲 NZ$27

INSIDER INFO

- Queenstown has lots of adventurous activities on offer: if you want to try **whitewater rafting** but aren't sure about the risks, opt for the **Kawarau River** rather than the Shotover. The Kawarau is a high-volume river with no exposed rocks in the rapids and is therefore gentler.
- **Queenstown's gardens** rarely feature in tourist brochures but they are worth a visit. Extensive lawns and rose gardens mix with sports grounds on a small peninsula on the eastern side of Queenstown Bay, off Park Street.
- Taste some of the award-winning wines from this southernmost wine-growing region. Pick up a **wine trail map** from the visitor centre.

⑥ Dunedin & Otago Peninsula

Dunedin's early wealth and Scottish heritage have left a tangible mark. The first impression is of a cityscape dominated by spires, gables and roofs bristling with turrets. This is also the gateway to the Otago Peninsula, a place of untamed natural beauty and a sanctuary for rare wildlife.

THE OTHER SIDE OF THE WORLD
Dunedin is the old Gaelic name for Edinburgh, but, apart from street names and the original architecture, it has little in common with the Scottish capital. Locals claim that Dunedin is hillier, smaller and closer to the sea – and that it has a better climate than Edinburgh.

Set between rolling hills and the rugged coastline, Dunedin is the capital of the southern province of Otago, which is best known for its pioneering gold-mining history, rugged scenery, and fertile orchards and vineyards.

The city clings to the walls of a natural amphitheatre, enclosing a harbour whose narrow channel extends to the tip of the Otago Peninsula and beyond **Port Chalmers**. Dunedin's prosperity in the second half of the 19th century resulted in a Victorian city in the middle of the southern Pacific and, despite modern intrusions, much of the original architecture remains intact. Historic buildings have been given a new lease of life, serving as public venues and municipal buildings. Many grand old homesteads have been restored and wooden villas are scattered through the hilly suburbs.

A statue of poet Robert Burns is just one example of the pervading Scottish influence seen around the city

ROBERT BURNS
25 JANUARY 1759
21 JULY 1796

Scottish Influence
Dunedin's Scottish heritage is also evident throughout the city. This is one of only a handful of places in New Zealand with a kilt shop, stocking more than 500 tartans. Dunedin also boasts its own pipe band, and still has haggis ceremonies and a population that speaks with a distinctly rolling accent. Much of Dunedin's architecture is modelled on Scottish and other British examples: New Zealand's first university, the University of Otago, resembles the University of Glasgow buildings; the college buildings of Otago Boys' High School have the air of a British public school; and the former prison was modelled on architect Norman Shaw's design for Scotland Yard in London.

The Wild South

The City's Sights

Start your exploration in the heart of the city, the eight-sided **Octagon**, through the middle of which runs Dunedin's main street, changing from Princes Street on the south to George Street on the north. Rather fittingly, a **sculpture of poet Robert Burns** overlooks the Octagon's small central park – "with his back to the kirk and his face to the pub". The Oban Hotel, which Burns once faced, is no more, but behind him towers **St Paul's Anglican Cathedral**. Walk up the marble steps to see its soaring limestone-vaulted nave. Apart from Italian marble floor tiles, most of the stone and timber used to build the cathedral came from New Zealand, most notably the near-white Oamaru limestone, which you will find in public buildings and sculptures throughout the country.

The ground floor of the **Civic Centre** next to the cathedral houses Dunedin's **visitor information centre**. On the other side of the cathedral is the **Dunedin Public Art Gallery**, which has a large collection of paintings by Frances Hodgkins, an artist who was born in Dunedin in 1869.

It is a short walk along George Street to the **University of Otago** campus. Dunedin is very much a university town – during term time its population of just under 120,000 swells by about 17,000, and students are one of the driving forces behind the city's vibrant café and cultural scene. The campus itself is constantly bursting at the seams, with new buildings going up on the fringes, but a walk through the inner group of historic slate-roofed bluestone buildings, huddled beside the Leith stream, will give a sense of its Victorian origins.

The bluestone buildings of Dunedin Universityw

If you're going to take the vintage train journey to the **Taieri Gorge** (➤ 184), allow time to inspect Dunedin's **railway station**, a monument to Edwardian architecture and testimony to the settlers' faith in railways. Inside, the Royal Doulton mosaic-tile floors and stained-glass windows depict railway motifs and the monogram of New Zealand Railways.

The Otago Peninsula

A tour of the Otago Peninsula is a must, even if you only have time to drive to **Taiaroa Head**. You should get a chance to observe albatrosses, penguins and seals in the wild, just a few minutes from the city. Taiaroa Head is the only mainland breeding colony of **royal albatrosses** in the world. Albatross chicks are raised here every year but can only be seen as part of a guided tour to the observatory.

Insider Tip

It takes about 45 minutes to drive to Taiaroa Head along the coastal route, which winds past many bays on the harbour side of the peninsula, each with spectacular views of the city. If you take the inland route, the views are even better, as you're overlooking the entire peninsula, with its rocky shores within the harbour and its steep cliffs and secluded sandy beaches on the seaward side. You can also inspect **Larnach Castle** (➤ 184) before you reach the peninsula's main settlement, **Portobello**, where the road continues to Taiaroa Head. A few minutes before you reach the albatross colony, a sign points to 🐧 **Penguin Place**, an ecotourism venture where visitors can observe yellow-eyed penguins from hides and trenches dug into the dunelands.

Visitors approach Taiaroa Head by water

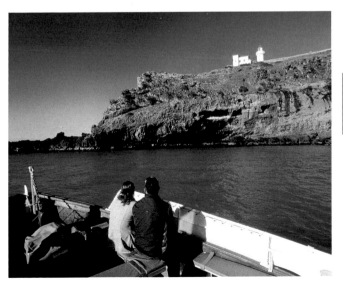

The Wild South

TAKING A BREAK

Visit **Glenfalloch Woodland Garden**, about 9km (6mi) from Dunedin along the coastal route to Portobello. The narrow walking tracks wind through shrubs, trees and herbaceous borders. The gardens have a café and wine bar, open Nov–April daily 11–3:30 (tel: (03) 476 1006; www.glenfalloch.co.nz).

➕ 221 F3

Dunedin Visitor Information Centre
✉ 50 The Octagon, Dunedin
☎ (03) 474 3300; www.dunedinnz.com
◷ Mon–Fri 8:30–6, Sat, Sun 8:45–6, public holidays 9–5

Dunedin Public Art Gallery
✉ 30 The Octagon, Dunedin
☎ (03) 477 4000; www.dunedin.art.
museum ◷ Daily 10–5 🎟 Free

St Paul's Cathedral
✉ The Octagon, Dunedin
☎ (03) 477 2336; www.stpauls.net.nz
◷ Services: Sun 8am, 10am, 7pm;
Tue, Fri 8am; Wed 10am; Thu 8am, 6pm;

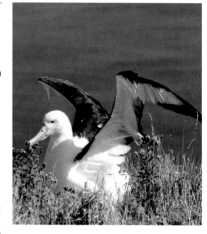

Taiaroa Head has a rare colony of breeding royal albatrosses

Royal Albatross Colony
✉ Taiaroa Head, Otago Peninsula ☎ (03) 478 0499; www.albatross.org.nz
◷ Visitor centre: Wed–Mon 9:30–5, Tue 10:30–5. Tours of the albatross colony:
24 Nov–March Wed–Mon 9am–sunset, Tue 10:30am–sunset; April–16 Sep
Wed–Mon 10am–sunset, Tue 10:30am–sunset; booking essential
🚌 Peninsula bus, tour buses 🎟 NZ$40

Penguin Place Yellow Eyed Penguin Reserve
✉ Penguin Place, Harington Point Road, Otago Peninsula
☎ (03) 478 0286; www.penguinplace.co.nz
◷ Oct–March tours every 30 mins 10:15am–90 mins before sunset; April–Sep
tours every 30 mins 3:15–4:45pm 🎟 NZ$50

INSIDER INFO

- Visit the **Toitu Otago Settlers Museum** (31 Queens Gardens, Dunedin; tel: (03) 477 5052; www.toituosm.com; daily 10–5; free) to find out more about the Scottish families who influenced Dunedin's development or to join a guided city tour.
- If you're interested in natural history or the area's Maori cultural heritage, the **Otago Museum** (419 Great King Street, Dunedin; tel: (03) 474 7474; www.otagomuseum. govt.nz; daily 10–5; NZ$10; Discovery World: inexpensive) has some good displays.

Insider Tip
- Don't miss **Sandfly Bay** with its magnificent beach that runs along the peninsula's seaside coast. Head there in the evening if you fancy watching yellow-eyed penguins returning to their nests to sleep.

⑫ Central Otago

Central Otago stretches out across a rugged plateau sheltered by the Southern Alps. The wide, open landscape is fringed only by rolling foothills and luminous skies. There is something romantic about "Central", with its Tuscan-style golden hills and tiny villages, old stone buildings and gold-rush relics.

GOLDEN OPPORTUNITY
Central Otago's gold rush isn't over yet, and the Macraes mining company still extracts about 5 tonnes of gold each year.

Summer temperatures can climb well over 30°C (86°F) and parch the landscape, while in winter they regularly drop below freezing and the foothills get a dusting of snow. The arid climate has helped preserve many gold-mining remnants, and provides ideal conditions for fruit growing and viticulture.

Hit the Road

Arrowtown and the rolling foothills of the Central Otago plateau

Plan at least a day to cover the 280km (174mi) between Queenstown (➤ 173) and Dunedin (➤ 175), allowing time for stops. Several old gold-mining sites along the way are worth exploring, as are some of the wineries and orchards. The banks of the **Clutha River** provide ideal picnic spots and short walks. On your way out of Queenstown, stop at the visitor information centre for a guide to **Central Otago's wineries** and a map of the **Otago Goldfields Heritage Trail**, which links more than 20 sites with gold-mining history.

From Queenstown, follow State Highway 6 along the Kawarau River. If you want to explore one of the best-

The Wild South

preserved Chinese gold-mining settlements, make a short detour to charming **Arrowtown** (➤ 183); otherwise, drive along the **Kawarau Gorge** to see the river's **Roaring Meg rapids** and stunning canyon. About 18km (11mi) from Queenstown you will pass another gold-rush legacy – a stone-piered suspension bridge, which was built in 1880 and today doubles as a platform for bungy jumpers (➤ 182).

Chinese prospectors once lived in these small huts

Visiting Cromwell and Clyde
The steep slopes of the gorge are in stark contrast to the flat valley area of **Gibbston**, planted with row after row of grape-vines, and the expansive **Cromwell Flats**. **Cromwell**, about 50 minutes from Queenstown, sits at the confluence of the Clutha and Kawarau rivers. When gold was discovered here in 1862, several thousand miners arrived within days and transformed the settlement. More recently, parts of Cromwell disappeared under Lake Dunstan, when the **Clyde Dam** was built as part of the Clutha River hydropower scheme. Many historic huts had to be painstakingly removed and re-erected in what is now called **Old Cromwell**, a popular attraction. Along SH6 is **The Big Picture**, which features an interactive film about local winemakers, tastings and lessons on how to distinguish between wine aromas.

From Cromwell, State Highway 8 will take you to **Clyde** and **Alexandra**, a pleasant town on the banks of the Clutha and the district's commercial hub (➤ 184).

Along the Clutha River
From here you can either follow SH8 or take SH85, nick-named **the Pigroot**, to Dunedin (➤ 175). The Pigroot winds through rolling hills and sleepy townships to reach the dramatic **Maniototo Plains.** The faster way to Dunedin is along SH8 and the mighty **Clutha**, New Zealand's largest river. The Clutha is 87km (54mi) shorter than the Waikato River in the North Island but it carries almost twice as much water. Between Alexandra and Roxburgh, the Clutha

flows through a narrow gorge that can only be seen from a boat or a foot track, but even a short walk provides some stunning views.

TAKING A BREAK

Speargrass Inn (tel: (03) 449 2192), between Alexandra and Roxburgh, offers rooms, food and crafts.

➕ 221 E4

Visitor Information Centre
➕ 221 E4 ✉ 21 Centennial Avenue, Alexandra
☎ (03) 448 9515; www.centralotagonz.com
🕐 Nov–March daily 9–6; April–Oct 9–5

Central Otago Vineyards
➕ 221 D4 ✉ Central Otago Winegrowers Association, Cromwell
☎ (03) 445 4499: www.cowa.org.nz (the website includes a detailed map of the wineries in Central Otago); www.cromwell.org.nz

A 19th-century stone cottage near the town of Alexandra

Old Cromwell Town
➕ 221 D4 ✉ Melmore Terrace, Cromwell
☎ (03) 445 0212; www.cromwell.org.nz
🕐 Shops and café: daily 10–3 💲 Free

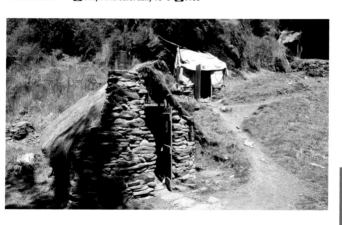

INSIDER INFO

- The most beautiful time to see Central Otago is **autumn**, when the poplars and willows turn amber and gold.
- Another good time to visit is when the Otago Goldfields Heritage Trust holds its **annual cavalcade**, usually in March, and hundreds of people re-enact history by travelling along the old gold-mining routes on horseback and in wagons.
- If you are taking the Pigroot, detour to St Bathans and have a snack at the reputedly haunted **Vulcan Hotel**, dating from 1882. The Blue Lake, near by, was formed after gold diggers sluiced away an entire hill.

The Wild South

At Your Leisure

63 Wanaka

Some 55km (35mi) northeast of Queenstown, lakeside Wanaka offers a couple of great family attractions. **Puzzling World** has mazes, optical illusions and plenty of hands-on puzzles to keep idle minds busy. Out at the airport, meanwhile, is the **Warbirds and Wheels Museum**, dedicated to the country's World War I and II air aces and with vintage aircraft on display. Some of the planes fly in the biennial Warbirds Over Wanaka air show (➤ 188).

🔳 221 D4

Puzzling World

✉ 102 Ardmore Street, Wanaka
☎ (03) 443 7489; www.puzzlingworld.co.nz
🕐 Nov–April daily 8:30–5:30, May–Oct 8:30–5
💵 Some attractions free, otherwise from NZ$8

Warbirds and Wheels Museum

✉ Wanaka Airport, SH6, Luggate
☎ (03) 443 7010; www.warbirdsandwheels.co.nz
🕐 Daily 9–4 (extended hours in Jan)
💵 NZ$20

64 Shotover River

The Shotover River gorges are the mini Grand Canyons of the south but some of their landscaping was done by hand, pick and shovel during the gold-mining days. The most stunning gold-rush relics are at **Skippers Park**, about 27km (17mi) from Queenstown. At Winky's Museum in the park you'll find rusty horseshoes, century-old bath taps, pots and bottles and – bizarrely – a miner's boot with the poor fellow's foot bones still in it. Try your luck with a gold pan and you will almost certainly take home a flake or two. The road to Skippers Park can

There are numerous places to take the plunge around Queenstown

be dangerous and hire cars are not insured for the route.

🔳 221 D4

Skippers Canyon

✉ Skippers Canyon, Shotover River
☎ (03) 442 9434, 0800 226 966 toll free; www.skipperscanyonjet.co.nz
🕐 Tours mid June–mid Sep daily 9, 1; Sep–June 8:30, 12, 3:30
💵 From NZ$129

65 Bungy Jumping

Thrill seekers inspired by the exploits of AJ Hackett (➤ 29) will be satisfied near Queenstown. The original bungy site is a bridge across the Kawarau River, 43m (141ft) high and the only place where jumpers can splash into the water. The next highest jump is The Ledge, adjacent to Queenstown's gondola station (➤ 174), at 47m (154ft), and with spectacular views across to the Remarkables mountains and down

Wet n' Wild: white-water rafting on the Shotover River

to Queenstown 400m (1,300ft) below. The highest jump in Queenstown is the Nevis Highwire, where you leap from a gondola suspended 134m (440ft) above the Nevis River.

AJ Hackett Bungy

🟦 221 D4

✉ Bungy Centre, corner of Camp and Shotover streets, Queenstown

☎ (03) 442 4008; www.bungy.com 🅖 Daily; courtesy transport to bungy jump location

🅤 From NZ$180; T-shirt included

66 White-Water Rafting

Rafting companies operate year-round on the Kawarau and Shotover rivers, except when the water levels are too high. Up to eight people – confident swimmers only – fit into each boat. There's a brief introduction on how to paddle, how to float safely down-river and how to help scoop others out. Generally, the Kawarau River is the safer option, with no exposed rocks. Book at the Queenstown information centre.

Insider Tip

Challenge Rafting

🟦 221 D4 ✉ Queenstown Visitor Information Centre, corner of Shotover and Camp streets, Queenstown

☎ (03) 442 7318, 0800 423 836 toll free; www.raft.co.nz

🅖 Daily 🅤 NZ$200

67 River Surfing

River surfing, or sledging, gives you a some control over how you navigate the rapids, equipped with a wetsuit, helmet, fins and a body board. Each trip starts in calm water with an introduction to the equipment and techniques. From there you can either stay in the quieter sections, slowly floating down the Kawarau River, or tackle four rapids of varying difficulty. Basic swimming skills are needed.

Serious Fun River Surfing

🟦 221 D4 ✉ 39 Camp Street, Queenstown

☎ (03) 442 5262, 0800 737 468 toll free; www.riversurfing.co.nz 🅖 Daily 9am, 2pm; booking required, courtesy transport to river

🅤 From NZ$195

68 Arrowtown

Arrowtown is a faithfully restored early gold-mining settlement, set against the backdrop of a majestic mountain range and the golden, tussock-covered high country. The town's main street, lined with historic houses, shops and saloons, could be mistaken for a Western film set. A few minutes from the centre, on the banks of Bush Creek, are the remains of a Chinese gold-mining camp, indicating the harsh life of Chinese diggers, who often came to work the tailings for any gold undetected by earlier miners.

🟦 221 D4

☎ www.arrowtown.com

The Wild South

A romantic setting: Larnach castle

69 Alexandra

Like most Central Otago towns, Alexandra sprang up virtually overnight after the discovery of gold nearby. While many of the historic buildings remain, Alexandra has developed into a tranquil but modern town and the commercial hub of Central Otago. It's now an oasis of orchards among rocky hills, owing its current prosperity to fruit production and the growing reputation of local wines.

🚏 221 E4 ☎ www.alexandra.co.nz

70 Larnach Castle

Built by the 19th-century banker and merchant baron William Larnach, this fancy castle was one of the most expensive buildings in the country when construction was completed. From 1871 Larnach employed more than 200 workmen and spent a reputed NZ$426,000. The castle's best-known features are its elaborate ceilings, carved by English and Italian craftsmen. After Larnach's suicide in 1898, the castle was used as a cabaret venue, a tourist resort and a psychiatric hospital. The Barker family bought it in 1967, restoring the buildings and gardens.

🚏 221 F3
✉ 145 Camp Road, Otago Peninsula
☎ (03) 476 1616; www.larnachcastle.co.nz
🕐 Castle: daily 9–5; gardens: Oct–Easter daily 9–7; Easter–Sep daily 9–5
💰 Castle and gardens: NZ$28.
Accommodation offered (➤ 185)

71 Taieri Gorge Railway

A vintage train takes passengers through the spectacular Taieri Gorge, inland from Dunedin. As the railway winds for 58km (36mi) to Pukerangi, the landscapes change from rolling pastures to steep cliffs of layered schist rock. In the narrowest part of the gorge, the train passes between sheer cliffs on one side and a sudden drop on the other. From Pukerangi, the land flattens into the Taieri river plains that continue to Middlemarch, a small rural settlement. The train has an open viewing carriage and makes stops at sightseeing spots. Most people take the four-hour return trip to Pukerangi or six-hour return to Middlemarch, but you can continue to Queenstown by bus.

🚏 221 F3 ✉ Dunedin Railway Station, Anzac Avenue, Dunedin
☎ (03) 477 4449; www.taieri.co.nz
🕐 To Pukerangi: Oct–April Mon–Thu, Sat 9:30, 2:30, Fri, Sun 2:30; May–Sep daily 12:30. To Middlemarch: Oct–April Fri, Sun 9:30. To Palmerston: Oct–April Wed, Sat 9:30; May–Sep occasional days
💰 From NZ$59

Taieri Gorge Railway

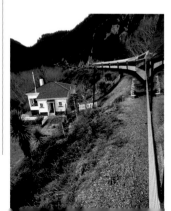

Where to...
Stay

Prices
Expect to pay for a double room per night:
$ under NZ$200 $$ NZ$200–$350 $$$ over NZ$350

QUEENSTOWN

The Heritage Queenstown $–$$$
This alpine-lodge style complex is a short walk from town and has lovely views over Lake Wakatipu and the Remarkables. Suites have kitchen facilities, and there are also 40 villas. In winter, there's a roaring fire in the restaurant; in summer you can dine on the balcony.

✚ 206 B3   ✉ 91 Fernhill Road
☎ (03) 442 4988; www.heritagehotels.co.nz

Novotel Queenstown Lakeside $$$
This 4-star hotel is just a few steps from the lake and downtown Queenstown – a peaceful, central location that's responsible for a large part its appeal. Only a handful of the 273 rooms have uninhibited views of the water. Elements, the restaurant, serves breakfast and modern New Zealand cuisine in the evenings. If the weather's good, you can eat out on the terrace.

✚ 221 D4   ✉ corner of Earl Streetan and Marine Parade ☎ (03) 442 7750; www.novotel.com

CENTRAL OTAGO

Mt Rosa Lodge $$$
This luxurious bed and breakfast is set in the Gibbston Valley and looks out over Mt Rosa Station, one of the largest vineyards in Central Otago. There are three tastefully decorated guest rooms, each with its own private access, outdoor terrace, ensuite bathroom, king-size bed and sitting area. There's a gourmet breakfast, and your hosts can provide picnic hampers and dinner on request. Aside from visiting wineries, you can take part in such outdoors activities as golf.

✚ 221 D4
✉ Gibbston Back Road, RD1 (near Queenstown)
☎ (03) 441 1484; www.mtrosalodge.co.nz

DUNEDIN

Larnach Lodge $–$$$
This re-created colonial wooden farm building in the grounds of Larnach Castle (► 184) has a stunning view of the harbour and the Otago Peninsula. Twelve rooms are ensuite and decorated in period style. Six more rooms, located in the converted coach house, have shared bathroom facilities. Guests can have dinner in the castle (arrange it by 5pm), and a free tour during opening hours. Breakfast is also included.

✚ 221 F3   ✉ Larnach Castle, 145 Camp Road
☎ (03) 476 1616; www.larnachcastle.co.nz

Lisburn House $–$$
This cosy bed and breakfast, three minutes' drive south of the city centre in the suburb of Caversham, was built in 1865 and is one of Dunedin's finest remaining examples of Victorian Gothic architecture. The interior features a wood-panelled dining room. There are three large bedrooms, each with queen-size four-poster bed and private bathroom. The Claddagh restaurant is open for both lunch and dinner.

✚ 221 F3
✉ 15 Lisburn Avenue, Dunedin
☎ (03) 455 8888; www.lisburnhouse.co.nz

Where to…
Eat and Drink

Prices
Expect to pay per person for a meal, excluding drinks:
$ under NZ$45 $$ NZ$45–$60 $$$ over NZ$60

QUEENSTOWN

The Bathhouse $$$
Built to commemorate the coronation of King George V in 1911, The Bathhouse is now a nostalgic café on the beach. Tables and chairs are set on the boardwalk, and the glass frontage gives views over the lake and mountains. This casual, relaxed café has beer on tap. It is open for breakfast, lunch, dinner and serves tapas-style dishes of New Zealand-inspired cuisine using lamb and salmon.
➕ 221 D4 ✉ 15 Marine Parade, Queenstown Bay ☎ (03) 442 5625; www.bathhouse.co.nz ⏰ Daily 9am–late

Gibbston Valley Winery $
One of Central Otago's pioneering vineyards, Gibbston Valley makes the most of its site in the scenic Kawarau Gorge. There's a stylish restaurant, a tasting facility and a shop. Local and seasonal ingredients are used in such dishes as the Mediterranean platter and pan-fried South Island salmon. Each dish has a suggested wine match. Wine tastings and cellar tours are also available. *Insider Tip*
➕ 221 D4 ✉ Gibbston, RD1, SH6 ☎ (03) 442 6910; www.gibbstonvalleynz.co.nz ⏰ Daily noon–3; wine tours: 10–4

ARROWTOWN

Saffron $$$
This friendly restaurant receives rave reviews. Try the scampi from Stewart Island to start, followed by a trio of Thai curries. The extensive wine list favours local wines, but there's a good selection of French vintages available too. Pesto, Saffron's sister restaurant next door, serves pizzas and pasta to families.
➕ 221 D4 ✉ 18 Buckingham Street ☎ (03) 442 0131; www.saffronrestaurant.co.nz ⏰ Daily 11am–late

DUNEDIN

Pier 24 $$–$$$
Located in St Clair Beach Resort, chefs Michael Coughlin and Greg Piner bring a touch of culinary genius to each dish. In the summer when the doors are open wide, this becomes coastal alfresco dining or in winter, hide behind the glass and watch the storms. The main menu changes regularly, but look out for Southland lamb with parmesan and rocket gnocchi and the always-popular crème brûlée.
➕ 221 F3 ✉ 24 Esplanade, St Clair Beach ☎ (03) 456 0555; www.stclairbeachresort.com ⏰ Oct–March daily 7am–late; April–Sep 8am–10:30pm

Plato $$
Housed in a former seafarer's hostel on the waterfront in Dunedin, Plato is a relaxed restaurant serving imaginative dishes using seasonal, local ingredients, especially seafood. Try pan-fried lamb's kidney to start, followed by sole with spinach and greenshell mussels. To wash it down, opt for any of the outstanding New Zealand wines on offer.
➕ 221 F3 ✉ 2 Birch Street ☎ (03) 477 4235; www.platocafé.co.nz ⏰ Daily 6pm–late; brunch: Sun 11am–2pm

Where to...
Shop

QUEENSTOWN

Queenstown is geared for tourists, with most shops in the **Queenstown Mall** area open till late and many offer packing and posting services. Prices may be on the high side.

Sports and outdoor equipment are readily available but try **Outside Sports** (9 Shotover Street; www.outsidesports.co.nz) or **Queenstown Sportsworld** (17 Rees Street).

Stroll down the pedestrian Queenstown Mall for rugby paraphernalia at **Champions of the World** (11 The Mall; www.champions.co.nz), a branch of **Louis Vuitton** (12 The Mall), and souvenirs, books and cafés. **O'Connell's Shopping Centre** (corner of Camp and Beach streets; www.oconnells.net.nz) has 25 stores under one roof, offering everything from food to fashion.

At the **Jade & Opal Factory** (22 Beach Street; www.jadefactory arrowtown.co.nz) you can watch carvers produce jewellery and sculptures in traditional and contemporary designs.

For picnic items head for the **Mediterranean Market** (53 Robins Roads; www.mediterranean.co.nz).

ARROWTOWN

Buckingham Street is lined with boutiques, galleries and souvenir shops housed in pretty cottages. **The Gold Shop** (No. 29; www.the goldshop.co.nz) sells original jewellery and boasts an extensive collection of natural gold nuggets that help to bring the town's gold rush history to life. If you want to buy an original piece of New Zealand art, head to the **Arrowtown Gallery** (26 Wiltshire Street; www.arrow towngallery.com). For knitwear, there's **The Wool Press** (No. 40; www.thewoolpress.com). **Ikon** (No. 50) sells New Zealand designer clothing. Follow the Wakatipu Arts Trail to buy direct from artists – ask for a leaflet at the **Lakes District Museum** (No. 49; www.museum queenstown.com).

DUNEDIN

George Street is the main shopping area, with a mix of chain stores and highly individual local stores. Dunedin celebrates its Scottish roots at **The Scottish Shop** (17 George Street; www.scottishshop.co.nz). **Meridian Shopping Mall** (267–287 George Street; www.meridianmall.co.nz) houses Arthur Barnett's department store, K-Mart, fashion chains and food outlets.

For designer clothing, head for **Plume** (310 George Street; www.plumestore.com). Browse for designer objects at **Things** (326 George Street; tel: (03) 477 4427) and **Acquisitions** (251 George Street; tel: www.acquisitions.co.nz). For collectables, try **Queens Gardens Antique Centre** (16 Queens Gardens).

Near the Octagon, is the **Lure Jewellery Workshop** (1st Floor, 130 Stuart Street), where you can watch five jewellers creating pieces of contemporary New Zealand jewellery. For work by New Zealand artists, try **Milford Galleries** (18 Dowling Street; www.milford galleries.co.nz), **Moray Gallery** (55 Princes Street; www.moraygallery.com) or **Brett McDowell Gallery** (5 Dowling Street; www.brettmc dowellgallery.com).

Up near the university, **Everyday Gourmet** (446 George Street; www.everydaygourmet.net.nz) is a good place to buy deli food. The **University Book Shop** (378 Great King Street; www.unibooks.co.nz) has two floors of books for all interests.

Where to...
Go Out

QUEENSTOWN

For listings of what's on, see the free *Mountain Scene*, published every Thursday, or call in at the Queenstown visitor information centre (corner of Shotover and Camp streets; www.queenstown isite.co.nz).

Skiing
Queenstown is a major ski resort, with two fields on its doorstep: **Coronet Peak** and **The Remarkables** (both; www.nzski.com/queenstown). Others are about an hour away near Wanaka. You can hire gear in the city or on the field.

Wine Trails
Central Otago, the world's southernmost wine-making region, has more than 30 vineyards. Pick up a wine trail map from the visitor centre or ask about guided tours.

Golf
There are five golf courses around Queenstown: **Millbrook Resort** (www.millbrook.co.nz), **Queenstown Golf Club** (www.queenstowngolf. co.nz), **Frankton Golf Club** (sportrec. qldc.govt.nz/golf), **Arrowtown Golf Club** (www.arrowtowngolf.co.nz) and **The Hills** (www.thehills.co.nz).

Nightspots
SkyCity Wharf Casino (Steamer Wharf) is open till 3am and **SkyCity Casino** (Beach Street; both: www. skycityqueenstown.co.nz) till 4am. You may be asked for ID.

The city's coolest bar – literally – is **Minus 5° Ice Bar** (88 Beach Street; http://www.minus5icebar. com) and it is made entirely of ice.

Festivals
The **Clyde Wine and Food Harvest Festival** is held at Easter, while June/July brings the hugely popular annual **Queenstown Winter Festival**. The biennial **Warbirds Over Wanaka**, held at Easter, is the largest air show in the southern hemisphere (www.warbirdsoverwanaka.com).

DUNEDIN

Check Thursday's edition of the *Otago Daily Times* for listings or ask at the visitor centre (50 The Octagon; www.dunedin.govt.nz/ isite, www.odt.co.nz).

Arts & Entertainment
Dunedin's professional theatre company, **Fortune** (231 Stuart Street; fortunetheatre.co.nz), has regular seasons of plays.

Concerts of classical music are given regularly by the **Southern Sinfonia** (110 Moray Place; www. southernsinfonia.org).

Dunedin Casino operates in the restored 1880s Southern Cross Hotel (118 High Street; www. dunedincasino.co.nz). There's a dress code.

Sports
Otago waterways are perfect for fishing trout. Professional guides supply transport, gear, tackle and the necessary fishing licence. Golf is available at several courses: contact the visitor centre. **Carisbrook Stadium** is the city's major sporting venue. A new stadium is being built for the 2011 Rugby World Cup.

Festivals
The city's **Summer Festival** is held from Jan–Feb. It's followed in March by the **Fringe Festival** (for contemporary art and artists) and **Scottish Week** (bagpipe concerts and much, much more!) October welcomes the annual **Rhododendron Festival** and the biennial **Otago Festival of the Arts**.

Walks & Tours

Walks & Tours

1 WELLINGTON CITY TO SEA WALKWAY
Walk

DISTANCE 4km (2.5mi)   TIME 1.5 hours
START POINT Bolton Street Memorial Park ✚ 223 E4
END POINT Aro Street ✚ 223 D1
GETTING BACK From Aro Street, catch the No. 9 bus

Wellington skyline as seen from the botanic gardens

This walk, with its stunning views of the city and harbour, covers the first third of a 12km (7mi) route that leads from the heart of central Wellington to the capital's southern coastline and the picturesque suburb of Island Bay. You can pick up a detailed description and map of the entire walkway at the Wellington Visitor Information Centre (▶ 114).

❶–❷

Turn from The Terrace, one of Wellington's central arteries near Parliament (▶ 112), into Bolton Street. The **Bolton Street Memorial Park** is just a few metres uphill on your right. From 1840 to 1892 this was the only cemetery for non-Catholics in Wellington, unusually allowing all faiths in one burial ground.

Walk up the steps to the small **chapel**, a replica of the original

1866 Anglican mortuary. Inside are displays about the main killers of the 19th century – disease, fire, poverty, earthquakes, tides and battle – and burial records of prominent citizens, including some of the founders of Wellington, who are interred in the cemetery (chapel open daily 10–4).

When a motorway was built through the cemetery in the 1960s, the original chapel was removed and the remains of almost 4,000 early settlers were shifted to a mass grave below the current chapel. On the left side of the chapel, the Anglican part of the old cemetery is still mostly intact and you'll find some beautiful tombstones.

Follow the walkway on the right of the chapel to the **Denis McGrath Bridge**, which crosses the motorway. Turn right after the bridge to follow Robertson Way through a heritage rose garden and uphill past the Jewish cemetery to a lookout point over Thorndon (▶ 115). A few metres further uphill, at an iron gate, is the **Seddon Memorial**, a tall obelisk in honour of Richard John Seddon, who arrived in New Zealand as a gold-miner and eventually became the country's Premier in 1893.

❷–❸

From the Seddon Memorial towards the gate of Anderson Park. As you pass the sports grounds on your right you can already see the Lady Norwood Rose Garden and the

Denis McGrath Bridge

Jewish Cemetery

Anglican Cemetery

Chapel

1

Anderson Park

2 ■ Seddon Memorial

Begonia House ■

■ Peace Flame

Bolton Street

Wellington Urban Motorway

The Terrace

"Sundial of Human Involvement"

Salamanca Road

Carter Observatory ■

Meteorological Station ■

Cable Car Terminal **3**

Kelburn Park

0 ————— 300 m
0 ————— 300 yd

Kelburn Parade

Victoria University ■

Mount Street Cemetery ■

Waiteata Road

The Terrace

Te Aro School ■

Aro Park

Abel Smith St

Aro Street

Epuni St

4

↓ To the sea

Botanic Garden's **Begonia House** (open daily 9–5 in summer; 9–4 in winter). Here, the traffic noise finally subsides, particularly around the small Japanese-style Peace Flame water garden to the left of the rose garden. Leave the Begonia House and café on your right, and follow the Serpentine Way uphill (a sign points to the Cable

Walks & Tours

Wellington Harbour

Car) as it winds through remnants of native forest. After about five minutes, it meets a narrow track; turn left into the Junction Path towards the **Sculpture Park**. Path names are not always on raised signposts so look for flat plaques on the lawn. Pass several sculptures, then continue along Manuka Way for a few metres before turning right into Scrub Path. The path skirts around the hilltop, where you'll see the large **meteorological station**. Follow the markers along Scrub Path, then turn right onto Hill Path and climb up the steps (made of railway sleepers) and, at the top, turn right into Australian Path. This takes you to the top of the hill and the **Sundial of Human Involvement**, the **Carter Observatory** and the top terminal of the **Cable Car** with its museum (➤ 116).

🖪–🖩

The magnificent views from the Cable Car take in Wellington's central city, the waterfront, **Matiu/ Somes Island** (➤ 117) and the distant Rimutaka Ranges.

TAKING A BREAK

You're never short of a café to rest in when exploring Wellington. Round off your walk with a snack at the **Aro Café** (90 Aro Street; tel: (04) 384 4970).

Walk out onto the road and past a planted traffic island to turn left onto a footpath signposted to Rawhiti Terrace. Cross Rawhiti Terrace and continue down another footpath to Kelburn Parade and the **Victoria University** buildings. Veer left to Salamanca Road and cross it to enter **Kelburn Park**. Walk around the left side of the sports field and turn left at the large fountain. Follow the track through bush, past squash courts, through another part of Wellington's green belt and up a

Spectacular views can be seen from the Cable Car

few steps to Salamanca Road. Then turn left and cross the road, and walk back up on the other side to Mount Street.

At the top of Mount Street, at the Student Union Building, turn left and stroll through the **Roman Catholic Cemetery**. When you reach Waiteata Road, at the bottom of the cemetery hill, turn right and follow the markers past university buildings, around the back of a student apartment block, its car park and a gym to the Boyd Wilson sports field. Walk along the field and turn left down a path past Te Aro School to the southern end of The Terrace. From there, turn right to follow The Terrace for a few metres until it intersects with Abel Smith Street. Cross the street and walk to Aro Street Park and the Aro Valley.

Aro Street, with its colonial villas, shops and cafés, is one of Wellington's favourite historic streets.

2 LAKE MATHESON
Walk

DISTANCE 2.5km (1.5mi) for lake circuit   **TIME** 1.5 hours for lake circuit
START/END POINTS Car park at Lake Matheson ✚ 218 B4
GETTING THERE At Fox Glacier turn into Cook Flat Road and after about
5km (3mi) turn right to Lake Matheson car park

Lake Matheson is renowned for providing the best opportunity to see New Zealand's highest mountains without having to brave the harsh alpine environment. On a calm day, the reflections on the lake are magical, but even if the surface is ruffled, the views to the Southern Alps are magnificent. A short drive away is Gillespies Beach, which represents the wild essence of the West Coast, with pounding surf and enchanted landscapes of bleached driftwood.

➊–➋

The best time to see the reflections of Aoraki/Mount Cook and Mount Tasman on Lake Matheson is early in the morning or late in the evening. The lake circuit starts from a car park about 5km (3mi) from Fox Glacier village. The path skirts the entire lake, undulating between the swampy shoreline and forest, to three main viewing platforms.

At the start, the track crosses a **swing bridge** over Clearwater River and cuts through dense, low forest

Mount Cook and Tasman perfectly reflected in Lake Matheson

Walks & Tours

Stunning landscapes surround Lake Matheson

along the outlet stream, sometimes giving way to patches of towering flax bushes, until it reaches the lake and the jetty after about 20 minutes.

At the **jetty** lookout, the entire lake comes into view for the first time. Lake Matheson was carved out by the retreating Fox Glacier, which left a hole at the head of a small side valley about 14,000 years ago. It used to be an important food-gathering place for Maori people, who put out eel traps in the lake and hunted the forest for wood pigeons and the weka (wood hen). When the Europeans arrived, they cleared the grassy river flats for farmland, but the lake's forest fringe remains and is now part of **Westland/Tai Poutini National Park**.

As you continue from the jetty, the lake disappears from view briefly. After about 10 minutes, a raised

WALKING AT GILLESPIES BEACH

From Lake Matheson, drive along Cook Flat Road for 9km (6mi), turn right and follow Gillespies Beach Road (unsealed) for 11km (7mi), then turn right to the car park.

Walk through the dunes to the beach and head north. The beach has a wild beauty, with roaring surf and skeletal trees scattered along the high-tide mark. It's named after James Edwin Gillespie, who detected gold here in 1865. Rusting gold dredgers are still visible, but they are gradually sinking into the mire.

After about an hour you'll reach the estuary fed by the Waikowhai Stream. Cross the trestle bridge and either explore the lagoon's dark tidal swamps or follow the path further north to the tunnel and lookout point. From there you can drop back down to the beach and walk for 30 minutes to the fur seal colony at Galway Beach. This is mainly a winter haul out for immature males, so while there may be hundreds there in winter, it can be difficult to find any in summer.

boardwalk brings you to the water's edge, as it skirts around the lakefront and crosses the swampy outlet at the back of the lake. From there a few steps lead up to the **View of Views** platform, which overlooks the entire lake, across to the Fox valley and mountain ranges. You'll get good views of the mountains from any of the viewpoints, but this is the best spot to get the postcard image of the peaks reflected in the water.

Sheltered by dense forests, the lake's surface is calm most days. Reflections are particularly clear on the water due to the tannin leached from fallen vegetation and the humus-rich soil which has stained the water a dark brown colour that looks like black tea.

The wetlands around the lake are home to introduced waterfowl, as well as native songbirds such as the melodious bellbird, who you are likely to hear during the walk.

2–3

From the View of Views it is five minutes to the next lookout, **Reflection Island** – although not really an island but a small platform jutting out onto the water. The rest of the loop track keeps to the forest and eventually brings you back out to the farmland, punctuated by the tall kahikatea swamp tree. On frosty, misty mornings, these isolated, gnarled trees are another scenic setting for photographs of the mountain ranges.

Gillespies Beach with its ocean-worn tree stumps

195

3 EAST CAPE
Tour

DISTANCE 334km (207mi)
TIME 3–4 days for a leisurely tour (4–5 days with stops along the way)
START POINT Opotiki, eastern Bay of Plenty ✛ 213 D3
END POINT Gisborne ✛ 213 E2

The East Cape, first to greet the rising sun, remains isolated and sparsely populated. A tour along the Pacific Coast Highway (SH35) takes you along a string of azure bays and deserted beaches, interspersed with small Maori townships. The area is steeped in Maori history and you will find numerous meeting houses and churches. The jagged Raukumara Range provides a formidable backdrop to the coastal scenery.

A bird's-eye view of White Island

1–2

Start your journey at **Opotiki**, a small farming township at the confluence of the Waioeka and Otara rivers. The extensive coastline at this eastern end of the Bay of Plenty is lined with safe, sandy beaches and is punctuated by rocky volcanic outcrops. Opotiki marks the intersection between SH2, which continues to Gisborne through the Waioeka Gorge, and the more scenic SH35, which winds its way around the spectacular East Cape to the same destination.

As you leave Opotiki, you'll get good views out to **White Island** (▶ 97), 48km (30mi) offshore. About 6km (4mi) from Opotiki, at the sandy beaches of **Tirohanga**, there are remnants of terraces of an ancient and extensive *pa*, a Maori fortified village, clearly visible on Tirohanga Bluff. The partly unsealed Motu Road, now a popular mountain-bike track along the Waiaua River, turns off from SH35 about 11km (7mi) from Opotiki, climbing through rugged, bush-covered country to Matawai, on SH2, which is about two hours' drive away.

For the next 20km (12mi) the road follows the coast, opening up to views across the Bay of Plenty at Maraenui Hill, until you reach the mouth of the **Motu River**, renowned for white-water rafting and jet boating.

3–4

Te Kaha, 70km (43mi) from Opotiki, is a small town set in a delightful cove that was once the scene of inter-tribal battles. As recently as

2–3

After passing several stretches of sandy beaches and rocky inlets, you reach **Torere**, about 23km (14mi) from Opotiki. Holy Trinity Church, beside the meeting house, is worth a short stop in order to compare its relative simplicity with the ornate wooden St Mary's Church at Tikitiki, further along the route.

Walks & Tours

The Anglican Church at Raukokore

1930, open-boat whaling still operated here and whales were landed on the beach. It's now a holiday resort. Te Kaha's richly carved Tukaki meeting house features an intricate lintel. Pretty **Whanarua Bay**, about 18km (11mi) further along the Pacific Coast Highway, has a number of secluded beaches.

About 10km (6mi) from Whanarua Bay, at **Raukokore**, the Anglican Church stands imposingly on a lone promontory near the sea. Built in about 1894, it shows a strong European influence in its architectural design.

4–5

For the next 15km (9mi) the road snuggles into the curves of the coastline, looking out to the rocky inlets and glistening beaches of **Waihau Bay** and **Oruaiti Beach**, until it turns away from the coast at Whangaparaoa, near **Cape Runaway**, the eastern extremity of the Bay of Plenty. It was named by Captain Cook in October 1769 when five Maori warrior canoes paddled out towards his ship. Cook ordered grapeshot to be fired over the warriors' heads, scaring them into a quick retreat.

Whangaparaoa is a place of mythical significance to Maori as the landing place of two of the seven ancient canoes that brought the first people to populate Aotearoa (New Zealand). From Whangaparaoa, SH35 briefly leaves the coast as it skirts across to **Hicks Bay**, 148km (92mi) from Opotiki, offering viewpoints, bush walks and deep-sea fishing excursions. The grey shell of the derelict freezing works (an abattoir) near the old wooden wharf recalls the days of

Rocky inlets and sandy coves are dotted along the East Cape

intensive coastal shipping at the cape before the road was developed.

5–6

From Hicks Bay continue for another 12km (7mi) to **Te Araroa**, which has a visitor information centre, postal facilities, shops, a petrol station and, in its school grounds, reputedly the biggest pohutukawa tree in the country, thought to be 600 years old. It has a girth of over 19m (62ft) and is named Te Waha o Rerekohu after an old tribal chief.

At Te Araroa, you'll find the turn-off to the **East Cape lighthouse**, at mainland New Zealand's most eastern point. The detour, a 44km (27mi) return trip on an unsealed road, takes about 50 minutes, and you'll have to go up 700 steps from the car park to the lighthouse, but the effort is well rewarded with the views towards **East Island**. Originally, the lighthouse was on East Island but the rocky outcrop has no beaches, and when four men drowned trying to land supplies, the lighthouse was shifted to its present site.

Tikitiki, 25km (15.5mi) from Te Araroa, is a small settlement on the banks of the Waiapu River, best known for St Mary's Church, one of the most ornate Maori churches in New Zealand. It was built in 1924 as a memorial to World War I soldiers from the local Ngati Porou tribe, still the main tribe on the East Coast.

6–7

The centre for the Ngati Porou is the small town of **Ruatoria**, 20km (12mi) further on at the foot of the tribe's sacred mountain **Mount Hikurangi**. At 1,752m (5,747ft), Mount Hikurangi is the North Island's highest non-volcanic peak. You can get good views from the Ihungia rest area, about 20km (12mi) further along the highway;

because of the peak's sacred status you need permission to climb it.

Further along, **Waipiro Bay village**, reached via an unsealed loop road off the highway, was once the busiest town on the coast; today, it's a slow-paced settlement where most activity revolves around the *marae*. **Te Puia Springs**, 231km (143mi) from Opotiki, has a lake and hot pools near by, and **Tokomaru Bay**, 242km (150mi) from Opotiki, is a crumbling but picturesque town

The East Cape lighthouse

with a beach. For the next 40km (25mi) you'll pass several beaches before reaching **Tolaga Bay** and the **Cooks Cove Walkway**, south of the township. The easy 6km (4mi) return trip crosses private land to where Cook dropped anchor to repair the *Endeavour* and take on water supplies (allow 2.5 hours; the walk is closed during lambing season, August to Labour Weekend). For the rest of the 54km (33mi) journey to **Gisborne**, the road passes several tranquil beaches and settlements, including Whangara, where *Whale Rider* was filmed (► 22).

Walks & Tours

4 MILFORD ROAD
Scenic Tour

DISTANCE 120km (74mi) **TIME** 2.5 hours' driving time; allow about 4–5 hours to take in sights and short walks along the way
START POINT/END POINT Te Anau ✚ 220 B3

Driving on State Highway 94, the road to Milford Sound, is a journey of superlatives. It leads through the Te Wahipounamu World Heritage area, one of the greatest wilderness areas left in the southern hemisphere, with the highest mountains, largest glaciers, tallest forests, wildest rivers, most rugged landscape and deepest lakes.

❶–❷

For the first 30km (19mi) to Te Anau Downs, the road follows the edge of **Lake Te Anau**, a long, narrow lake with three side arms stretching out towards the peaks of the Southern Alps. From the small wharf, the road leaves the lake to wind gently through pastures with fenced paddocks, grazing livestock and pockets of native forest dominated by the small-leaved southern beech.

After about 50km (31mi), you reach the first lookout point out to the **Eglinton Valley**, a frequently mist-shrouded river valley. The ranges and forests close in as you reach **Mirror Lakes**, about 58km (36mi) from Te Anau. Stretch your legs on a five-minute boardwalk beside several small glacial lakes. The lakes provide reflective views of the **Earl Mountains**. Look out for the Mirror Lakes sign, which is upside down so that you can read the reflection. This is a favourite habitat for waterfowl and wetland plants. Beech trees are the main feature of Fiordland forests. From the Mirror Lakes, it's only 5km

The Earl Mountains are reflected perfectly in the aptly named Mirror Lakes

(3mi) to Knobs Flat, which has campsites and toilets.

❷–❸

Take a break at **Knobs Flat** to see the displays on local nature and on the history of the road to Milford, particularly the construction of Horner Tunnel, which you'll enter later (see box below).

As you leave Knobs Flat, the landscape starts changing from hilly pastures to an increasingly dense native rainforest and soaring, partly snow-covered peaks.

About 78km (48mi) from Te Anau, just before the road meets Lake Gunn, a 45-minute **nature walk** provides an opportunity to see typical vegetation before the road climbs beyond the tree line.

Milford Road

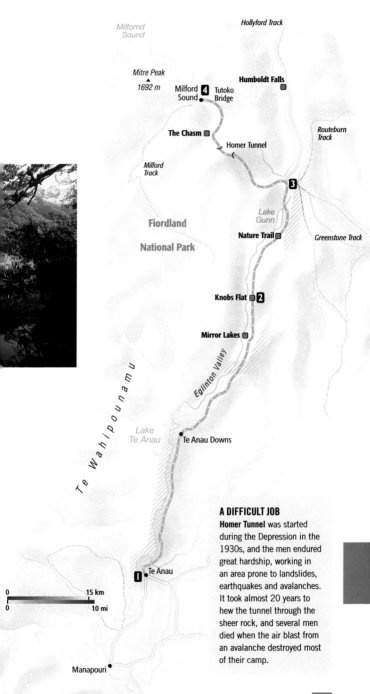

Hollyford Track

Milford Sound

Mitre Peak
▲ 1692 m

Milford Sound **4** Tutoko Bridge

Humboldt Falls

The Chasm

Homer Tunnel

Routeburn Track

Milford Track

Fiordland

National Park

Lake Gunn

Nature Trail

3

Greenstone Track

Knobs Flat **2**

Mirror Lakes

Eglinton Valley

Te Wahipounamu

Lake Te Anau

Te Anau Downs

1 Te Anau

0 _____ 15 km
0 _____ 10 mi

Manapouri

A DIFFICULT JOB

Homer Tunnel was started during the Depression in the 1930s, and the men endured great hardship, working in an area prone to landslides, earthquakes and avalanches. It took almost 20 years to hew the tunnel through the sheer rock, and several men died when the air blast from an avalanche destroyed most of their camp.

Walks & Tours

A few minutes into the nature walk, a 500-year-old beech log has a mark on one of its year rings to indicate its size when Captain Cook made his first visit to New Zealand.

Several longer walks fork off Milford Road, including the popular **Routeburn** and **Greenstone tracks**, before you reach the junction with the unsealed no-exit Lower Hollyford Road. This leads to the **Humboldt Falls** and the head of the Hollyford Track.

🖸–🖪

The last few kilometres before Milford are the most scenic (though the risk of avalanche means you can't stop until you get to the Chasm). You should turn your lights on as you approach **Homer Tunnel**, about 19km (12mi) from Milford. Here, the mountains form a solid rock wall in front of you, free of vegetation but awash with hundreds of waterfalls fed by snowfields and glaciers. The water

The beautiful Milford Sound lies at the end of this scenic drive.

runs through the rock and drips down inside the tunnel, as the hand-hewn passage was left unlined. Sections of the 1,207m (3,959ft) tunnel now have large sheets of metal to divert the water down the sides, where it forms two small creeks running alongside the traffic. As you come out of the tunnel the view opens out to a narrow U-shaped valley and the road continues on a steep downhill run to Milford, through a precipitous zigzag past imposing mountains streaming with water. The road frequently narrows to one-way bridges to cross creeks that can swell to roaring rivers. One ⟨Insider Tip⟩ of the best short walks along Milford Road is **the Chasm**, about 9km (6mi) from Milford, a 20-minute walk along the Cleddau River to two footbridges with views of a series of waterfalls.

From the Chasm, the road passes a stretch of steaming beech forest and a river viewpoint at the Tutoko Bridge, before finally reaching **Milford Sound** (➤ 170), with Mitre Peak dominating the view.

BEFORE YOU SET OUT...

- Milford Road can be **busy in high season**, so it's a good idea to set off from Te Anau before 8am and take the boat at around 11am before all the buses arrive.
- The road **may be closed due to winds or avalanches** (mostly June to November); check roadside information signs in Te Anau.
- Fill your tank and buy food and drink before you leave Te Anau. **There are no petrol stations or shops** on the road to Milford Sound. ⟨Insider Tip⟩
- Buy the annotated Milford Road World Heritage Highway Guide map (NZ$1; available from Fiordland National Park Visitor Centre, Te Anau).
- For **up-to-date road advice** and weather reports: Transit Highway Information Line: 0800 444 449 toll free; www.milfordroad.co.nz; www.fiordland.org.nz

Practicalities

Practicalities

WHAT YOU NEED

● Required ○ Suggested ▲ Not required	Some countries require a passport to remain valid for a minimum period (usually at least 6 months) beyond the date of entry – check before booking.	UK	USA	Canada	Australia	Ireland	Netherlands
Passport/National Identity Card		●	●	●	●	●	●
Visa (regulations can change – check before booking)		▲	▲	▲	▲	▲	▲
Onward or Return Ticket		●	●	●	●	●	●
Health Inoculations (tetanus and polio)		▲	▲	▲	▲	▲	▲
Health Documentation (► 208, Health)		▲	▲	▲	▲	▲	▲
Travel Insurance		●	●	●	●	●	●
Driving Licence (national, plus translation for Spanish nationals)		●	●	●	●	●	●
Car Insurance Certificate (included if car is hired)		▲	▲	▲	▲	▲	▲

WHEN TO GO

Auckland

High season   Low season

JAN	FEB	MAR	APR	MAY	JUN	JUL	AUG	SEP	OCT	NOV	DEC
23°C	23°C	22°C	20°C	18°C	15°C	13°C	14°C	16°C	18°C	19°C	22°C
73°F	73°F	72°F	68°F	64°F	59°F	55°F	57°F	61°F	64°F	66°F	72°F

Sun   Sunshine and showers   Wet

The temperatures given above are the **average daily maximum** for each month. New Zealand's main travel season is during the warmer months, generally from November to March, but ski resorts like Queenstown are busy throughout the year. The warmest months are December, January and February, and the coldest are June, July and August.

The north of New Zealand is often described as "Mediterranean", with short winters and long summers. The south has long winters with plenty of snow. The best time to travel is after January, as the weather in late summer and autumn tends to be more stable than during spring. Winter and spring have more rain, which can cause floods in some areas.

WEBSITES

- www.tourismnewzealand.com (Tourism New Zealand)
- www.tourism.net.nz
- www.aucklandnz.com (Tourism Auckland)
- www.rotoruanz.com (Tourism Rotorua)
- www.christchurchnz.com (Christchurch and Canterbury Tourism)
- www.wellingtonnz.com (Positively Wellington Tourism)
- www.queenstown-nz.co.nz (Queenstown Tourism)

Practicalities

GETTING THERE

By Air Auckland and Christchurch both have large international airports. There are two ways to fly to New Zealand: along the eastern route (via the Middle East and Asia) or across the western route (via America/Canada). The eastern route is much busier and a little shorter (approx. 22 hours versus approx. 24 hours in the air). Air New Zealand (check out the "Skycouch" from London via L.A.) and Cathay Pacific (try Premium Economy Class via Hong Kong) are very comfortable. **Travel times** New Zealand is a 3.5-hour flight from eastern Australia. A direct flight to New Zealand takes around 12 hours from the west coast of the United States. Flights from Europe to New Zealand head either via the US or destinations in Asia, from where they take around 10 hours.

Ticket prices Many airlines now cooperate with one another, meaning you'll rarely find any truly cheap deals. You might save some money on the Internet by buying multi-leg flights with different airlines, however – e.g. to Singapore (Lufthansa, KLM, Air France, etc.) then to Auckland with Jetstar (a subsidiary of Quantas, www.jetstar.com). Make sure to leave enough time for connections.

Stopovers: Singapore Airlines offer some very cheap stopover deals in Singapore, and Changi airport is as close a travel hub can get to being a pleasurable experience. **Cathay Pacific** also offer some cheap hotel deals (www.cxholidays.com). Asian cities are around halfway to New Zealand, making them perfect for a relaxing break in your trip.

TIME

New Zealand Standard Time is 12 hours ahead of Greenwich Mean Time (GMT), and 2 hours ahead of Australian Eastern Standard Time.
Daylight Saving Time Clocks are put forward by one hour on the last Sunday of September and wound back on the first Sunday of the following April.

CURRENCY AND FOREIGN EXCHANGE

Currency The unit of New Zealand currency is the dollar; $1=100 cents. Notes are issued in 5, 10, 20, 50 and 100 dollar denominations, coins in denominations of 10, 20 and 50 cents (all silver), 1 and 2 dollars (gold). Although the New Zealand dollar (also referred to as the kiwi dollar) has gained against major overseas currencies in recent years, the country remains a fairly low-cost holiday destination. There is no restriction on the amount of foreign currency that can be brought in or taken out, but every person who carries more than $10,000 in cash in or out is required to complete a Border Cash Report. **Foreign currency** can be exchanged at banks, some hotels and Bureau de Change kiosks, which are found at international airports and most city centres. The best **exchange rates** are given by the trading banks: BNZ, National Bank, ANZ, Westpac. You can withdraw money from **ATM machines** with international credit cards and ATM cards as long as they have a four-digit PIN encoded. All major **credit cards** can be used. **Travellers' cheques** are accepted at hotels, banks and some stores. All goods and services are subject to 15 per cent **Goods and Services Tax** (GST), included in the displayed price. You can't claim this tax back.

Camping
- www.goseenewzealand.co.nz (Camping tips)
- www.camping.org.nz & www.nzcamping.co.nz

NZ Automobile Association
www.aatravel.co.nz

- www.radionz.co.nz/podcasts (NZ Radio)
- www.tvnz.co.nz (NZ news)
- www.stuff.co.nz (NZ news)
- www.teara.govt.nz (Encyclopedia of NZ)
- www.maori.org.nz (Maori culture)
- www.nzs.com (links to NZ sites)

Practicalities

NATIONAL HOLIDAYS

1 Jan	New Year's Day
2 Jan	New Year's Holiday
6 Feb	Waitangi Day
Mar/Apr	Good Friday*, Easter Sunday
25 Apr	Anzac Day*
1st Mon Jun	Queen's Birthday
Last Mon Oct	Labour Day
25 Dec	Christmas Day*
26 Dec	Boxing Day

* Many restaurants and attractions close on these days

ELECTRICITY

New Zealand operates on a 230V AC, 50 hertz mains supply, three-pin plug system. Most hotels provide 110V AC sockets for shavers only, and hardware or electronics shops stock adaptors.

OPENING HOURS

○ Shops
● Offices
● Banks
● Main Post Offices
● Museums/Monuments
● Pharmacies

8am 9am 10am noon 1pm 2pm 16pm 5pm 7pm

☐ Day ▨ Midday ☐ Evening

In addition to the opening hours shown left, **pharmacies** and **stores** are open on Saturday 9–12 or 9–4 and some shops are open on Sunday. Bigger towns may have **late-night shopping** on Thursday or Friday until 8:30 or 9pm. Some **smaller shops** close at lunchtime on Saturdays. Local **convenience stores** (dairies) are usually open 7am–8pm seven days.

TIPS/GRATUITIES

Tipping is not generally expected, but may be given to reward excellent service:

Restaurants, cafes, bars	Not expected
Tour guides	Not expected
Taxis	Not expected
Hairdressers	Not expected
Chambermaids	Not expected
porters	Not expected
Toilets	Not expected

MAORI WORDS TO TRY

Maori is the second official language in New Zealand behind English. Try these words and the locals will love you:

Kia Ora	Hi, g'day
Haere Mai	Welcome
Ka Pai	Good, fine
Haere Ra	Goodbye

TIME DIFFERENCES (SEP–MARCH)

New Zealand (NZDT)	London (GMT)	New York (EST)	Los Angeles (PST)	Sydney (AEDT)
12 noon	← 1am	← 8pm	← 5pm	← 10am

Practicalities

STAYING IN TOUCH

Post Auckland's main post office is at 24 Wellesley Street (tel: (09) 379 6710). The main office in Wellington is at 7–27 Waterloo Quay (tel: (04) 496 4999); in Dunedin, it's at 233 Moray Place (tel: (03) 474 0932). The location in Christchurch changes due to the earthquake.

Public telephones Telecom operates the public telephone service. Most call boxes (some of which are equipped with WiFi) use Telecom phone cards available from shops. For directory enquiries dial 018, and for international directory enquiries dial 0172.

International Dialling Codes
Dial 00 followed by

UK:	44
USA/Canada:	1
Ireland:	353
Australia:	61
New Zealand:	64

Mobile providers and services Major cell phone providers are Vodafone, Telecom and 2 Degrees. SIM cards for each network are available for purchase at electronic stores and mobile phone retail stores. Pre-paid SIM cards start at around NZ$20. Using a local phone number, incoming calls are free.

WiFi and Internet Internet speeds are not as fast in New Zealand as other countries. Maximum download speeds can be up to 24Mbps. WiFi is now fairly standard all over the country. In many cases access is free – or for the price of a coffee at a local café. When you log on you will be shown the networks in your immediate area and can pre-pay for an hour, day or month.

PERSONAL SAFETY

New Zealand is generally safe. Thieves are attracted to areas where tourists congregate, so take care with valuables.
- Don't leave valuables in your car within plain sight. Opportunistic thieves only need a few seconds to take a handbag, laptop or even luggage.
- In the outdoors, the weather can change quickly from one extreme to the other.
- Prepare carefully for outdoor excursions: take appropriate clothing for any kind of weather, protect yourself from the sun and bring a first-aid kit. For weather forecasts see www.metservice.com.
- Hitchhiking is not illegal but strongly discouraged. If you do plan on hitchhiking, go in pairs or a group and leave your contact details and travel plans with friends/family or trusted locals you have met.

Police assistance:
☎ 111 from any phone

POLICE	111
FIRE	111
AMBULANCE	111

Practicalities

HEALTH

 Insurance A doctor's visit costs about $55. Make sure your travel insurance covers hospital care. Accidents are covered by the Accident Compensation Corporation (ACC), which ensures that tourists are not charged for any medical treatment required as a consequence of an accident suffered in New Zealand. This covers both physical and psychological damage. The ACC scheme means you can't sue anybody for damages. In cases of minor injuries you may have to contribute to the cost of the initial doctor's visit and physiotherapy.

 Dental services Dentists are expensive, so make sure your travel insurance covers dental treatments.

 Weather The sun can be harsh in New Zealand, even through cloud. Make sure you apply sunscreen and wear a hat.

 Drugs Painkillers can be bought over the counter at pharmacies, but antibiotics have to be prescribed.

 Safe water While tap water is safe to drink, some streams are infected with giardia and E-coli, which can cause serious illness.

RESTRICTED GOODS

Many types of goods such as food, wooden items and outdoor gear need to be declared on entering New Zealand. Check the list on your Passenger Arrival Card.

CONCESSIONS

Students/Children Most museums offer discounts for children (5–14, under-fives can usually get in free) as well as university students. There are also family concessions, which cover two adults and up to 4 children.
Senior citizens Discounted prices are available for some attractions, public transport and accommodation.

TRAVELLING WITH A DISABILITY

Wheelchair access and toilet facilities for people with disabilities are a legal requirement for new accommodation establishments. Quarantine laws prevent overseas visitors from bringing guide dogs. Cities have a Total Mobility (wheelchair transporter) taxi service. Some tour companies can adapt adventure activities for people with disabilities. For further information visit the New Zealand Federation of Disability Centres' website: www.weka.net.nz

CHILDREN

Most attractions, particularly museums, have hands-on activities designed for kids. Hotels and restaurants are generally child friendly, but some B-&B's are designed for couples rather than families. Special attractions for kids are marked out with the logo shown above.

RESTROOMS

All attractions have public toilets, which can also be found in many public areas, such as city squares, parks and playgrounds. Most public toilets have access for wheelchairs and many have baby-changing facilities.

EMBASSIES & HIGH COMMISSIONS

UK
(Wellington)
☎ (04)924-2888

USA
(Wellington)
☎ (04)462-6000

Ireland
(Auckland)
☎ (09)977-2252

Australia
(Wellington)
☎ (04)473-6411

Canada
(Wellington)
☎ (04)473-9577

Road Atlas

For chapters: See inside front cover

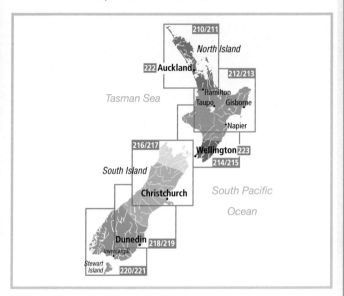

North Island

210/211

222 Auckland

212/213

Hamilton
Taupo Gisborne

Napier

Tasman Sea

216/217

South Island

Wellington 223

214/215

Christchurch

South Pacific

Ocean

Dunedin 218/219

Invercargill

Stewart
Island 220/221

Key to Road Atlas

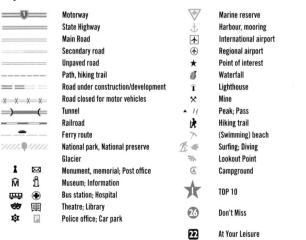

Motorway	
State Highway	
Main Road	
Secondary road	
Unpaved road	
Path, hiking trail	
Road under construction/development	
Road closed for motor vehicles	
Tunnel	
Railroad	
Ferry route	
National park, National preserve	
Glacier	

♂	✉	Monument, memorial; Post office	
Ⓜ	ℹ	Museum; Information	
🚌	⊕	Bus station; Hospital	
🎭	📖	Theatre; Library	
☼	P	Police office; Car park	

▽	Marine reserve
⚓	Harbour, mooring
✈	International airport
⊕	Regional airport
★	Point of interest
⋰	Waterfall
♆	Lighthouse
✕	Mine
▲)(	Peak; Pass
🧗	Hiking trail
🏊	(Swimming) beach
🏄 🤿	Surfing; Diving
🔭	Lookout Point
⊙	Campground

⭐ TOP 10

㉖ Don't Miss

22 At Your Leisure

1 : 1.850.000

0	40	80 miles
0	40	80 km

Pacific Ocean

Bay of Plenty

White Island
(Active volcano) ★
White Island
32

Cape Runaway
Whangaparaoa Pt.
Whanga-
paraoa
Lottin Pt.
Matakaoa Pt.
Orete Pt.
Waihau Bay
Oruti Beach
Whanarua Bay
Potaka
Hicks Bay
Natural Solution ★
Te Araroa
East Cape Lighthouse
East Cape
Waikawa Pt.
Te Kopua
Whanarua Bay
Raukokore
Pukeamaru
992 m
Awatere
4
Te Kaha Pt.
Whanarua Bay
Pacific Coast
Macademias Farm
Raukumara
1413 m
Rangitukia
Awanui
Te Kaha
Whitianga
Pariokara
Omaio
Waiomatatini
Reporua
Moutohora I.
Omaio Bay
Houpoto
Whanokao
1618 m
Tikitiki
Thornton
Torere
Ruatoria
Mahora
Edgecumbe
Ohope
Opape
Hikurangi
1752 m
Hiruharama
Whareponga
Paroa
Omarumutu
Kopuaroa
Waipiro Bay
Whakatane
Takaputahi
Takapau
Ihungia
Te Puia Springs
Awakeri
Wainui
Kutarere
Otara
Koutunui Head
Te Teko
Taneatua
Nukuhou
North
Waioeka Pa
Whitikau
Huiarua
Waima
Opotiki
Tokomaru Bay
Mawhai Pt.
Tuatini
Waimana
Toatoa
Hikuwai
Motu Falls
Arero
Cook's second landing 20.10.17 ★
3
Waikirikiri
Tanatana
Motu
Waipaoa
Anaura Bay
Oponae
Wairata
Maungahaumi
▲ 1213 m
Tauwhareparae
Mangatuna
Tauwhare
Moutohora
Huanui
Tolaga Bay Cashmere Company
Kaiaua Bay
Hopeone
Trafford's Hill
Matawai Whatatutu
Rakauroa
Wharekaka
Tolaga Bay
Pourewa I.
Te Urewera
Maungapohatu
1366 m
Arakihi
613 m
Takapau
Haurii
Waihau Bay
Koranga
Oamaru
Wharekopae
Puha
OOrmond
Waimata
Puatai Beach
Te Whaiti
Ngaputahi
Murupara
Te Karaka
Gable End Foreland
National
Rere
Ngatapa
Matawhero
Makaraka
Ruatahuna
Manuoha
1403 m
Pehiri
Whangara
Pouawa
Park
Taupeupe
Saddle
Aniwaniwa
Waerengiokuri
Gisborne
Hangaroa
Manutuke
Okitu
L. Waikaremoana
Waikaremoana
Ruakituri
Muriwai
Poverty Bay
Kaitawa
Tuai
Te Reinga
Waingake
Young Nick's Head
Lake
Waikaremoana
Track
Tarapatiki
Marumaru
Maraetaha
Ardkeen
Bartletts
Rangiahua
Ohine-
paka
Frasertown
Morere
Mahanga
Willow Flat
Tuhara
Opoutama
Pukenui Beach
Kopuawhara
Kotemaori
Raupunga
Wairoa
Nuhaka
Waikokopu
Oraka Beach
Mahia
Table Cape
Putorino
Kihitu
Mahia Beach
Mohaka
Waihua
Long Pt.
Te Kapu
366 m
Tutira
Whakamahi Beach
Mahia
Peninsula
Ahuriri Pt.
Hawke Bay
Portland I.
Tangolo
Waipatiki Beach
Whirinaki
Eskdale
Bay View
Rissington
Westshore
Taradale
NAPIER **35**
Fernhill
Flax-
mere
Clive
Haumoana
Gannet Colony
Cape Kidnappers
HASTINGS
Clifton
Havelock North
Te Mata Peak
399 m
Ocean Beach
Waimarama
215
Kairakau Beach

213

Tasman Sea

Seal Rocks
Neils Beach
Cascade Pt.
Halfway Bluff
Cascade River
Cascade River Valley
Dagon 1693 m
Awarua Pt.
Pyke Big Bay Track
Big Bay
Long Reef
Mt. Aspiring 3030 m
Martins Bay
National
Mt. E 2586
Hollyford Track
McKerrow
Rees/Dart
L. Alabaster
Yates Pt.
Mt. Tutoko 2746 m
Mt. Earnslaw 2819 m
Centaur 2518 m
Milford Sound
Mitre Peak 1692 m
Milford Sound
"Isengard" "Lothlorien"
Seabreeze Pt.
Poison Bay
Routeburn Track
"Amon Hen"
Paradise
Jetboating
Sutherland Sound
Sutherland Falls
Homer Tunnel
Mt. Christina 2502 m
Hollyford
Mt. Bonpland 2348 m
Sk
Bligh Sound
The Divide 532 m
Kinloch
Glenorchy
George Sound
Milford Track
L. Gunn
Caples Track
Coro
Two Thumb Bays
Cascade Creek
Elfin Bay
Mount Creighton
Mt. McDougall 2036 m
Knobs Flat
Greenstone Track
Spoth Pk. 2050 m
Arthur Fernhi
Caswell Sound
Mirror Lakes
Queensto
Fiordland
Charles Sound
Walter Peak Station
Nancy Sound
Thompson Sound
Te Ana-Au Caves
Mt. Irene 1879 m
Secretary I.
Mt. Lyall 1905 m
Te Anau Downs
Jade Peak
Doubtful Sound
Snowdon 1577 m
Mt. Forbes 1305 m
National
Kepler Track
"Fangorn Forest"
Mt. Soaker 1593 m
Spire Peak 1696 m
The Dail
Dagg Sound
Towing Head
Te Anau
Mt. Kellard 1210 m
Manapouri Power Station
Wilmot Pass
"Dead Marshes"
"River Anduin"
Breaksea I.
Mt. Ward 1719 m
Flat Mt. 1768 m
The Key
Breaksea Sound
L. Manapouri
Resolution I.
Mt. Clerke 1070 m
Manapouri
Five Fingers Point
Cooper I.
Mt. Solitary 1454 m
Mossburn
Anchor I.
Long I.
Green L.
Monowai
Castlerock
Josephville
Caroline Pk. 1722 m
Monowai
Wairah
Etal Creek
Caroline
Dipton West
Dipton
Park
Ohai
Opio
Benmore
West Cape
Otahu Flat
Wreys
Bush South
Kauana
Cape Providence
Treble Mt. 1049 m
Blackmount
Nightcaps
Hillend
Otapi
Chalky I.
Clifden
Orawia Gap
Scotts
Wairio
Limehills
Winton
Brow
Chalky Inlet
Mt. Aitken 1189 m
Jetboating
Piko Piko
Aparima
Pukemaori
Oreti Plains
Preservation Inlet
Hump Ridge Track
Tuatapere
Drummond
Lochiel
Coal I.
Papatotara
Otautau
Northope
Isla Bank
Ryal Bush
Puysegur Point
Hakapoua
Te Waewae
Ringway
Fairfax
Thornbury
Makarewa
Long Pt.
South Coast/Waitutu Track
Te Waewae Bay
Gummies Bush
Wallacetown
Monkey Island Beach
Waihoaka
Riverton
Lornevile
INV
Pahia
Orepuki
Pahia Pt.
Colac Bay
Lomg-wood
The Rocks
Oreti Beach
Wakapatu
Centre I.
Pahia
Otatara
New River Estuary
Escape Reefs
Greenhills
Greenpoint
Solander I.
Foveaux Strait
Ocean Beach
Bluff

Bishop and Clerks Is.
Black Rock Pt.
Ruapuke
Rugged Is.
Mt. Anglem 980 m
North West Circuit Track
Rakiura
Hazelburgh Group
Codfish I.
Rakiara Track
Halfmoon Bay (Oban)
Bench I.
Mason Bay
Ulva Island Bird Sanctuary
Mt. Rakeahua 681 m
Kiwi Watching
Ernest Is.
Doughboy Bay
National
South Red Head Pt.
Mt. Allen 749 m
Park
Big Moggy I.
Port Adventu
Shelter Pt.
Breaksea Is.
Stewart I.
Big South Cape I.
Pearl I.
Port Pegasus
South West Cape
Broad Bay
South Cape

A — B — C

Auckland

Index

Index

Index

Index

Picture Credits

Credits

1st Edition 2017

Worldwide Distribution: Marco Polo Travel Publishing Ltd
Pinewood, Chineham Business Park
Crockford Lane, Chineham
Basingstoke, Hampshire RG24 8AL, United Kingdom.
© MAIRDUMONT GmbH & Co. KG, Ostfildern

Authors: Veronika Meduna, Mavis Airey ("Where to… Stay/Eat and Drink"), Susi Bailey, Bruni Gebauer and Stefan Huy
Editor: Christiane Wagner
Revised editing and translation: Jon Andrews, jonandrews.co.uk
Program supervisor: Birgit Borowski
Chief editor: Rainer Eisenschmid

Cartography: © MAIRDUMONT GmbH & Co. KG, Ostfildern
3D-illustrations: jangled nerves, Stuttgart

Printed in China

Despite all of our authors' thorough research, errors can creep in. The publishers do not accept any liability for this. Whether you want to praise us, alert us to errors or give us a personal tip – please don't hesitate to email or post:

MARCO POLO Travel Publishing Ltd
Pinewood, Chineham Business Park
Crockford Lane, Chineham
Basingstoke, Hampshire RG24 8AL
United Kingdom
Email: sales@marcopolouk.com

FSC
www.fsc.org
MIX
Paper from responsible sources
FSC® C124385

10 REASONS
TO COME BACK AGAIN

1. Whenever the northern hemisphere's freezing in winter, it's **summertime Down Under**.

2. New Zealand has the **largest number of Kiwis in the world** – both the people and the birds!

3. NZ's vast stretches of **unpopulated wilderness** are just waiting to be discovered on foot.

4. Where else will you get to eat **fresher fish and seafood** than this?

5. The little country boasts a **huge range of land-scapes**, from mountains to volcanic steppes.

6. New Zealand is **a peaceful natural paradise** devoid of any really dangerous animals.

7. Quaffable **wines**, tasty **beers**, perfect Italian **coffee** and **tea** to make an Englishman proud.

8. Enjoy learning about **Maori Culture** – it's interesting, exciting and full of surprises.

9. **Friday night** is party night – come and paint the town red into the early hours!

10. One trip isn't enough to answer the age-old question: **which island is more beautiful?**

Map Included